MW01069253

With contributions by:

Sandra van Assen
Tijs van den Boomen
Marco Broekman
Guido van Eijck
Eric Frijters
Marieke Kums
Willemijn Lofvers
Saskia Naafs
Thijs van Spaandonk
Ady Steketee
Franz Ziegler

Urban Challenges, Resilient Solutions

Design Thinking for the Future of Urban Regions

TRANCITY×VALIZ
FUTURE URBAN REGIONS

The Strength of Design

The new *Architectuurnota* (Memorandum on Architectural Policy) was the subject of profound discussion.[1] As the central government withdrew, the cultural dimension of spatial planning was in danger of fading to the background. Content, research and imagination seemed far away.

Fewer rules, more space and work on a local and regional level whenever possible – that was the idea. Because planning takes place where things happen, on the ground, in the neighbourhoods, the streets, the districts. And at a higher level, it is where the system functions: regionally. The region is a functional notion in this context; deltas and energy networks are not bound by national borders.

Locally, therefore, strong and inspired. And, hence, using design. Because design is special. Design, as an instrument and process, has the strength to identify development opportunities and use them in viable innovations. Design can combine regional dependencies and local challenges and thus connect people and places, and refer to the future in concrete terms, in a practical and ambitious way. Design is crucially important in the representation of the added value of investments, because it can integrally connect the interests of sectors – across scales, across time.

Design is vital to the inclusive process of collaboration because it brings parties together in the strong coalitions that are so very important to real change. And not by negotiation, but by actually bridging differences. Design bridges the gap between quality and safety, between local needs and political capacity, between regional dependencies and the strength of the community, between economy, society and the environment. Design touches upon both the cultural process and sustainable impact.

Connections among the field, urgent challenges, politics and local strengths are crucial. Who can sustain these connections? That was, and still is, the crucial question. Because without design, the design process and the designers, it simply cannot be done!

Since I am convinced that the Academies of Architecture in the Netherlands are 'major and distinctive laboratories', I contacted them and we began to explore that agenda together, focusing on my question of whether they – from their position amid the challenges and midway between parties – could convert those challenges into a programme linked to the new *Architectuurnota*.

The offer of the Academies of Architecture comprised a research group that focused on this dynamic in which all Academies would operate nationally and simultaneously develop programmes both regionally and locally.

Now, during the prelude to the next *Architectuurnota*, it is time to look back and look ahead. The value of the Academies in this game is obvious, the strength of design has never been this poignant, the relationship with politics is crucial given the huge social challenges we face on a local, regional, national and international level. What's the next step? I can sure think of one!

Henk Ovink
Water Envoy, Kingdom of the Netherlands
Principal of Rebuild by Design

1

The *Architectuurnota* (Memorandum on Architectural Policy) – the *Action Agenda Architecture and Spatial Design 2013-2016 – Working on the Strength of Design* in full – was presented to parliament in September 2012. It is a joint publication by the Ministries of Infrastructure and the Environment; Education, Culture and Science; Interior and Kingdom Relations; Economic Affairs; Agriculture and Innovation; and Defence.

Content

Introduction

Traditionally, urban planning solves problems through cool deduction and a top-down approach. But only a few people still believe that this works. The current generation of architects, urban planners and landscape architects knows that making our urban regions more healthy and vital takes a more collaborative and intelligent approach, argues Tijs van den Boomen.

Ideas rather than ready-made designs: that is what designers need to 'loosen the nuts and bolts of the modernistic system'.

The research group Future Urban Regions (FUR), set up in 2013 and led by Eric Frijters, conducted a three-year study on healthy urbanity.[2]

2

FUR is a collaboration of the six Dutch Academies of Architecture and was financed by the Ministry of Infrastructure and the Environment.

This book presents the results of that study on the basis of three questions: What is healthy urbanity? (Part 1) How can we conduct research by design? (Part 2) Who do we need to realize ideas about healthy urbanity? (Part 3)

Each part opens with a substantive analysis; subsequently, its question is addressed on the basis of practical examples.

Each part broaches six themes that underpin the broad notion of 'healthy urbanity', namely: resilient infrastructure, renewable energy, material cycles, vital economy, healthy living and sociocultural solidarity.

Each theme includes, first, the discussion of a national or international practical example and second, one or in most cases two succinct design proposals that academy students produced in the FUR design ateliers. All in all, this book contains more than 50 cases.

Anthropocene

There is no doubt about it: humanity's future is urban. More than half of the world's population already lives in cities – cities that will not stop growing for a long time: in just over three decades, two-thirds of the world's inhabitants will be urbanites. In the West, a whopping 85 per cent of the population will be living in cities by that time.[3] This is, in fact, good news. Cities make us 'richer, cleverer, greener, healthier and happier', to quote economist Edward Glaeser.[4]

This glorious future will not unfold by itself, however, far from it. Growth is accompanied by serious issues that are added to the avalanche of problems we already face. In modern jargon, they are called *challenges*, but that term veils the seriousness of problems such as climate change, social inequality, large-scale migration, depletion of resources, terrorism, rising sea levels, declining biodiversity, segregation, shrinkage and adverse development, to name but a few.

Cities play an important part in addressing these problems. Naturally, cities cannot be understood as isolated systems: they are closely connected to both each other and to the rural areas that surround them. After all, even taigas, rainforests and oceans are inextricable bound up with our world-wide urban system. Biofueled power plants that produce clean energy for our electric cars, for example, may cause the destruction of rainforests on the other side of the globe. The digital world is also closely interwoven with the physical one: energy-guzzling servers keep our data in the cloud, and without conflict minerals such as coltan, there would be no smart phones and laptops.

We live in the Anthropocene, the age in which the climate and atmosphere are strongly influenced by human activity. This 'Human Age' has been going on for quite some time – there are paleo-climatologists who date the Early Anthropocene to about 8,000 years ago, when humans took up intensive arable and cattle farming – and started the deforestation of the planet.

In any event, we live in a world that we increasingly design ourselves, whether deliberately or unwittingly. Our activities are part of a global metabolism, a continuous exchange of resources, water, energy, food, biomass, and so on. The boundaries between culture and nature and between cities and ecological systems are fading. We are creating conditions that provide us with livelihood opportunities: conditions that may at the same time herald our end.

The chains of cause and effect are widespread and connected at many levels. The linear approach, in which issues are isolated and subsequently unravelled into bite-sized problems to solve, no longer works. It leads to increasingly complex and therefore fragile systems and the combating of unexpected side effects takes more and more energy and money. In the low-lying Netherlands, for example, we have to keep the pumps running to keep our feet dry; but the pumping causes subsidence and therefore simultaneously aggravates the problem.

3

The proportion of urbanites in 'the more developed regions' will grow from 78 per cent in 2013 to 85 per cent in 2050, an increase of 130 million people. At the same time, rural populations will decrease by 90 million people. Source: *World Urbanization Prospects, Revision 2014*, United Nations, Department of Economic and Social Affairs, Population Division, 2014.

4

Triumph of the City: How Our Greatest Invention Makes Us Richer, Smarter, Greener, Healthier, and Happier, Edward Glaeser, 2011.

Dynamic systems that move in sync with nature offer more solace than the isolated combating of undesirable consequences. Some cases require a small-scale approach, others a large-scale one, for example building grids to store and distribute solar or wind energy. Or the construction of the Great Green Wall, a 15-km-wide strip of forest to the south of the Sahara that is meant to put a stop to the encroaching desert, creating local employment at the same time. After all, local embeddedment and bottom-up influence are indispensable in large-scale projects.

The call for the construction of a robust, dynamic system does not equal a plea to simply 'live in harmony with nature'. The idea that 'primitive peoples' have a small ecological footprint is a romantic misconception: the inhabitants of North America managed to extinguish the majority of the large mammals that lived there many millennia ago, disafforesting the entire continent as they went along. It is the city – the apex of human inventiveness – that provides opportunities for solving the problems that face the ever-growing population of the world.

Under the flag of ecomodernism, a group of 19 leading green thinkers and scientists even makes out a case for human beings to withdraw into the cities to give nature free rein: 'Urbanization, the intensification of agriculture, nuclear energy, aquaculture and desalination are all processes with a proven potential to reduce human pressure on the environment and create more space for non-human species.'[5]

American-Lebanese philosopher Nassim Nicholas Taleb even carries things one step further: though he believes robustness and resilience will improve the systems in question, they remain focused on the absorption of shocks. Instead, he advocates 'anti-fragile' systems, systems that take advantage of chaos, unpredictability and disorder because it makes them stronger. Like evolution itself.[6]

The problems outlined above require a break with deductive modernism; we need to find sustainable solutions, circular and resilient, renewable and efficient, socially inclusive and diverse.

A one-sidedly technological approach that improves efficiency is not enough, we need smart urban planning that contributes to pleasant habitats, safe and tasty food, fast Internet, lively streets, inexpensive and reliable transport, clean water, meaningful employment, mixed neighbourhoods, and another thing or two. This smart urbanism goes beyond the smart cities many people have pinned their hopes on.[7]

The difference? A smart city will dynamically coordinate the provision of public transport, rental bicycles and parking spots, whereas smart urbanism focuses on the underlying system. In this example, it would require not only the construction of offices and shops near stations to ensure that people could get about on foot or

[5]
The starting point of the eco modernists is: '*A good Anthropocene demands that humans use their growing social, economic, and technological powers to make life better for people, stabilize the climate, and protect the natural world.*' See: www.ecomodernism.org.

[6]
Antifragile: Things That Gain from Disorder, Nassim Nichaloas Taleb, 2012.

[7]
Smart about Cities: Visualising the Challenge for 21st Century Urbanism, Ton Dassen and Maarten Haijer, PBL, 2015.

by bike, but also a mix of uses, densification and a fine-meshed structure.[8]

Many books have been written about the desired new direction, using ever-changing terms. These include Cradle to Cradle, but also Circular Economy, Transport Oriented Development, Efficient and Renewable Energy Systems, Closed-Loop Ecosystems and the by now widely established triplet People, Planet, Profit.

It is easy to add to this list, but the approach is essentially one that simultaneously sets its hopes on the physical and on the social system, one that has an eye for both the metabolism of the urban regions and for the way the people use these urban regions. Hans Bruyninckx, director of the European Environment Agency in Copenhagen, recently summed it up concisely: 'The debate about a sustainable society is also about the flow of Syrian refugees.'[9]

What's the what?

This book presents the results of the research group Future Urban Regions (FUR) in three parts, addressing the 'what', the 'how' and the 'who'. FUR chose the umbrella term 'healthy urbanity' and makes it concrete by distinguishing six themes: three physical and three social ones. Like any classification, this senary division is somewhat arbitrary: there could also be eight themes, or five, or seven. Their cohesion and interdependence make splitting hairs over the classification uninteresting: improvements in one area help in other areas, the cogs of the machine interlock.[10]

Part 1 focuses on the idea of healthy urbanity and its six themes: What is healthy urbanity?[11] The first three themes are derived from the physical domain: Resilient Infrastructure, Renewable Energy and Material Cycles.

1. Resilient Infrastructure. Like a head of lettuce or a human being, you can describe a city or a region as a metabolism, with inlet and outlet flows, transformation processes and by-products, rhythms and feedback processes. It is only possible to make a city function under extreme circumstances if you understand how the flows of water, waste, energy, traffic and food work. After hurricane Sandy, the city of New York decided not to ensconce itself behind a high dike, but to work with a combination of 'resistance, delay, storage and drainage' →p. 138.

2. Renewable Energy. Coal and oil made the industrial revolution possible, but even now, when we have long been in the grip of the next revolution, the digital one, we are still largely dependent on the use of finite energy sources. The realization of sustainability goals – both in terms of renewability

---

8

Meanwhile, three levels of smart cities are distinguished. The smart city 3.0 looks beyond technology and focuses on the participation and emancipation of citizens. Also see the practical example 'Smart City – Copenhagen' →**p. 58**.

9

'We're now exhausting 1.4 planet, it can't go on this way', *nrc Handelsblad*, 16 April 2016.

10

The 18 Practical Examples this book discusses also witness the relationship between the themes. They are classified according to the main theme to which they relate, but other topics to which they make a positive contribution are always indicated as well.

11

Each of the participating Academies of Architecture developed one of the themes: Amsterdam – Vital Economy; Arnhem – Healthy Living; Groningen – Renewable Energy; Maastricht – Sociocultural Solidarity; Tilburg – Resilient Infrastructure; Rotterdam – Material Cycles.

and in terms of limiting greenhouse gas emissions – is essential. The German municipality of Saerbeck, which produces renewable energy bottom-up, demonstrates one way to achieve this →p. 64.

3. <u>Material Cycles</u>. The earth may be an open system in terms of energy, but it is not in terms of resources: they are 'only available until they run out'. A circular economy, in which chains are closed and resources reused is therefore necessary. Difficult? Tropical swimming pool Tropicana in Rotterdam stood empty for years, until some entrepreneurs with an anti-squatting contract moved in and began cultivating mushrooms in its abandoned, damp basements. It proved the starting point for a completely circular enterprise →p. 160.

As was mentioned above, FUR also distinguishes three aspects of healthy urbanity's social component: Vital Economy, Healthy Living and Sociocultural Solidarity.

4. <u>Vital Economy</u>. Modern urban planning is based on the separation of functions: just before the Second World War, the Congrès Internationaux d'Architecture Moderne (CIAM) prescribed that dwelling, work, leisure and circulation each needed its own domain. That was perhaps a logical response to the polluted, overcrowded cities of the industrial revolution, but unfortunately the solution turned out to have serious side-effects, such as the disappearance of production from the city. Now that both production techniques and traffic have become much cleaner, the path to more mixed cities lies open. The example of the London High Streets shows the vitality that hides in organically grown, 'old-fashioned' city streets →p. 170.

5. <u>Healthy Living</u>. Now that the city has definitively become the habitat of humans, it is expected to offer not only employment and protection, but also a healthy habitat in both the physical and the psychological sense. Healthy for people, furthermore, as well as healthy for the animals and plants that increasingly take refuge in the city. A green city encourages movement and recreation, provides tranquillity and relaxation. In Roombeek, the Enschede neighbourhood that was destroyed by a fireworks disaster in 2000, this was a reason to restructure the local school's kiss-and-ride area as a running track →p. 100.

6. <u>Sociocultural Solidarity</u>. The anonymous metropolis – such as Franz Biberkopf's Berlin – is as much a cliché as the working-class area where people share life's joys and sorrows – 'Sometimes you want to go / Where everybody knows your name / And they're always glad you came / You want to be where you can see / Our troubles are all the same;'[12] It is clear, however, that social contacts improve

12
'Where Everybody Knows Your Name', Gary Portnoy.

liveability and stimulate citizen participation. The example of the *Baugruppen* in Berlin shows that the creation of collective spaces can spontaneously contribute to the integration of refugees →p. 108.

As the above examples show, the focus of FUR so far has been on the Western world, or rather on cities in developed countries that have a sizeable urban middle class.[13] The problems of Third World countries and their slums proved so different that it was not useful to integrate them in the study. Still, there are plenty of ambitions left. What contribution can we expect research by design to make?

How?

It is possible, however, to outline the contours of the design research using a small thought experiment: 'If a building is the answer, what was the question?'

Designers are traditionally presented with clear questions: once a programme of requirements has been formulated, designers use their talent and experience to come up with an answer – a building, a park, a structural plan, a piece of furniture, a motorway. However, the tough problems the world faces today do not come equipped with a programme of requirements. Worse still: there are often not even any commissioners involved, at least, not in the traditional sense of the word: people with the position and the means to realize promising solutions.

Research by design is therefore primarily research; the design is merely the instrument used to carry out that research. The aim is to not only find the right solution and the accompanying programme of requirements, but to also find (coalitions of) commissioners. Whereas traditionally, designs come into play in a very late stage of the process, research by design can be used when many aspects are still diffuse and uncertain.[14]

Research by design boasts a long tradition in the Netherlands. The exhibition 'Nederland Nu Als Ontwerp' (NNAO) is considered the kick-off of this approach.[15] In the middle of the economic crisis of the 1980s, when spatial planning had deteriorated into a technocratic jigsaw puzzle, the foundation also named NNAO commissioned the creation of four scenarios for the development of the Netherlands towards 2050. Suddenly it became clear that there were options and that by using design, ordinary citizens could also form an image of that future.

As it turned out, using research by design was the best possible way of showing people 'what they *could* want', a visualization of the future that could be used to mobilize people. According to Dirk Sijmons, former Government Advisor on Landscape and one of the designers that participated at the time, this exhibition 'harshly reminded planning of its design background'.[16]

13
'Word-wide, the urban middle classes will grow from 1.8 billion people in 2010 to 4.9 billion in 2030. Source: *The Emerging Middle Class in Developing Countries*, OECD Development Centre, Working Paper No. 285, 2010.

14
See the left-hand section of the DTP Diagram →p. 128.

15
A systematic, philosophical exploration of the differences and similarities between research by design and traditional research is found in the treatise *Een kleine methodologie van ontwerpend onderzoek* (1992) written by urban planner Taeke de Jong.

16
IABR-2016-*The Next Economy*, George Brugmans, Jolanda van Dinteren, Maarten Hajer, 2016.

It was the International Architecture Biennale Rotterdam (IABR) that further developed and sharpened the design research instrument.[17] From an exhibition that presented research, it grew into a continuously growing research by design process aimed at an 'inclusive agenda' that opposes unbridled liberalism and urban development that is dictated by the real estate market.

According to Maarten Hajer, head curator of the IABR 2016, designers are good at formulating 'imaginaries'. The Dutch word for imaginaries fascinated him, because in this language they are called 'mental images': the images produced by mental processes, the images that colour our thought. Mental images allow a common view of reality, a framework within which to think, and they create a vision to pursue. In short, they create 'meaning, longing and confidence'.

Mental images can be grand and comprehensive – the view that man was the radiant centre of the world marked the beginning of modernity, the earth photographed from the moon represented the realization that the earth is fragile and finite and paved the way for the environmental movement. But they can also be a lot smaller and more local: the second-hand houseboats that members of De Ceuvel, a breeding ground in Amsterdam, had towed onto a contaminated dock site immediately show that time and temporality are fundamental charac-teristics of their approach.[18]

Mental images can produce change precisely because they connect the present and the future. 'I am convinced that we will need the inspiration of the designer to loosen the nuts and bolts of the modernistic system,' Hajer writes, and his words chafe all the more because he is the first IABR-curator who is a scientist rather than an artist.[19]

FUR not only examined healthy urbanity (What is it?), but emphatically also investigated the instrument of design research itself (How is it conducted?). The meth-ods and techniques that are discussed in Part 2 have been tested in practice. What is special about FUR is that both the lecturer and the researchers, who each took an Academy of Architecture under their wing, work as architect/urbanists and have their own offices.[20] And being fed by the field is essential to design research in which, after all, professionalism, experience and intui-tion play an important part.

As sociologist Richard Sennett shows in a comprehen-sive study, craftsmen are more capable of connecting the mind and the body – more specifically, the hand – than anybody else.[21] They perfect their work for its own sake, not to earn money or prestige. Indeed, rather than com-placently looking for solutions to the problems at hand they – intentionally or unintentionally – look for new,

17
The theme of the IABR 2016 is The Next Economy. Previous editions addressed Urban by Nature (2014), Making City (2012), Open City (2009), Power (2007), The Flood (2005) and Mobility (2003).

18
See: www.deceuvel.nl.

19
Maarten Hajer is Professor of Urban Futures at the University of Utrecht and was the director of the PBL Netherlands Environmental Assessment Agency from 2008 to 2015.

20
They are introduced by means of short portraits on page →p. 21 and the following. In these portraits, they explicitly address their professional experiences with research by design.

21
In The Craftsman (2008) Richard Sennett uses a broad definition of craftsmanship: it includes playing the cello and repairing cars as well as the programming of computers and the raising of children.

underlying problems to continue to unravel the essence of their work. You see the same enthusiasm at the Academies of Architecture, where architects and urban planners transfer their experiences with research by design to fellow professionals who want to develop their careers, after all, the students themselves are professionals.[22]

This book shows both concrete designs for healthy urbanity and explains how design research works in the field. 'Using new research methods, we can figure out how space is used, what performance we expect of it and which smart connections and alliances we need to achieve that performance,' says lector Eric Frijters. 'You don't design a building, at least not to begin with, you design a better research question.' Researcher Thijs van Spaandonk says it is the essence of design research: 'To use the design to question, to investigate, to be surprised and to overcome your own aesthetical preferences.'

Design research implies that designers are involved in the process much sooner than is traditionally the case, long before there is an actual commission, which in some cases fails to materialize at all. Still, research by design is very much about the here and now. FUR researcher Willemijn Lofvers: 'Designing is traditionally about the future, about what could or should be. However, it is much more important to examine what there is now and what we need today. We need to bring the future closer.' Colleague researcher Ady Steketee adds: 'You imagine visions and use them to assess a possible future. That means it is a way to feed political decision making, because research by design is by definition local and political.'

Research by design is a way to unearth a commission and at the same time forge a coalition that can do something with it. It is not only a search for the hard, spatial side and for the metabolism of flows that are relevant to that side, but also for the way people use the space. And for the right scale to circle the problem before attacking it.

It is dangerous to focus only on the problematic side. Not only because it deters potential partners – too difficult, too negative, too big – but also because it narrows the mind. A more positive outlook not only opens the mind, it also widens ones perspective of the system as a whole.

In addition to collecting data and analysing current problems, it is therefore necessary to identify opportunities and trace anecdotes – short stories that cannot yet be captured in hard data, but that promise change.[23] And this process keeps repeating itself, for research by design is iterative: the output of step one is the input of step two.

This requires perseverance as well as humility. Steketee: 'Even when they carry out research by design, designers will be designers – rather than researchers. There is no way we can say anything about the global economy, but you can expect us to document our sources properly, to explain what we base ourselves on.'

22
To be admitted to an Academy of Architecture, students need to work in the profession. They can pursue a Master's degree in architecture (MARCH), urban planning (MURB) or landscape architecture (MLA). During their studies they participate in a design atelier each semester. The ateliers that relate to FUR are described in Appendix 1 →**p. 296**.

23
The DOCA method (Data, Opportunities, Challenges and Anecdotes) is explained in Part 2 →**p. 131**.

Who?

Coalition forming is one of the most elusive and complex aspects of
design research. Who do you need to carry out research by design and
subsequently transform its outcomes into action? Part 3 presents the
'who' question and is, precisely because it is a pre-eminently contextual
question, unable to answer it univocally. Instead, the question is defined,
the process explored.

The range of possible partners is wide and a thorough analysis of
interests may yield unexpected ones. Such as insurance companies,
which can combat obesity and other health problems by investing in
residential environments and in the long term reduce their expenses
that way. Or car rental companies with electric cars that make their
batteries available for the storage of energy from the grid – a way to
connect the transport and energy networks.

The reverse is also possible: architects can appropriate tasks such as
project development and financing and act as their own commissioners
to realize their designs, perhaps forming a CPO or collective private
commissioning party in combination with other self-builders. Voilà:
the architect/developer is born, or rather makes a comeback.

Stakeholders are identified on the basis of both the subject of the
research by design in question and the phase it is in. Over time, parties
drop out and new ones join in. In the best-case scenario this selection
process slowly produces an increasingly well-defined group that has
sufficient enforcement power and the sense of urgency to tackle the
problem.

FUR researcher Sandra van Assen warns that designers tend to look
for an inspiring, innovative solution to each problem, while this is
often unnecessary. 'If the stakeholders are not convinced of the need
for change, you should focus your design activities on that level.' She
likens the process to Maslow's hierarchy of need: first the necessity,
then the functional demands, subsequently the spatial integration, next
the adding of value and right at the top is innovation. 'Good designers
don't need to be at the top of the ladder, they figure out what is needed.'

The 'problem-looking-for-an-owner' process does not necessarily
lead to a commission for the designers involved: they can be superseded
over time. FUR researcher Marco Broekman: 'In our research project
about the possibilities of small-scale vocational education in Amsterdam, we found that 80 per cent of the demand was actually not spatial
at all. After the final discussion with the commissioner, I thought
perhaps we should not get involved. Now the roles are reversed: if the
client wants a festival and to that end needs to set up a couple of buildings, he calls us in to bat ideas around.'[24]

Lofvers, too, emphasizes that designers are not
necessarily pivotal in research by design: 'The focal
point is always changing, the hierarchy disappearing,
is it increasingly about relating to society.' That also
means insecurity: 'Architects lose their "artistic
engineer" foothold.'

24

The research involved, into
small-scale vocational education,
was commissioned by the Creative Industry Fund NL and was
presented during the IABR 2016.

Sometimes design research emerges unprompted, without the intervention of a designer. In the Betuwe, an initiative for the production of renewable energy grew into a group of 120 involved entrepreneurs, citizens and governments active in the fields of wind cooperatives, private disability insurance funds, the reuse of an abandoned swimming pool and even large-scale area development. The group is called Dirk III, after the eleventh-century count Dirk the Third who gave his serfs land in exchange for a modest share in their crops – a kind of cooperative agriculture.

And research by design can also simply mean that you do not intervene, as French architecture office Lacaton & Vassal demonstrated in the mid-1990s after it had been commissioned to beautify the Place Léon Aucoc in Bordeaux. The firm's research showed that the square was perfect. The architects' advice was: do nothing, or rather, do nothing new, use the available budget for maintenance.[25] They got their way, and Lacaton & Vassal presents the design on its website marked 'completed'. So research by design does not have to result in a design.

Critical Notes

Putting topics on the agenda, explaining, inspiring, representing, innovating, connecting, exploring, uniting – design research's list of claims is a long one. But naturally it is not a universal remedy. Research by design comes with serious risks.

Finding the right scale, for example, is not an easy task to say the least. Collective provisions for renewable energy, for example, are much cheaper than individual solutions, but at the same time frustrate experimentation, innovation and commitment. Take district heating: to heat dwellings, the residual heat of companies is led through a separate network of underground pipes. This sounds ideal, but the network's long cost recovery period and the mandatory participation create a monopoly and cause residents to lose interest. Interestingly, a group of self-building residents in Buiksloterham, a collective-private development in Amsterdam-Noord with a particularly sustainable agenda, managed to shirk the mandatory connection to the district heating system.[26]

Mental images can also acquire a connotation that is very different from the one the designer had in mind. The MVRDV study into intensive cattle farming yielded valuable insights, for example that it is necessary to close production cycles. But even 15 years after its launch, the image of the more than 600-m-high 'pig flats' on the Maasvlakte is still the weapon of choice of factory farming opponents'.[27]

Problems also arise if governments give commissions without actually planning to use the results. In such cases research by design can degenerate into a reason for endless studies and decision postponing and thus

25

'Not doing/Overdoing: "Omission" and "Excess"', Robin Wilson. In: *Architectural Design, Special Issue: The Architecture of Transgression*, Volume 83, Issue 6, 2013.

26

The municipality of Amsterdam wants to quadruple the number of dwellings with district heating to 230,000 in 2040. To achieve this, connection is mandatory in Buiksloterham as well, 'unless the ground lessee realizes a more sustainable alternative or builds energy-neutrally'. Also see Part 3, Chapter 'A Metabolic Square' →p. 208.

27

See: www.bit.ly/2avhnoK.

lead to stagnation. The deserved fame Dutch research by design has acquired contrasts sharply with the meagre results the country achieves in terms of liveability and sustainability.[28]

But these criticisms and pitfalls do not negate the need to tackle the problems the world is facing, nor the options designers have to contribute to solutions. Strikingly, Robbert Dijkgraaf, one of the most renowned scientists in the Netherlands, even advocates the design approach for 'hard' scientific research. 'The scientist becomes a kind of designer,' he recently said in an interview, 'you design using the building blocks of nature, and you go back to studying your design.'[29]

28

The Monitor Duurzaam Nederland 2014 compares the Dutch performance with that of other European countries. It uses 14 domains. Especially in terms of climate and energy, biodiversity and landscape, of local environmental quality and on trade, aid and resources, the Dutch scores are lower than the European average. See: www.bit.ly/1NJs5b8.

29

Robbert Dijkgraaf currently heads the Institute for Advanced Studies at Princeton University. The interview Lex Bohlmeijer had with him on 27 February 2016 is broadcast at www.bit.ly/1Y6lTvK.

The Team

Sandra van Assen

'A good design supports the process and that's all right with me: I'm process-oriented rather than object-oriented. I don't mind whether or not I design the most beautiful railway zone in the world, I'd rather focus on strategic questions. The essence of a design or vision has to be both clear and abstract to ensure that it can exercise influence for a long time.'

She introduced the undivided landscape as a guideline for the infrastructure of the central axis of Friesland ten years ago: 'Recently, someone explained to me how important that is. That means things have come full circle.'

The solitary designer? Not her cup of tea, researching and counselling in a team fascinates and stimulates. 'I was instructed to draft a guideline for the design of solar fields in the countryside. Rather than pick up a pencil, I organized solar tables with initiators, planners, sustainability experts and designers. During the first six months, this requires patience – Why does it have to be so complicated? – but now there's laughter at the table. So we work our way through things and create a guideline that everybody owns.'

She has noticed that designers often find it hard to face undesirable outcomes of research by design, while these in fact offer interesting insights. 'A major question for me is how objective research by design is. Subjectivity is not a problem, but it does have to be explicit: communicate that there are other options.'

Sandra van Assen (1973) is an architect and urban planner. Her urban planning networking office focuses on research by design and counselling, locally and internationally. She is pursuing her PhD on interdisciplinary spatial quality counselling at Delft University of Technology. She is collaborating with northern research centres and is a visiting lecturer at Windesheim Zwolle and the Politecnico di Milano. She is a researcher and lecturer at the Academy of Architecture in Groningen.

Van Assen was responsible for the theme *Sustainable Energy*. She led the design ateliers *Energy Transition Region Groningen*, *Energy Transition and Healthy Ageing* and *Energy: Transition and Transformation 2016*. Together with Eric Frijters and Willemijn Lofvers she wrote the main text of Part 3 as well as the Practical Examples *Klimakommune – Saerbeck* →p. 64, *'What If' Scenarios – Leiden* →p. 148 and *Energy Workplace – Friesland* →p. 226.

Tijs van den Boomen

'The amount of information designers can gather from a drawing or sketch never ceases to amaze me. I see the lines and roughly understand what it will look like, but the depth of the thinking, the choices that have been made and especially whether it is actually possible are beyond me.'

He has noticed that the way designers think is different from the way language-oriented people think: 'Sometimes it's like designers come from Venus and we come from Mars, or vice versa. If you point out to them that there are contradictions or ambiguities in a text, they say: "Hold on, I'll draw it so you'll understand".'

'Just like words, designs can carry people away and stir them up and also just like words, designs can be untruthful. That carries both the strength and the risk of research by design. This book is about its strength.'

Tijs van den Boomen (1960) is a journalist and city researcher. He focuses on the public space, on the everyday spaces to which your citizenship grants you access. In addition to his work for *NRC Handelsblad*, *De Groene Amsterdammer* and *Het Parool* his titles include *Asfaltreizen* and *De mobiele stad* (with Ton Venhoeven).

Van den Boomen edited the book. He also wrote the introductory essay and the portraits of the team members, except those of co-editors Guido van Eijck and Saskia Naafs – who of course wrote theirs themselves.

Marco Broekman

'My office works at the interface of urban design, strategy and research by design. The first is classic: there's a clear commissioner, a clear site, a clear challenge and a clear timeframe. Strategic projects involve an unclear challenge, but you still know who you're doing it for and where. In research by design, nothing is clearly defined: neither the site nor the commissioner or problem owner, nor the time frame, nor the type of solution.' He likes it nevertheless – or perhaps that is precisely why he likes it: 'Research by design is pre-eminently suitable to provide different stakeholders with an understanding of the opportunities and problems of challenges. You can use scenarios to force choices and connect parties.'

He has found that the different challenges his office accepts mutually influence each other. 'In urban plans, we use elements of research by design to increase the scope of the project. Or we use more abstract ideas from the field of energy transition, urban economy or vocational education in ongoing concrete projects.'

Sometimes research by design implies forcing commissioners to choose: 'A shrinking region in the east of the country asked us how they could best advertise their vacant real estate. We soon found out that every core in the region had new-build projects in the pipeline and were therefore indirectly drawing away all potential strength. In such a case you need to confront people: ultimately, research by design is also politically charged.'

Marco Broekman (1973) is an architect and urban planner. He owns marco.broekman urbanism research architecture, an internationally operating office with ten employees. He is a visiting lecturer at the Academies of Architecture of Amsterdam, Rotterdam and Maastricht, rmit University in Melbourne and the University of Lund.

Broekman was responsible for the theme *Vital Economy*. He led the design ateliers *Ontwerplab Vrieheide*, *Zaans Next Economy* and *SouthWest Works!* Together with Eric Frijters he wrote both the main text of Part 1 and the Conclusions. He also wrote the Practical Examples *Inhabited Industrial Area – Barcelona* →**p. 88**, *High Streets – London* →**p. 170** and *Industrial Curator – Arnhem* →**p. 248**.

Guido van Eijck

'When I started to work on this book, I had quite straightforward ideas about designers. I just imagined they were people that sat behind drawing boards churning out sketches for buildings or urban areas. I had no idea they also dealt with complex issues like the transition to renewable energy or combating climate change and flooding. Or with small-scale initiatives that contribute to a healthier city at the level of the neighbourhood or the building.'

'These themes are too big to simply bring to the drawing board, yet too urgent to only discuss at the conference table. As researchers, designers have a pivotal role: they collect the various information flows and subsequently convert them into concrete plans. The task that fell to me was to reduce all that information into clear chapters for this book.'

As a journalist, Guido van Eijck (1987) writes for, among others, *De Groene Amsterdammer* and *de Volkskrant* and as an editor, he was involved in the journalistic start-up Yournalism. He was co-editor of *Het Oostblokboek* (2014), a historical travel guide about architecture and other remains of socialism in Eastern Europe.

Van Eijck edited all of the practical examples of *Resilient Infrastructure* →**p. 58**, →**p. 138**, →**p. 216**, *Renewable Energy* →**p. 64**, →**p. 148**, →**p. 226** and *Material Cycle* →**p. 76**, →**p. 160**, →**p. 236**.

Eric Frijters

'I believe in complexity: good research by design will continue to expand, you make it complicated. Cycle after cycle, your knowledge improves. This process of endlessly puzzling your way through every scale level is what fascinates me.'

Frijters discovered design research by chance as he was working on his thesis. 'Rather than a museum on a mountain, I wanted to design something that had social impact, so I immersed myself in the reorganization of Dutch agriculture. I kept asking professors at Wageningen University to shoot holes in my design proposals and that way, I got a feel for the metabolism of the agricultural system. '

His fascination for research by design lasted and he began to explore the metabolism of cities, regions and entire countries. 'Urban planners have always relied on assumptions and regulations, but we are going to have to learn to deal with hard data. We have to shift from "location, location, location" to "use, performance, location". That doesn't mean presentations shouldn't be poetic, after all, that helps us come to grips with this strange beast called metabolism. It's especially the connection between knowledge and art that fascinates me.'

He sees his research group and this book as forms of research by design: 'When I applied for the job of lector there was nothing. We started looking for our research subject together with the academies, researchers, regional stakeholders and students. We've endlessly refined the models.'

Eric Frijters (1972) studied architecture at Eindhoven University of Technology with side trips to Karlsruhe and Amsterdam (philosophy). He wrote for magazines such as *Archis* and *de Architect* and contributed to books such as *Tussenland* and *The Metabolism of Albania*. He and Olv Klijn founded Fabric, an office with five employees that specializes in research by design and won, among other awards, the *Prix de Rome*.

Frijters is the lecturer responsible for Future Urban Regions. He developed the research by design models, wrote the main text of Part 1 together with Marco Broekman and that of Part 2 with Willemijn Lofvers. He wrote the main text of Part 3 together with Sandra van Assen and Willemijn Lofvers and, finally, wrote the conclusions together with Marco Broekman.

Marieke Kums

'You only get to know the preconditions of a project when you use design to test them. That's how you find out whether you can work with them or want to counter them. It's a crucial issue, for you often have to change preconditions to really tackle a problem. Just like scientists break conventions to make progress. In my case the process is sometimes rational but also often very intuitive. I think that in that sense, research by design and design research are similar.'

Wouldn't that be considered callous among researching designers? 'Well no, "research" represents the creation of new insights and "designing" the creation of new objects or spaces. To me, changing the order of the words doesn't change their meaning.'

Research by design can also be used to attract new stakeholders and thus new budgets: 'Designing and visualizing ideas allows different parties to efficiently participate in the process. Dutch designers are good at this, because they think in broad terms and are sensitive to the interests of other parties. Call it the polder model, if you like.'

Marieke Kums (1979) studied architecture and urban planning at Delft University of Technology, MIT and Harvard. She worked in Japan and has had her own office in Rotterdam since 2010: Studio Maks. Together with international teams of designers, she works on projects on scales ranging from product design to urban planning. She conducts research at the Academy of Architecture of Tilburg.

Kums was responsible for the theme *Resilient Infrastructure*. She led the ateliers *Water Works* →p. 297 and *Eindhoven 2050* →p. 297.

Willemijn Lofvers

'Even though research by design is my office's core business, it's still difficult to pin down what it is.' As an example, she mentions the Wallis block in the neglected Rotterdam district Spangen, where new residents were given rundown properties for free on the condition that they renovate them and live in them for a number of years. 'Once they'd finished their homes, they began doing up the gardens, then the public green and they're now working to improve the fringes of the district. Is that still research by design? And does it really matter?'

She thinks it's essential that designers have a modest attitude: 'We have to go beyond aesthetics; it's about starting with nothing, trying things out. As designers we don't have primacy, this is about widely shared processes and so you're getting to know the existing force field. What we can do, thanks to our expressive skills, is focus those processes: that constitutes our added value.'

Willemijn Lofvers (1965) studied at the Willem de Kooning Academy and at the Academy of Architecture of Rotterdam. She conducts research into urban renewal and rural restructuring, for example in the form of 'Stadsklassen'. In addition, she is pursuing her PhD at the Delft University of Technology, studying the ownership of urban developments, and lectures at the Academy of Architecture of Rotterdam.

Lofvers was responsible for the theme *Material Cycle*. She led the design ateliers *Food Hub Spaanse Polder*, *The Resource Factory* and *Waste as a Resource*. She wrote the main text of Part 2 together with Eric Frijters and that of Part 3 together with Sandra van Assen and Eric Frijters. She also wrote the practical examples *Urban Farming – The Hague* →p. 76, *Blue Economy – Rotterdam* →p. 160 and *Do it Yourself – Liverpool* →p. 236.

Saskia Naafs

'I once had the opportunity to witness the redevelopment of a square in Amsterdam-Oost at close range. I saw how hard it was for the designer to take everything into account: the city wants a beautiful yet vandal-proof and maintenance-friendly square; the elderly want to quietly sit on benches surrounded by greenery; the young want to play football and basketball at the same time; local residents don't approve of all that noise. Then there are the mothers who want their children to be able to play safely and the loitering teens that always break things.'

Because all factors had been identified properly in advance, the designer managed to realize an attractive and well-used square, 'but of course not before the neighbourhood had harshly commented on the plan a couple of times'.

'It's just a small example, but it does indicate that good design benefits from research. And yet there will be a point, in both research and in design, and in editing alike, when you have to cut the knot and say: "Now, I know best".'

Saskia Naafs (1984) is a journalist and researcher; she focuses on urban development, housing and real estate. She is part of the platform for investigative journalism Investico and regularly writes for *De Groene Amsterdammer* and *Het Parool*. For the International New Town Institute she co-wrote, among other publications, *New Town Roots* and *De Vinexmensen*.

Naafs edited all the practical examples of *Vital Economy* →p. 88, →p. 170, →p. 248, *Healthy Living* →p. 100, →p. 178, →p. 258 and *Sociocultural Solidarity* →p. 108, →p. 188, →p. 268.

Thijs van Spaandonk

'A good designer produces a product that meets the expectations of the client, that is the "expected".

A very good one creates the "expected unexpected"; only the best manage to create the "unexpected unexpected". The latter is the potential of research by design.' Like *The Smog Free Tower* by Daan Roosegaarde, that transforms polluted air into jewellery? 'No, that's a very cool project, but it doesn't tackle the underlying causes.'

He thinks social systems that come to an end need research by design to give them a new impulse. 'It doesn't have to lead to a new building or design. Sometimes a "serious game" is better, for example to provide entrepreneurs with an action perspective in the uncertain global force field: what it is they can do when a spanner is thrown into the works.'

He doesn't see this open attitude in all designers by a long shot. 'Many designers only join in to eventually win the commission for the building. This doesn't do justice to research by design.'

Thijs van Spaandonk (1981) is an architect. His company BRIGHT is part of the internationally operation design group The Cloud Collective. He often collaborates with non-traditional parties in the field of spatial planning. He is a visiting lecturer at the Academies of Architecture of Arnhem and Tilburg and at Hong Kong University.

Van Spaandonk wrote the practical examples *Smart City 3.0 – Copenhagen* →**p. 58** and *Rebuild by Design – New York* →**p. 138**, as well as all of the 33 design proposals plus the descriptions of the 18 design ateliers.

Ady Steketee

'Salvador Dali, Rem Koolhaas and the Das brothers,' he volunteers when asked for research by design pioneers: 'Designers bring imagination, that's their gift. They can imagine possible futures, which stakeholders can subsequently assess. Because the question what future is the best is a political question.'

Research by design isn't all that new, he says: 'Under normal circumstances designers would always examine the wider context to determine the scope of a problem. For this they used tools such as thinking in scenarios and mapping. This used to be called analysis; the difference is that it is done much more systematically these days. This not only improves the quality, but also the transparency and the verifiability. And that's essential.' Also new are the high expectations in administrative circles. Somewhat sceptical: 'What matters is whether we can forge coalitions, otherwise we have nothing but hot air.'

Ady Steketee (1960) sees every building challenge, including new construction, as a transformation process. The traces and movements of people, goods, ideas and cultures are central in this respect. In addition to his work for Marx & Steketee architecten he is active as an author, lecturer (at almost every academy and university in the Netherlands) and supervisor of quality teams.

Steketee was responsible for the theme *Healthy Living*. He led the design ateliers *The Ecological City*, *Sports and Exercise in Public Places* and *Sports and Exercise II* and wrote the practical examples *A Place to Play – Enschede* →**p. 100**, *Serious Game – Oosterwold* →**p. 178** and *Biodiverse City – Eindhoven* →**p. 258**.

Franz Ziegler
'I'm an analytical designer
originally, that means
design research, which
is something very dif-
ferent from research by
design. I only learnt the other properly at
FUR.' It improved his knowledge: 'Design
research hands you the tools to inter-
rogate the commission: Is it right? But
research by design takes things one step
further, it challenges you to ask fundamental questions and to explore latent
challenges.'

He's still critical, though: 'My FUR
theme, Sociocultural Solidarity, quickly
draws attention to participation and
bottom-up developments. But in Zuid-
Limburg, where I often work, everything
was always top-down, so you have to
integrate that in your approach and strategy. Also, in research by design, you
always look closely at the context, without ideological bias.'

Ziegler puts into practice what he
professes with words. When the office
building next to his office came on the
market, he founded the Residential Coop
'Buur zoekt Buur', the starting point of
an open process to enrich the centre of
Rotterdam with a collective residential
block. And in a district of Maastricht he is
the foreman of Vrienden van Pottenberg,
inspired by his great example, Friends of
the High Line.

Franz Ziegler (1966) is an architect and urban
planner with a taste for redevelopment and
transformations of existing buildings and
urban fabrics. The eight employees that work
at his Rotterdam office once again regularly
draw by hand. He teaches at the Academies of
Architecture of Amsterdam and Maastricht.
   Ziegler was responsible for the theme
Sociocultural Solidarity. He led the design
ateliers *Connected in Parkstad* and *Parkstad
Connects*. He wrote the Practical Examples
Baugruppe – Berlin →**p. 108**, *High Line –
New York* →**p. 188**, *Natuurderij – Deventer* →**p. 216**
and *Broedstraten – Amsterdam-Noord* →**p. 268**.

Part 1 – What

Traditionally, spatial designers – as the name implies – focus on space. However, to understand healthy urbanity it is essential to also look at the metabolism of urban regions. Not only at physical flows, but at social and societal ones as well. This double metabolism leads to the formulation of six themes: three physical and three social ones.

In Part 1, FUR researchers argue in favour of examining the urban regions in systemic terms: What boundaries do such regions encounter and which laws govern them? It is an account that may sound apocalyptical and depressing to some: What in the world can we do about that?

But don't despair, studying the flows of the urban metabolism provides opportunities for improvement. Working on healthy urbanity, FUR not only takes the flows of energy, resources, water and waste into account (the traditional domain of the metabolism approach), but also the flows of people, goods, data and ideas.

In conclusion, the six substantive FUR themes are separately discussed and explored in depth.

30

Earth overshoot day, the day on which we have used up more natural resources than the planet can renew in a year, falls earlier every year. In 2016 we already reached that point on 8 August. See: www.overshootday.org.

Flows as a New Dimension

The world population continues to grow and by 2050, there will be more than 9.5 billion people. That is a third more than there are now, while we are already structurally depleting the earth.[30] Swedish scientist Johan Rockström warns against the insidious destruction of our planet. He defines critical boundaries for nine processes that determine

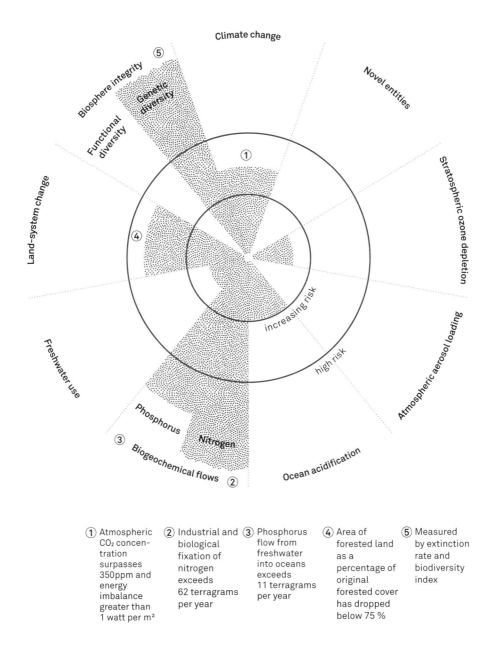

① Atmospheric CO₂ concentration surpasses 350ppm and energy imbalance greater than 1 watt per m²	② Industrial and biological fixation of nitrogen exceeds 62 terragrams per year	③ Phosphorus flow from freshwater into oceans exceeds 11 terragrams per year	④ Area of forested land as a percentage of original forested cover has dropped below 75 %	⑤ Measured by extinction rate and biodiversity index

fig. 1 — The nine planetary boundaries

its liveability.[31] Three of those – biodiversity, climate change and the global nitrogen cycle – have certainly been crossed already. Of a number of others, such as chemical pollution or atmospheric aerosol loading, we know nothing. That does not mean we are nowhere near those boundaries, just that we have no information about them.

Crossing these boundaries creates the risk that the earth's system, or the complex of interactions between life and environment, is put off balance permanently. When exactly that will happen is difficult to predict, especially since the processes involved are interconnected and mutually reinforcing.[32] Moreover, many of the earth's systems respond abruptly: a development can elapse apparently continuously for a long time, only to reach its tipping point and suddenly change. That is why it is important to set boundary values at a safe distance from so-called threshold values.

If we continue to consume resources, materials and energy at today's speed, Rockström predicts, we will rapidly reach the boundaries of the possibility of life on earth. Given the fact that urban regions contribute hugely to that pollution, they are the obvious places in which to intervene.

Economies of Scale

The city is one of the most successful human phenomena and it does not look as if its hegemony is about to end any time soon. Cities continue to grow; the 600 largest cities already house a quarter of the world's population. However, this immense growth has a downside. Many cities are in deltas because from time immemorial, that is where there has been sufficient energy, water and food. But it is precisely in those deltas that the growth of urban regions causes a lot of pressure on the amount of available arable land, vital green spaces and clean drinking water. Urban regions also gobble up huge amount of materials and energy and are responsible for three quarters of all greenhouse gases from fossil fuels.

The famous British scientist Geoffrey West is a theoretical physicist who studies the mathematical laws that govern biological and urban systems. His research has produced some interesting insights. For example, the cells of mice have to work harder to process nutrients than those of dogs, humans, elephants or whales. The connection is *sub*linear: if an animal is twice as big, it will use *less* than twice as much energy.

As it turns out, this economy of scale applies to cities as well. As a city doubles in size, the number of petrol stations only needs to increase by 85 per cent. That same percentage applies to the length of roads, the number of electricity cables and so on.

31

The nine critical processes are climate change, loss of biodiversity, the nitrogen and phosphorus cycles, atmospheric ozone depletion, ocean acidification, freshwater use, land use, chemical pollution and atmospheric aerosol loading. 'A safe operating space for humanity', J. Rockström et al. In: *Nature* 461, 472-475, 24 September 2009.

32

The nine boundaries are not undisputed. Scientists such as Linus Blomqvist and Erle Ellis argue that though there are tipping points, they are local and there is no evidence that overrunning them will put the earth's entire system off balance.

Among socioeconomic effects, West finds another connection: here, the relationship is *super*linear rather than *sub*linear. In other words: as the city doubles in size, the number of highly educated people *more* than doubles. The gain is always 15 per cent, whether you look at wages, the number of patents, or at urban facilities such as theatres. Unfortunately, this law also applies to less pleasant matters: crime and influenza epidemics also receive a 15 per cent bonus and therefore grow more than average.

Due to this superlinear connection, socioeconomic systems like cities evade the growth curve of organic beings. We humans are subject to the sublineair connection and grow excessively in early life, then growth slows down and finally, we die. Cities are different, they grow exponentially: their size skyrockets, ever faster and ever steeper. That is not good news, because it means they are destined to collapse. The only solutions, says West, is innovation: we have to start new curves over and over again in order not to perish, leap forward though nobody knows where we will end up.

Flows

Spatial design (read: architecture, urban planning and landscape architecture) is thus facing a number of additional challenges to say the least. Besides fulfilling the classic task of providing spaces for people, businesses and recreation, it is now emphatically expected to provide a spatial answer to the question of how we should deal with finite supplies of resources, materials and energy in rapidly growing cities. In other words, to answer the question of how to organize the urban (eco) system more efficiently. This requires a shift from an exclusively spatial approach to the development of spaces to an approach that pays more attention to their functioning.

The field of activity of designers is defined by two forces: the top-down agendas and ambitions of governments, public organizations and major market parties on the one hand and the bottom-up ideals and wishes of citizens and local organizations on the other. In this area of tension, the designer traditionally only disposes of spatial instruments: buildings and squares, shops and streets, parks and car parks.

But designers no longer only face the challenge of examining the physical side of the city: more and more often, the performance of the city as an (eco)system is the subject of design challenges. To be able to say something about the way the city is used, designers add an extra angle to the field of activity diagram, namely *flows*.

Landscape architect Dirk Sijmons thinks that ensuring that urbanites have access to the basic necessities of life, such as water, food and energy, is among the most important challenges designers face.[33]

Using smart design strategies that are based on efficiency and collaboration, the metabolism of the urban

33
Dirk Sijmons was head curator of the International Architecture Biennale Rotterdam 2014. Its theme was *Urban by Nature*.

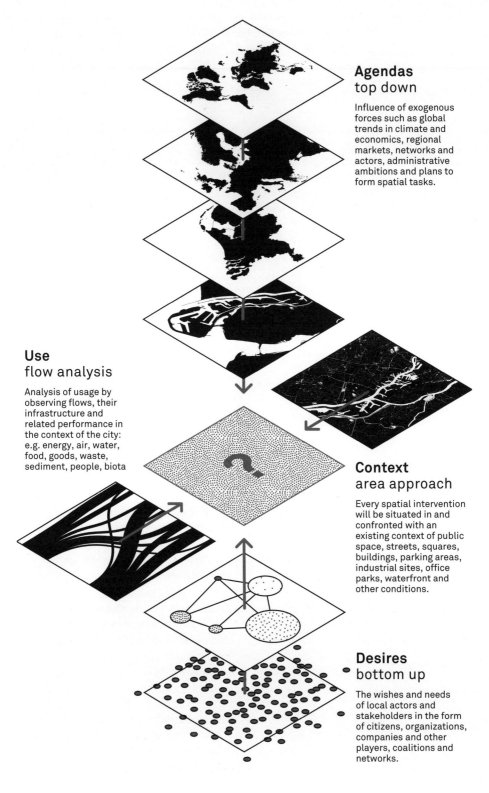

Agendas
top down

Influence of exogenous forces such as global trends in climate and economics, regional markets, networks and actors, administrative ambitions and plans to form spatial tasks.

Use
flow analysis

Analysis of usage by observing flows, their infrastructure and related performance in the context of the city: e.g. energy, air, water, food, goods, waste, sediment, people, biota

Context
area approach

Every spatial intervention will be situated in and confronted with an existing context of public space, streets, squares, buildings, parking areas, industrial sites, office parks, waterfront and other conditions.

Desires
bottom up

The wishes and needs of local actors and stakeholders in the form of citizens, organizations, companies and other players, coalitions and networks.

fig. 2 — The field of activity – four angles

landscape can be improved and a circular economy can come to fruition.[34]

Coherence

Every flow has its own infrastructure and represents the process side of the urban landscape. It is of key importance to achieve a greater coherence between urban flows, rather than merely optimize the infrastructure of each separate flow on a technical level. An example of the latter are the *glow in the dark*-roads created by Daan Roosegaarde and Heijmans: they are nice and useful, but you would rather have mutually connected flows, such as, for example, the use of car batteries (the traffic system) to store the electricity produced by solar panels (the energy system).

Thinking in terms of flows means being able to shorten and connect them. Using the output of one flow as the input for another can close cycles.

The aim is to better use the spatial plan of the urban landscape. This is substantially influenced by infrastructure, such as mobility and utility networks and heat networks. In addition to innovation and optimization of existing networks or the creation of new networks for compaction, the design of urban infrastructure on the basis of flows can be used deliberately to guide major urban expansions.

While coordination between the construction of infrastructure and urban development is often lacking in practice today, smarter infrastructural planning will contribute to a better spatial planning and a better-functioning, ecologically healthier urban landscape.[35]

As FUR is working on healthy urbanity it not only takes the flows of energy, resource, water and waste into account (the classic domain of the metabolism approach), but also the flows of people, goods, data and ideas.

The Physical Metabolism Map

The metabolism approach introduces an analogy between the city and live organisms. The idea goes back a long time, to the nineteenth century when Georges-Eugène baron Haussmann said of the sewers that were being constructed beneath his famous Parisian avenues: 'The underground galleries are an organ of the great city, functioning like an organ of the human body, without seeing the light of day . . . the secretions are taken away mysteriously and don't disturb the good functioning of the city and without spoiling its beautiful exterior.'[36]

In her thesis *Urban Metabolism of Paris and Its Region*, Sabine Barles shows how nineteenth-century Paris was the first to close phosphate cycles by using sewage as a fertilizer in the food production taking place along the River Seine.[37] This resulted in hugely increased food

34
'Changing the city is, first and foremost, changing the way we look at it. It means: understanding it as a collection of extensible strengths and powers rather than as a mass that inheres in design.' Lacaton & Vassal, 2015.

35
Sustainability and Cities: Overcoming Automobile Dependency, P. Newman, J. Kenworthy, 1999.

36
Le Paris d'Haussmann, P. de Moncan, 2009. Haussmann himself, incidentally, was not responsible for the metabolic handiwork to which the city was subjected. Lodewijk appointed another baron, namely Belgrand, to provide the city of Paris with sewers and a water infrastructure.

37
'Urban Metabolism of Paris and Its Region', S. Barles. In: *Journal of Industrial Ecology*, Vol. 13, 2009.

supplies that were used to feed the people of Paris: urban metabolism *avant la lettre*.

In the 1950s and 1960s, a group of leading Japanese architects headed by Kenzo Tange called itself the Metabolists. They dreamt of autonomous, floating cities that would independently develop without any definite shape or form.

In 1965, it was the American inventor and professor Abel Wolman who explored the analogy in depth. He was at the inception of an environmental technology tradition that centres on the issue of the functioning of the physical urban metabolism. Important instruments are the *Material Flow Analysis* (MFA) and the *Life Cycle Analysis* (LCA). The former mainly aims to scrutinize urban regions and to understand how the urban (eco)system transforms resources. The latter has a broader scope and analyses the overall environmental impact of urban activity.

Mapping

Despite all the work of the past decades, this approach is still not commonplace. While the metabolism of the human body is now fully mapped and we can accurately describe which materials enter and exit our bodies, large parts of urban systems are still uncharted territory. We know the 7,400 chemical reactions of our bodies, but we cannot possibly describe the processes of the urban system with comparable accuracy and reliability.

There are exceptions: in many regions it is, for example, possible to roughly map the water system from source to sink. But it is much harder to map waste flows – research is still in its infancy. The MIT invented an original way to map the distances waste travels.[38] Some objects covered more than 1,500 km to their final destinations.

This study makes us aware that flows have a spatial dimension and are therefore part of the spatial design domain. After all, each flow has its own infrastructure, as our own bodies teach us. We also see that every infrastructure allows different flow rates.

The speed at which our nervous system transports signals bears no relation to the speed with which our digestive tract processes food. Obviously, the same is true of urban flows. The blood in our vascular system resembles the surface water flowing through the region; buildings – actually temporarily solidified flows of building materials – strongly resemble our skeletons.

Thus it is possible, albeit rather primitively, to begin mapping the flows that traverse the city. The aim of the visualization of the spatial expression of flows and more particularly of their infrastructure is to identify inefficiencies or urban waste. This wastage may involve losses as well as unused opportunities. It can give rise to a spatial challenge: to transform linear (residual) flows into circular processes and connect them with other spatial interests.

38

Trashtrack, MIT SenseLab, 2011. For this experiment, 500 students took an item they had wanted to throw away to the library. This could be a written A4 page or a banana peel or even a mobile phone. These items were placed in different categories (*trash types*). Subsequently, the items were equipped with a GPS tracker and thrown into regular trash cans.

Looking for Synergy

The improvement of the physical metabolism roughly allows two approaches. The first aims to reorganize production-consumption cycles. Leading principles are reuse, redesign, innovation and substitution.[39] The second approach uses the geographical proximity of material and other flows and deliberately looks for synergy between the different flows by connecting them locally or by facilitating more exchange between the flows.

Spatial design can contribute to this second approach by creating the conditions necessary to combine flows and improve their coherence.[40] For example, safety standards rule out living, working or going to school underneath or near high-tension networks, but temporary stays are harmless to people as well as animals. Though the space that legislation creates beneath high-tension networks is in fact empty, it may very well be used for other purposes. It is possible, for example, to enhance both the Dutch main ecological structure and biodiversity by opening up that space to ecological and recreational co-use.

Another concrete example is the large-scale dumping of industrial heat in the Port of Rotterdam. This is a form a wastefulness that is now banned in Scandinavian countries. As this is a reality we are also about to face, it is now time to think about ways to use this residual product of cooling water systems to heat homes and businesses in the region. This process has now been started and has resulted in the growth of a regional heat network for greenhouse farming and district heating.

Social Metabolism and the Doughnut

The scientific study of the urban metabolism is dominated by the physical, environmental-technological perspective, but there is another perspective that is equally important, namely the social perspective.[41]

Oxford economist Kate Raworth points to the one-sided approach of Rockström's nine planetary boundaries.[42] Yes, we have to stay within those boundaries in order to not destroy the system, but, she wonders, what about the people inside this system? How do you ensure that everyone has access to employment, income, food, water, health and energy? How do you guarantee social capital, gender equality, resilience and freedom of expression?

In addition to Rockström's nine-boundary ceiling, she formulated a foundation of 11 values to which every person is entitled 'to be able to exercise their human rights'. And she drew this in the shape of a doughnut: stay inside the outer ring and outside the inner ring.

Alongside the highly technologically-oriented approach of metabolism, staying inside the doughnut requires a more sociological orientation that analyses why the

39

Towards the Circular Economy;
Economic and Business Rationale
for an Accelerated Transition,
Ellen McArthur Foundation, 2013.

40

Urban Metabolism, Sustainable
development of Rotterdam,
J. Borsboom et al., Rotterdam, 2014.

41

Ibid.

42

'A Safe and Just Space for
Humanity: Can we live within the
doughnut?', K. Raworth, Oxfam
Discussion Papers, 2012. Also see
www.bit.ly/2aMMDRb.

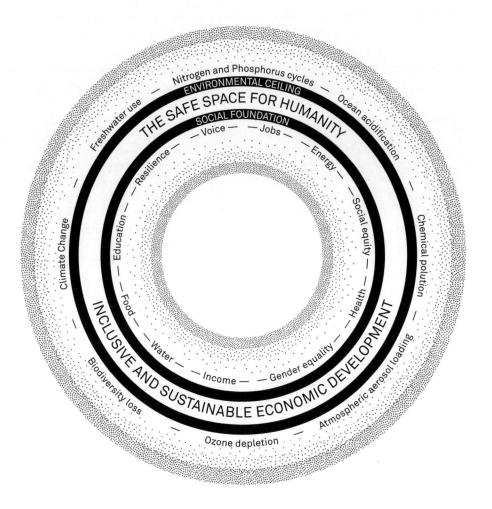

fig. 3 — Eleven essential values

system works and what life it allows. How do the ingenious, inter-locking flows and systems of the complex, interactive urban system continuously work to meet the needs of its inhabitants?

How do the cycles of production and consumption work? What are their effects on the local economy, the urban quality of life, inequality and sustainability?

How do the elements form the whole? What are the social and polit-ical contexts of the metabolism? What are the social costs and obstacles that face the improvement and adjustment of the physical domain, and are they feasible and desirable?

This human behaviour-oriented and use-oriented approach mainly sees the urban metabolism as a descriptive framework that can be used to achieve more sustainable communities and cities. Technological developments ensure that this approach is gaining importance. Thanks to the GPS signals of mobile phones, for example, we know more and more about communication and pedestrian flows in the city and this provides us with insights about changing patterns of use.

Towards a Combined Metabolism
Studies of the urban metabolism have to balance its physical and its social side. Designers can only substantially improve urban produc-tion and consumption systems if they have a thorough understanding of these flows and of the relationships between anthropogenic urban activities and natural processes.

Though the metabolism approach tends to scale up, via the local and the regional level, to the global level, it always remains closely interwoven with the human scales of land use, settlement, infrastruc-ture and ecology.[43]

Swiss urban planners Oswald and Baccini attempt to combine the physical and the social metabolisms in a single design approach.[44] To this end they name four principles for the redesign of the city (shapability, sustainability, reconstruction and responsibility) and four major urban activities (to nourish and recover, to clean, to reside and work, and to transport and communicate). These are assessed in terms of the four main components of urban metabolisms: water, food (biomass), building materials and energy.

FUR, too, aims to unite these two ways to approach the urban metabolism. The question FUR asks itself is: How can design best use the urban (eco) system to improve urban living and enhance spatial quality?

The Six Themes
On the basis of comprehensive literature studies, FUR has explored the major challenges cities face. These were crossed with the priorities of the six regions that each accommodates a Dutch Academy of Architecture. This way, FUR has coupled six challenges that urban regions face to the policies of six Dutch regions.

43
The idea that ecosystems are theoretically self-sufficient systems needs differentiation. Each ecosystem requires the continuous input of energy and nutrients in the form of sunlight and nitrogen, CO_2 and oxygen. Cycles inside the ecosystem are only 'closed' at the level of the biosphere, and on this scale, too, they always remain totally dependent on energy in the form of sunlight.

44
Netzstadt. Einführung in das Stadtentwerfen, F. Oswald and P. Baccini, 2003.

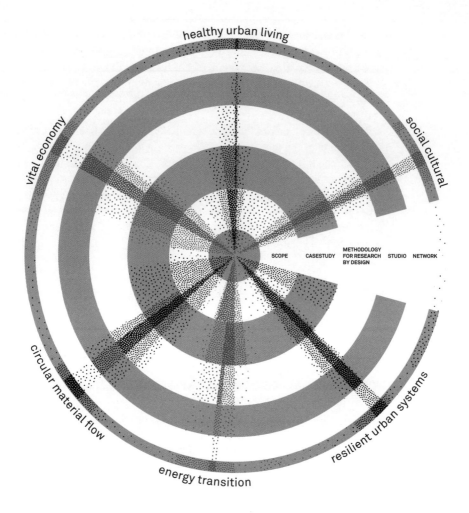

healthy urban living

social cultural

vital economy

circular material flow

energy transition

resilient urban systems

SCOPE   CASESTUDY   METHODOLOGY FOR RESEARCH BY DESIGN   STUDIO   NETWORK

fig. 4 — The six FUR themes

The six themes are: Resilient Infrastructure (Zuidoost-Brabant), Material Cycle (Rotterdam), Renewable Energy (Groningen), Vital Economy (Amsterdam), Healthy Living (Arnhem-Nijmegen) and Sociocultural Connectivity (Zuid-Limburg). Together, these six themes form healthy urbanity's research area.

The upper three challenges are rooted in a sociological approach of the urban metabolism and concentrate on urban use. They are about the three Ps: People, Planet, Profit. The bottom three challenges are primarily connected with the environmental-technological approach of the urban metabolism. They focus on the flows water, food and energy (together also called the nexus due to their strong interrelations). But no matter how you divide or arrange the themes, it is essential not to lose sight of their coherence.

Resilient Infrastructure

Resilience is the ability of systems to respond to changing circumstances or disruptions in such a way that its essential qualities are restored.[45] Working on resilience therefore means improving the performance of a system that is being threatened by risks, rather than preventing or limiting losses.[46]

Resilience is closely connected to the urban infrastructures that developed across the centuries and reflect social and historical evolutions. Sometimes such infrastructures developed gradually, with attention to the interrelation of the different systems, but more often they developed at an astonishing rate, without planning and without harmonization of spatial growth and the underlying system. It was furthermore implicitly assumed that the sources of water, energy and food were inexhaustible.

At the beginning of the twenty-first century, urban regions face new global challenges. The number of people living in urban regions continues to increase but paradoxically, the density in which they do so is decreasing. This makes demands on the infrastructure that facilitates the urban system.

Authorities will have to find space for the new infrastructure that will allow the transition from fossil to renewable energy sources. The current infrastructure, moreover, has to be improved. Sewer systems will be renewed, railroad tracks widened and copper cables replaced by fibreglass ones.

In addition, there are threats such as climate change, population growth, economic fluctuations, pandemics, terrorism and cross-border pollution that cause increased pressure on our urban infrastructure. On the one hand, threats such as these are growing because the world population is still growing; on the other they owe their growth to globalization and to the interrelatedness

45
See: www.aquo.nl.

46
City Resilience Framework,
Ove Arup & Partners, 2014.

of our infrastructure: more and more people use the same urban systems and thus increase the pressure on their immediate surroundings.[47] In the urban infrastructure, this leads to problems including the overload of mobility networks, both coastal (rising sea levels) and inland (increased precipitation) flooding, chronic under-capacity of energy networks, the accumulation of waste and air pollution and the simultaneous, complete breakdown of multiple networks.

The vulnerability of our cities became evident when hurricane Sandy hit New York on 29 October 2012. During the storm 71 people were killed and around 100,000 dwellings damaged, 38 billion litres of sewage water flowed into the ocean, 2 million people no longer had electricity and the underground network was largely flooded.[48]

The damage to the city of New York amounted to 19 billion dollars. Expectations are that this kind of disaster will only increase in size in the future. Should New York fail to take action, the financial damage of a similar storm around 2050 will be five times higher due to rising sea levels and the warming of the oceans: some 90 billion dollars.[49]

Designing a resilient infrastructure for the transport of people, goods, water, energy and material, both aboveground and underground, is crucial to improve both the performance of the urban system and its spatial expression. However, it is technologically and financially impossible to make an urban infrastructure that is immune to pressures and external dangers. We can, however, try to increase its resilience to limit failure or make failure safer at least. To achieve this, we need to change our model of spatial planning at a fundamental level.

A first step would be to anticipate the expected dangers and challenges rather than respond to failures after the fact. Hence, risk assessment plays an increasingly important part in the design and planning of cities. This takes more than the ICT tools of the Smart City movement.

Companies such as IBM, Cisco and Siemens provide municipalities with packages to make the existing city smarter. The ultimate goal, however, is not to come up with smart solutions to 'stupid' urban designs, but to reflect on ways to incorporate more resilience in the infrastructure of complex systems such as transport networks and those of water, energy and ICT, and how spatial design can contribute to this. That is, by smart spatial designs that require fewer technological solutions.[50]

The Benthemplein in Rotterdam is an example of an intelligent spatial design that provides a solution for the increase in heavy rains in the city.[51] This 'water square' includes storm water storage for nearly 2 million litres of water, which precluded expansion of the existing sewer system.

47
'European Green City Index | Executive summary', Economist Intelligence Unit, 2009, p. 6.

48
See: www.bit.ly/1FR2XI4.

49
A Stronger, More Resilient New York, The City of New York, 2013.

50
Ubiquity & the Illuminative *City. From Smart to Intelligent Urban Environments*, A. van Timmeren, 2015.

51
Benthemplein, De Urbanisten, design 2011-2012, completed 2013. Also see Part 3, Chapter 'A Metabolic Square' →p. 208.

A second step would be to design the systems in such a way that, should they fail, the consequences of that failure would only cause a minimal disruption in the total of all urban systems.

After Sandy had swept across New York, it turned out one area had resisted her successfully: Arverne by the Sea, south of JFK Airport. Rather than being based on minimal construction requirements, the design of this district took the possibility of a tropical storm into account. It includes beaches and dunes that make natural buffers as well as a sturdy boardwalk to break the waves. The entire residential area, furthermore, is built on an elevation and the dwellings are made of extra durable, solid materials. Here, unlike in other parts of New York, the electricity lines are installed underground.[52]

A final step necessary to increase the resilience of urban systems is the creation of a broad basis for its development and management. Traditionally, the urban infrastructure is the domain of the government. However as president of the Rockefeller Foundation Judith Rodin writes: 'The resilience of a company or an entire business sector is connected to the resilience of a community. Therefore the private sector has a clear interest in taking its financial responsibility.'[53]

But (smaller) local stakeholders can also be important cornerstones. A good example of creating new support is 'Room for the River'. To make the Dutch delta safer, more room is needed for water storage along the banks of rivers. To find that room, the research by design launched a less linear and less traditional procedure. Eventually, a farm proved the ideal party to realize nature conservation along the river.[54]

Working on a resilient infrastructure is a pre-eminently spatial task. Many systems are, for example, equipped for peak loads. The question is how we can change designing for that peak into designing to link systems together. Is it possible, for example, to use the excess capacity of the railroad network to absorb the peak load of the electricity network? How can this solution contribute to spatial quality and does it create opportunities for other parties?

In terms of transport networks, it is no use to start from a single type of transport; the starting point is a collection of well-connected modalities. This creates a resilient transport system. A combination of light rail, public transport bicycles, subsidized public taxi services and shared cars, say five major Dutch public transport companies, will make it possible in the foreseeable future to travel from door to door within one hour inside the Randstad.[55]

52

The developers were very aware of the effects of a tropical storm because they were involved in the reconstruction of New Orleans after Hurricane Katrina. See 'A Much Criticized Pocket of the Rockaways, Built to Survive a Storm', *The New York Times*, 20 September 2012, p. 24.

53

In 2013, the Rockefeller Foundation launched the *100 Resilient Cities Centennial Challenge*, a package of services to support cities to develop a resiliency plan. Urban infrastructure was a central part of such a plan.

54

See practical example 'Natuurderij – Deventer' →p. 216.

55

NS, Qbuzz, GVB, RET and HTM presented the memorandum 'Contouren voor een nieuw Nederlands mobiliteitsplan' on 7 July 2016.

New technologies make it possible to link up networks and offer bespoke services per region. Rather than megalomaniacal infrastructural projects, resilient infrastructure requires the better harmonization of infrastructure and use, coupled with spatial interventions at crucial points (Transit Oriented Development).

Renewable Energy

The world is addicted to oil, gas and coal. The supplies are finite and nearing exhaustion. The race for the last cheap fossil stocks evokes ecological disasters. Despite doomsday scenarios, we collectively pretend nothing is wrong. American urban planning, for example, is still equipped for a people unwilling to walk more than 200 m from their cars.[56]

Our freedom, prosperity and culture are connected with fossil energy; locally and globally, this impacts the urban landscape in all sorts of ways. Martin Pasqualetti distinguishes direct and indirect influences of the energy system on the environment.[57] Think about the environmental damage caused by the excavation of mountains for mining activities, for example, or the pollution of surface water and soil and the emission of CO_2.

Cities are responsible for 70 per cent of the worldwide energy consumption and for 40 to 70 per cent of all CO_2 emissions.[58] Thinking about energy and climate crises, one cannot get around thinking about the city. It plays a crucial part in the energy transition and in the improvement of the climate. The city is not only the problem, it also provides the solution.

The way a city is organized is in fact crucial. Amsterdam, for example, has a relatively low per capita energy consumption. The people of Amsterdam live in small, often stacked dwellings, cycle from home to work and own fewer cars than people that live outside the city. The city has a close-knit public transport network, with shops and cafés at walking distance. The concept of the compact city already represents a big step towards a post-fossil era. The study explains which urban densities and typologies lead to minimal energy consumption in the city.

Paradoxically, the direct spatial impact of our current energy system is very limited. The energy intensity of coal and oil is so high that small areas can cater to much larger areas.[59] This is especially true of the Netherlands, where no fuels are produced aboveground. Each energy transition (from wood and wind to peat; then from peat to coal, oil, gas and electricity) meant energy faded further from the public eye.

56
Een plan dat werkt; Ontwerp en politiek in de regionale planvorming, M. Hajer, D. Sijmons and F. Feddes, 2006.

57
Sustainable Energy Landscape: Implementing EnergyTransition in the Physical Realm, S. Stremke, 2015.

58
If you only look at CO_2 production, then the number is 40 per cent, if you take the total consumption in the city into account it is 70 per cent. *Inspiring Examples of Energy Efficiency in Cities,* UN Habitat, 2011.

59
Energie is ruimte, H. Gordijn, F. Verwest and A. van Hoorn, PBL Netherlands Environmental Assessment Agency, 2003.

An analysis in the *Kleine Energieatlas* shows that the current spatial system is largely separated from considerations concerning energy.[60] Energy supply and demand do not necessarily have to be proximate. Numerous considerations are involved in the construction of new roads and the development of cities, but energy is hardly ever among them.

However, the tide is turning. After all, renewable energy sources have a much greater impact on the available space. Spatial pressures in and around rapidly expanding urban areas naturally ensure that the new energy challenges become part of the spatial agenda. And the construction of energy-neutral neighbourhoods, villages, cities and regions will have spatial effects as well.

Unfortunately, so far the spatial discussion is more about the physical space that renewable energy claims than about the integrated harmonization of various spatial claims, of which energy is but one. Research by design carried out in Leiden shows what opportunities arise when you link the challenge of an energy-neutral region to regional water issues, agricultural strengthening and the improvement of the cycling infrastructure.[61]

According to Dirk Sijmons, there are three main motives for the transition from fossil to renewable energy sources: fossil fuels are running low, they cause geopolitical instability, and they accelerate global warming.

Gas extraction in the region of Groningen is having negative effects on the quality of life, but especially on people's sense of security. Years and years of gas extraction causes earthquakes with disastrous consequences for buildings. Moreover, the supply will be depleted within 35 years. It is therefore important that the Netherlands switches to new primary energy sources as soon as possible. This region has great potentials for solar, wind, hydro, wave, tidal, osmotic, geothermal and biomass power.

Transitions proceed incrementally. They require changes at all scale levels and that calls for new solutions and new perspectives. Alternatives to fossil energy are available. Given our technical knowledge, we can change to renewable energy tomorrow. But they do require major investments and it also takes time to prepare infrastructures and networks. A renewable energy system calls for a total makeover of cities and landscapes and will affect our behaviour. Compare it with a dwelling renovation that takes place while residents continue to live in the house and simply carry on as usual. The residents do not want to be surprised by power failures or lack of gas, they want functioning central heating.

The energy sector tends to see spatial issues as matters of development, whereas spatial designers usually see energy supply as a technical matter, which is outside

60

Kleine energieatlas – *Ruimtebeslag van elektriciteitsopwekking,* Ministry of Housing, Spatial Planning and the Environment, 2008.

61

See practical example 'What If'-scenarios – Leiden →p. 148.

the scope of their actual design work.[62] There are still very few spatial designers involved in renewable energy projects. This is due to the energy sector, but also to the designers themselves – they have too little knowledge of the energy system to play a part in it so far. But they could and should play a part, given their ability to connect interests and knowledge to solutions and action perspectives at the level of the street, the city and the region.

Many parties need something to hold on to, they want to be able to imagine the energy transition. The visual analysis of the challenges allows players to understand what the energy transition demands of them. This brings concrete action closer. Without overseeing every last detail of the energy system, designers can assist the parties involved by outlining solutions and linking them to the physical environment.[63]

The spatial context of the energy transition has both a qualitative and a quantitative side. Qualitative aspects are laws, rules and agreements that preserve the existing landscape and complicate the development of energy landscapes. Safety zones around infrastructure, buildings, nature reserves and mill biotopes preclude the placement of wind turbines, while solar panels are not welcome in historical districts with listed buildings. In addition, values, emotions and narratives connected to landscapes, cities and villages add to the resistance to renewable energy.[64]

Quantitatively, the energy density – the amount of space required per unit of energy – plays a central part, because that of renewable energy is many times greater than that of fossil energy. Lumping together qualitative and quantitative arguments, space turns out to be the critical factor: there is literally not enough of it for the necessary new energy landscapes. This calls for innovative spatial design that goes beyond 'fitting things in': it requires research into the potential of renewable production as a new urban landscape typology.

This not only concerns production places, but certainly also the infra-structure for the transport and storage of energy. An interesting spatial challenge is awaiting at the point where multiple flows come together, where energy production is linked to energy storage or where a resid-ual flow can be used for a recreational or social function in the district.

In the future, energy routes may shape the urbaniza-tion process. The Leiden study into the energy transition illustrates how the new infrastructure of the heat net-work can contribute to a new bicycle infrastructure for the city. To this end, heat pipes are combined with an attractive system of cycle bridges that provides shorter connections, prevents the freezing over of cycle paths and precludes major interventions in the existing infrastructure.

62
Landschap is energie,
D. Sijmons, 2015.

63
Convivial Toolbox, E. Sanders
and P.J. Stappers, 2013.

64
Landschap is energie,
D. Sijmons, 2015.

The energy world is in a state of flux. Not only the types of energy we use will change, but the roles we will play will change as well. In the new situation, consumers are sometimes producers and former producers are sometimes consumers.

Individual citizens, collaborations of citizens, and an increasing number of companies and water boards are already involved in the decentralized production of energy. This trend will continue. The connection between top-down approaches on the basis of smart technologies and large-scale solutions and bottom-up initiatives is essential. With respect to the city it is therefore necessary that those who work on the energy transition pay attention to the question: What kind of city do people want to live in, and what values are important to them in that context?

Material Cycle

Our economy is linear and the urban regions are the end of the line: food, energy and materials are imported from far beyond the city limits and, once inside, consumed and largely downcycled or wasted eventually.[65]

The growth of the world population and its rising standard of living ensure that the speed with which the stock of materials is depleted is accelerating. In contrast to the energy supply, the amount of materials available on earth is finite and it is not being replenished. In the case of some raw materials, we are already scraping the bottom of the barrel.

Particularly in Europe, this presents a geopolitical challenge as well. Though economically, the old continent is a global player with a huge consumptive footprint, at the same time it has a strikingly small natural stock of raw materials.

The aim is therefore to make the economy circular with regard to both active and passive materials. 'Active' are materials that have been stored or transformed, for example in the form of buildings. In addition, urban systems have a large amount of 'passive' natural materials: water, gas, minerals, phosphates, and so on.

To stamp out the idea that waste is the end point of a linear process, it is important to gain an understanding of the origins of materials and of the ways they are captured in economic chains. A chain comprises the entire process of production, transport, consumption and waste, with value being added or lost in different steps across the process.

Of old, cities are dependent on available natural resources. Unlike self-sufficient natural systems that use the sustainable mechanisms of recycling, cities are rarely sustainable. Yet cities do offer possibilities and opportunities for resilient development. This requires that we radically reverse our ideas about waste: as long as our mountain of waste is growing, so is our stock of raw materials. Each component in a

65
Circular Buiksloterham;
Transitioning Amsterdam
to a Circular City, E. Gladek
et al., 2015.

product then suddenly presents itself as a potential raw material for a
future product. Nature itself can serve as a source of inspiration. There
is no such thing as waste in nature. Each product is a source for a new
process.

Cradle to Cradle (c2c) distinguishes two cycles of materials: the
biosphere and the technosphere.[66] Materials in the technosphere allow
endless reuse, for example in industrial applications. The products in
the biosphere are organic materials that are compostable. Working in
accordance with the c2c principle means that every material is fully
reused without any loss of value. This means that there is no more
downcycling.

A priority of recycling is that the materials must retain the highest
possible level of complexity. Preserving entire products therefore
trumps disassembling products into component parts or separate
materials. Preferably, materials are not combined or mixed and, in
principle, they not recovered in an energetic form.

Now, the key question is how these general performance principles
for a circular economy can be translated into principles applicable on
an urban or regional level. And which spatial interventions are necessary to make these economic and ecological benefits possible. One of
the most important questions concerns the scale on which one has to
work. For it is not possible by a long shot to realize every principle of
the circular economy at any scale.

Ideas about waste centre on the three rs: Reuse, Reduce, Recycle, that
is: reuse as a product, reduce use, recycle as a material. Applied to
construction challenges, the first r refers to an existing building that
is redeveloped for a new function. The second r means that demand
is reduced as much as possible. In the New World of Work, for example, buildings are used more efficiently so that companies require
fewer square metres of office space. If both the preceding options are
excluded, there is still the demolition and recycle option, which means
that all the components and materials in a building are meticulously
separated with a view to reuse.

This calls for several contributions by designers. In the case of the
reuse of an existing building – the first r – it means adapting the building to the new function that it will accommodate. An example of this
is the transformation of the Tropicana swimming pool in Rotterdam
into laboratory space for companies. Here, experiments
with waste products have resulted in a network of
entrepreneurs that gear raw materials, residual materials,
production chains and business plans to one another.[67]

In the case of the reduction of use, the designer aims
for a building with a flexible structure: employees do not
have fixed work spaces and the building especially facilitates collaborations in varying combinations. Preferably,
the building is designed to accommodate as many forms

66

The Cradle to Cradle concept
was developed by German
biologist M. Braungart and
American architect W. McDonough.

67

See practical example
'Blue Economy – Rotterdam'
→p. 160.

of use as possible. This requires higher floors and a good internal infrastructure – necessary extra investment that will pay off in the long run.

In the case of the third R, reuse of the building as a source, the designer thinks like a miner. Villa Welpeloo by Superuse Studios is a residence that is almost entirely constructed of reused materials and raw materials taken from the nearby area. Thus, the designers not only dealt with waste sustainably, they also saved on transport costs.

Belgian collective Rotor uses recycled building materials to realize a unique aesthetic. Their starting point for the (re)development of buildings, spaces and objects is the value of the existing.

The introduction of a so-called commodity passport is a concrete measure to provide insight in the material composition of buildings. That way, the building itself becomes a registry of building materials, its passport the accompanying catalogue.

During the demolition of buildings, reusable products and materials are separated to ensure they retain their physical characteristics and economic value.[68] During the separation a special place is set aside for the storage of materials that can immediately be used for the construction of new and the renovation of existing buildings.

To apply these principles on a much larger scale requires a materials database that is coupled with an online marketplace. Materials can be stored in physical storage facilities (for example, on vacant lots) close to demolition or new construction projects. Integrated planning is essential for the realization of such a circular future. Building and demolition of buildings are harmonized. Thus, the use of new materials is limited to a minimum.

This requires buildings that are constructed as modularly as possible, but bio-based construction materials and 3D printers can play a part in this process as well. In addition, chain collaboration and financing are important to ensure that justice can be done to the long lifespan of buildings.

The role of spatial designers is not limited to the construction chain. Other flows and economic chains have valuable materials and commodities as well. According to Gunter Pauli, a member of the Club of Rome, we have to look closely at natural systems and copy them to realize sustainable ways of production and consumption.[69]

At the heart of this circular vision are biological processes in which flows of nutrients and water are efficiently directed and residual flows revalued. This also makes it possible to achieve significant economic, environmental-technological and social benefits.

In food production, for example, phosphate is the main ingredient for the production of fertilizers. Expectations are that inside 50 years, we will have extracted every phosphate we can get to from the earth so we will have to rely on phosphates that circulate in the

68

Vademecum voor hergebruik buiten de bouwsite, Rotor, 2016.

69

Blauwe Economie 10 jaar, 100 innovaties, 100 miljoen banen, G. Pauli, 2012.

urban ecosystem. It is therefore of key importance that we learn how torecover these resources.

Separating and processing the waste flows of producers, consumers and retailers provides opportunities to win back important nutrients that can be reused in the agricultural sector. This also places demands on the spatial organization of the city. A deeper understanding of urban nutrient flows will clarify where a centrally organized sewer system is needed and where citizens and businesses can purify their own water and recover valuable resources bottom-up, using a small-scale and independent infrastructure.

To shorten the food chain, it is essential that consumers get easier access to local food sources. Cooperative (urban) farms and growers in the immediate surroundings of cities can provide a direct supply of fresh, seasonal produce to consumers.

This calls for a radical change in the spatial organization of food production. One of the possibilities is the use of underused urban, roof and communal spaces for urban agriculture and urban gardens.

Hence, design has a part to play at every scale. Designing dwellings, architects can, for example, include standard recycle spaces. To begin with, urban designers of industrial areas can analyse the ways businesses can benefit from each other's residual flows. And on a regional scale level, understanding the metabolism helps them determine whether a stream is best closed centrally, or rather locally.

Vital Economy

Urban regions can only be economically vital if they make room for flows of people, knowledge and goods. A vital economy furthermore requires diversity, quality education, innovation and good governance. Only then will urban regions be able to adapt to changing circumstances.

According to Maarten Hajer, the 'new economy' primarily has to add local value and be circular and socially inclusive.[70] This new economy does not exist: it is a work in progress that is being developed in the field by people who, each on the basis of their own expertise, want to contribute to the solution of environmental and social problems. They strive for a circular and reciprocal economy, an economy that gives as well as takes and that is an organic part of a vital public domain.

The city contains a wide range of economic infrastructure: factories, offices, shops and schools as well as post, industrial areas, offices, parks and shopping streets. The fundamental question is how the city is going to accommodate the new economy: How can it simultaneously facilitate entrepreneurs, maintain a balanced workforce and attract talent through high spatial quality and a pleasant environment? Because a city has to accommodate both globalized knowledge

70

Maarten Hajer was head curator of the Internationale Architecture Biennale Rotterdam 2016. The Next Economy was the theme of this edition.

workers and beer brewing hipsters, hard-working nurses and unskilled labourers.

The city drives the economy. By 2025, the 600 largest cities of the world will house 2 billion people, that is a quarter of the total world population. Together, these people will produce some 49 trillion euros, that is 60 per cent of the total gross product generated on earth.

Despite this immense interest, it is still relatively unclear how the relationship between the economy and the city actually works. International comparative studies are nuanced on the subject of the city as a driver of economic growth: some cities show growth in both population and number of jobs, others do not.

The success of the Silicon Valleys and Brain Ports of this world cannot simply be copied in other regions. For it is not the space or the infrastructure that generates economic activity, it is the people who use that space.

An economic ecosystem is a complex system of which the components are interconnected: physical space and economic and social processes, spatial systems at different scale levels, individual actors, companies and institutions. Unravelling the economic metabolism of urban regions is a first step towards understanding these complex processes.

In the 1990s, the clout of companies was measured by their ability to specialize. However, things are changing: investors are more and more interested in the place that companies occupy in their chain. The appreciation of companies thus relies on the entire economic ecosystem. Something similar applies to urban regions: cities such as Eindhoven are successful because they have a spatial-economic strategy in which businesses, educational establishments and governments work closely together (the triple helix), but in which the city itself is also used as a laboratory for social and technological innovation.

The outsourcing of production to low-wage countries seems subject to change as well. It appears innovation works better if you do not only focus on the development of knowledge, but also make products yourself. In addition, outsourcing often turns out to be more expensive than expected, the production quality is disappointing, transport costs are high and turnaround times long. And wages are rising in the Third World, too.

Western cities are examining how they can use reindustrialization (reshoring) to reshape their urban areas. This means that various products are made closer to home once more and that there is a stronger connection within companies between the production and R&D departments. The boundaries between the (manufacturing) industry and the service sector are also blurring. Isolated industrial areas will make way for urban fabrics with more hybrid forms of living, working, learning and so on.

Cities such as Hamburg, Brussels, London, New York, Barcelona and Rotterdam are exploring how manufacturing processes and small-scale industry can be reintroduced into the urban fabric. In Brooklyn Navy Yard (New York), for example, innovative clusters have emerged that include production, R&D, education, start-ups and local entrepreneurs.

We cannot live more sustainably without tackling the current economic system, which focuses on growing consumption and growing economic inequality. This system largely leads to a non-sustainable exploitation of human beings and the planet.

The challenge of a vital economy is to find a proper balance between economic growth, local value, social inclusiveness and circularity. To this end, the economy has to become more layered and this in turn involves educational requirements. The Scientific Council for Government Policy advocates a learning economy in which people continue to renew and adapt themselves, because reality is continuously and rapidly changing as well.

The scale level at which we have to examine economic ecosystems is regional at the least and it is important to keep the chains of R&D, logistics, production, services and consumption in mind. Understanding a regional economic ecosystem requires a new organization of data, because the new economy is much more difficult to categorize than the old one. Previously, spatioeconomic policy limited itself to large-scale investments in infrastructure and main ports, whereas today attention is focusing on the harmonization of the existing infrastructure and a variety of economic, interconnected environments.

A vital economy requires the enhancement of innovation, entrepreneurship, adaptability, labour market flexibility and the heterogeneity of economic activities.

If diversity is indeed a condition for a vital economy, then the question is how spatial designers can strengthen that diversity and how they can improve the coherence and interaction between different economic sectors, actors and work areas. The answer involves various scale levels.

The designers of atelier SouthWest Works! warn that the metropolitan region of Amsterdam ought to avoid too strong a focus on the main port and that it had better cherish diversity. They advocate a varied region, in which the different qualities of the city, the landscape, the port, the airport and the green port are connected by physical and virtual infrastructure and by interaction environments that allow cross-pollination.[71]

In the study Blind Spot, the Vereniging Deltametropool and West 8 show that the landscape is an increasingly important settlement condition both for companies and for attractive talent.[72] Southwest Works! develops this notion for the Amsterdam region, where

71
See design proposal 'Cycling Commuters' →p. 224.

72
Blind Spot - Metropolitan Landscape in the Global Battle for Talent was published in April 2016 and is co-produced by the Vereniging Deltametropool, Wageningen UR and West 8, together with the Cultural Heritage Agency, the Ministry of Economic Affairs and Staatsbosbeheer.

Schiphol has created a strong fragmentation of the landscape. It is precisely robust, productive landscapes that are able to withstand the economic forces of Schiphol.

Designers can also help to fathom the existing ecosystem of a region and identify missing links. Designers in the atelier Zaans Next Economy couple Zaandam's strong food sector with 3D printing techniques. Algae that grow in the peatland area are processed on a FoodCampus in Zaanstad which includes not only factories but also educational establishments and consumption areas.[73]

At a lower scale level, urban typologies are needed that mix living, working, manufacturing, learning and consuming, coupled with strong a public space. In addition, we can learn a lot from the qualities of existing city streets that, though under pressure, still harbour a wide range of diversity and employment. In London, half of the employment outside the centre is concentrated along the 600 High Streets.[74]

A related spatial task is to interweave various forms of education in the urban fabric. An example in Amsterdam was the temporary FabCity Campus at the head of Java Island, just like the plan to redevelop part of all library buildings into public city work spaces.[75]

Finally, designers can transform economic environments such as shopping streets and industrial areas. Industriepark Kleefsewaard in Arnhem thus transformed from an industrial area into a modern work landscape and interaction environment.[76] This example shows that you can innovatively bring together people, goods and knowledge by combining a strong spatial component (hardware) with an idiosyncratic organizational model (orgware) and active programming (software).

73

See design proposal 'Algae Printer in Peatland Area →**p. 99**.

74

See practical example 'High Streets – London' →**p. 170**.

75

FabCity took place during the EU summit that was held in the first half of 2016 under Dutch chairmanship in Amsterdam. The library plan is an initiative of the Amsterdam University of Applied Sciences, the Public Library of Amsterdam, the municipality of Amsterdam and the De Waag Society.

76

See practical example 'Industrial Curator – Arnhem' →**p. 248**.

Healthy Living

People in cities live crowded together by definition, with all of the commotion and problems that entails. Air pollution, noise pollution, stress and personal danger greatly affect the health of humans, animals and plants. Furthermore, such negative effects are often not distributed evenly: the neighbourhoods in which the environmental conditions are bad are where the have-nots live, the unskilled and the socially weak who already suffer poorer health.

However, this health helix can also rotate in the opposite direction: people who live in a compact city move more than people who live in the suburbs, for example, where cars play a dominant part.

Designers can help encourage 'healthy living', combat the excesses, and improve air, water and soil quality. But that is not all, they can also encourage a healthy lifestyle by creating attractive public places that foster encounter, combat anti-social behaviour and reduce isolation. In short, by designing spaces that further the recovery and healing of both body and mind.

A good system of pedestrian and cycling trails helps, for example. There is a clear connection between people living in a city with a highly developed pedestrian infrastructure and their health. There are even indications that greenery has a positive effect on pregnancy and babies. An analysis of 64,000 births shows that women living within 300 m of a green space in the city have healthier babies: in this group, the proportion of extremely preterm births is 20 per cent below average.[77]

The research is part of a growing corpus that suggests that greenery has a positive effect on health. The researchers are not yet sure how the relationship between green space and health works: Does the additional green space provide more social opportunities and a stronger sense of social cohesion, for example, or does a psychological effect reduce stress and depression? Yet senior researcher Michael Brauer is sure: 'Given the high cost of health care, the fact that modification of urban characteristics, such as the strengthening of the green space in cities, can be an extremely cost-effective strategy to prevent disease while it also produces far-reaching environmental benefits at the same time is an attractive perspective.'[78]

The promotion of healthy living in the city has deep historical roots. In the early 1920s, movements that wanted to improve the health and wellbeing of city dwellers emerged in the Western world in response to the rampant industrialization. America had the City Beautiful movement, England had the Garden City movement and later the CIAM took over.[79] We are now facing the emergence of a similar movement, though it will be rather more complex than the previous ones.

The development of a healthy city of the future requires a new approach to urban development and to the design of healthy buildings, streets, cities and regions. This is not just about the protection of public health and the meeting of legal parameters, but about an integrated approach to the concept 'health'. This requires an early involvement of actors and alliances that work on the healthy city: health care organizations, the central government, the private sector, knowledge institutes, neighbourhood communities and (civil) organizations.

The aim is to programme and organize urban functions in such a manner that everyone not only has access to a healthy environment, but also to good health care. The current extramuralization policy, for example, raises a number of major spatial and social issues.

In the coming years, many residential care facilities will lose their current function. This will not only lead to a transformation challenge, but also have a major

[77]
'Residential Greenness and Birth Outcomes: Evaluating the Influence of Spatially Correlated Built-Environment Factors'. In: *Environmental Health Perspectives*, Vol. 122, 2014.

[78]
See: www.bit.ly/29K9NYA.

[79]
Congrès Internationaux d'Architecture Moderne (CIAM) was the name of a series of international conferences about modern architecture and urban planning that was held between 1928 and 1959.

impact on the quality of life in our neighbourhoods. Designers can help gear supply and demand of care to the scale of the city, as well as develop programmatic scenarios for the integration of care in the city.

Using the catch phrase '50 m² is the drug', Wouter Veldhuis of urban office Must advocates investments in accessible meeting places in neighbourhoods.[80] Isolation is a grave danger to public health and governments and market parties should therefore invest in walk-in centres, local living rooms and other meeting places. New technologies can help people make contact.[81]

The theme Healthy Living is about more than providing people with good spatial conditions, it is also about biodiversity. The aim is to create a balanced ecosystem that includes human beings.

Because of climate change, increasing urbanization and pressure on the amount of available space, the biodiversity of flora and fauna is diminishing rapidly. And yet biodiversity is not only an important condition for the survival of the earth, but also essential to, for example, the production of food. No bees, no pollination. In addition, cities are increasingly dependent on so-called ecosystem services, such as the production of clean water by helophyte filters and clean air by trees and plants.

Designers can contribute to the creation of conditions that provide all life (humans, animals and plants) with plenty of room in a clean environment (water, soil, air). Since the city hosts many spatial claims, it needs smart hybrid solutions. A good small-scale example of a spatial intervention is De Ceuvel in Amsterdam-Noord, which combines improvement of the living environment (soil) with a contemporary work environment for creative and social entrepreneurs.

At a higher scale level, a city such as Copenhagen has an integrated green strategy that ensures greenery is available in the immediate environment of every inhabitant.[82] And design atelier 'The ecological city' shows four design strategies to connect an impoverished Arnhem district from the 1960s with the river and to nature reserve the Veluwe.

A good ecosystem can also help to cool cities. In urban areas, the average temperature is a few degrees higher than in the surrounding rural areas. This is called the Urban Heat Island effect (UHI).[83] The main causes of these heat islands are the absorption of sunlight by dark materials and the relatively low wind speeds in the city. More greenery and construction measures can temper the heat. Passive techniques for the cooling of buildings and public spaces through wind chimneys, a method used in the Pakistani city of Hyderabad, can also lower temperatures.

80

Must, together with Architecture Workroom Brussels and De Smet Vermeulen, was responsible for the research by design *The Healthy City* for the IABR 2016.

81

Also see design proposal 'The Elderly Take to the Streets' →p. 267.

82

See practical example 'Smart City 3.0 – Copenhagen' →p. 58.

83

Klimaatverandering in stedelijke gebieden: een inventarisatie van bestaande kennis en openstaande kennisvragen over effecten en adaptiemogelijkheden, M. van Drunen and R. Lasage, 2007.

But it would be even better if urban designers coupled the approach of heat islands with a better use of residual heat in a smart and circular system.

Sociocultural Connectivity

A lively, dynamic, inclusive city filled with engaged and enterprising citizens, where old and new eras overlap yet remain recognizable, with room for new development and redevelopment – who would not want this perfect city?

Of old, urban planners have always taken the social and cultural components of spatial planning into account. In that sense, their ambitions were great: for a long time, they held the belief that connectivity could be created top-down. With the best of intentions, they made huge mistakes on the basis of highly coloured ideological views of society. The Dutch concept of a socially engineered society, for example, resulted in the notion of the 'neighbourhood idea', a typical excrescence of a failed top-down approach.

Citizens increasingly call for more influence on the design of the space. At the same time, the decentralization of spatial policy enables people to influence their own living environment and living conditions more directly. The fact that governments want to involve citizens and businesses in spatial developments has a background that is not only ideological. Governments also have financial motives: there is less and less public money available for large spatial investments. As a consequence, they focus on the organization of new, collective alliances.

Since the beginning of the economic crisis, traditional urban design and the planning profession have firmly been challenged by the new practice of what has become known as 'city making'.[84]

City makers are new initiators in the field of urban development that create their own space in the urban arena. They venture off the beaten track, invent new earning models, are highly committed socially, often use cultural means to achieve their goals and they are above all very practical. Though their approach bears a strong resemblance to that of research by design, they are not necessarily designers.

Spatial designers can contribute to city making because they can provide spatial perspectives and upscale ideas. Connecting the power of bottom-up initiatives and the new city makers with top-down challenges such as the energy transition, health care and mobility is an important task.

This new city making is a bottom-up solution to problems caused by urban planning. However, this solution is not without problems itself, because apparently the participation society and the interactive democracy mainly appeal to highly educated and well-connected people.

84
Het nieuwe stadmaken –
Van gedreven pionieren naar
gelijk speelveld, S. Franke,
J. Niemans and F. Soeterbroek
(Eds.), 2015.

And the lead this group has will only grow, due to the complex physical processes that will result from future environmental legislation.

According to the director of The Netherlands Institute for Social Research Kim Putters, the divides in society are becoming increasingly visible in the spatial domain as well.[85] He calls this the 'multiple divide', caused by the various ways people are connected to their environments. There are divides between the high-skilled and the low-skilled, between original inhabitants and newcomers, and between the 'influentials' and the 'deplorables'.

Designers therefore face the task of helping groups of people that do not have the necessary skills and contacts to organize and allowing them to create genuinely collective spaces and sociocultural interaction environments.

It may not be necessary for the different groups to live closely together, but they should at least meet each other in public places such as schools and libraries. And this is a spatial challenge as well. It is not enough to implement a standard of at least 30 per cent public housing; this must be complemented by a requirement of at least 30 per cent social programme.

An example of such an approach is the 'Broedstraten' concept that was developed in Amsterdam-Noord. A 'broedstraat' (breeding street) brings local residents and artists together around a theme, makes their creativity visible and connects it to the neighbourhood to foster more social cohesion as well as the positive development of the community.[86]

Technological innovations can help solve social problems, but only if accompanied by social innovations that use the strength of all members of society, whatever the social role or function they fulfil.

New social connections and organization forms in spatial processes create a different use of the city. Examples are *Voor je Buurt*, a platform for the crowdfunding of neighbourhood initiatives, *Design to improve life* in which children solve the social challenges of a region and *Liter of Light*, a low-tech solution for lighting in slums.[87]

Social innovation is also a precondition for the implementation of technological innovation, because without broad social acceptance and commitment it will be impossible, for example, to implement the energy transition.

Sociocultural connectivity also has a much looser – but not less important – relationship with spatial planning. People want to be connected with each other and the place in which they live, work and recreate.

They are not only interested in the here and now of a place, they also want something to make them aware of a historical connection. This can range from the recognizability of urban spaces such as squares or the

85
Voorbij de tweedeling, werken aan maatschappelijke waarde, K. Putters, Enneüs Heerma Lecture, 2015.

86
See practical example 'Broedstraten – Amsterdam-Noord' →p. 268.

87
See, respectively:
www.voorjebuurt.nl,
www.bit.ly/2atmNiw and
www.literoflight.org.

scale of the buildings, to typical local architecture. The characteristics of a landscape can also help people to relate to their surroundings, as do animals and smells.

The endless grassy landscape with Frisian dairy cows makes the Frisians feel at home. Brabanders love the bocage with its intimate, forest-lined, green rooms, long beech-lined avenues and heaths with flocks of sheep. The quays and bridges of river cities are much more than necessary infrastructure: they are the places that enable people to orient themselves, the places that make them feel at home.

If cities neglect or erase the landscape they are built on, they are left with anonymous urban structures. It is precisely the landscapes in which they are embedded that provide an anchor for sociocultural connectivity.

resilient infrastructure
Smart City 3.0 — Copenhagen (DK)

Smart, what city would not want to be just that?
Copenhagen is often seen as a shining example,
but what does it actually mean to work on a smart city?
How does a city prepare for the future? By using
resilience as a guiding principle to clear a path for
smart citizens.

Many Western cities continued to grow long after the
Second World War had ended, until they came apart
at the seams. Now that their growth is less explosive,
attention is shifting to the way people use the city. These
days, people travel a lot more inside the city than they
did in the past, for example, and the number of tourists that visit is rising sharply as well. How can traffic
congestions and the deterioration of the air quality be
prevented?

Cities have to respond to a large number of developments. How can they deal with the consequences of
climate change in the long term, for example, or with
sudden violent incidents that turn them upside down?
The smart city of Copenhagen introduces us to an
unusual combination of smart technology and highly
practical measures.[88]

On 2 July 2011, 15 cm of rain fell in Copenhagen a couple of hours' time. The estimated damage amounted to
nearly 1 billion euros. Partly in response to this extreme
downpour, the city published a plan to climate-proof the
city. This involved higher dikes, smarter water storage
and new pumping stations. A year before, Copenhagen
had already introduced a measure that made vegetation
on top of all new buildings with a flat roof mandatory, as
such roofs are better able to process rain water.

But Copenhagen wants to do more than merely battle
flooding. The city wants to be climate neutral by 2025.
To that end, it has to become more energy efficient, use
more renewable energy and make better use of residual
heat. The city wants to plant 100,000 trees to double the
current number and invest extra money in sustainable
mobility, for example by constructing a striking bicycle
bridge that meanders across the harbour like a red snake.

[88]
Copenhagen ranks high on the list
of smart cities found at the website
www.fastcoexist.com, a leading
news site in the area of ethical
economy, innovation, technology
and design. It tests smart cities on
the indicators smart environment,
smart governance, smart economy,
smart living, smart mobility and
smart people.

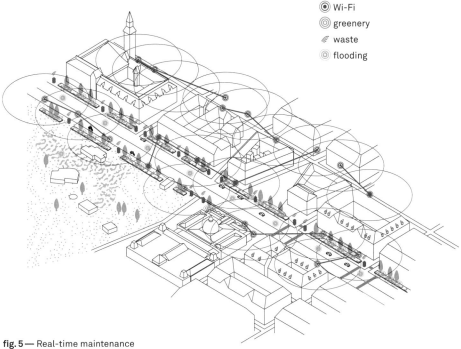

Wi-Fi
greenery
waste
flooding

fig. 5 — Real-time maintenance
of public facilities

fig. 6 — Ambitions CO₂ neutrality

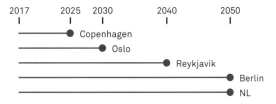

89

Copenhagenize, an international
consultancy that helps
governments make their cities
bicycle-friendly, biannually
publishes a list of the most
bicycle-friendly cities in the
world. In 2015, it was headed
by Copenhagen, followed by
Amsterdam and Utrecht.

It has allowed Copenhagen to consolidate its position
as the world's number one cycle city in recent years.[89]

No matter how practical these interventions are, the
contribution of information technology is essential.
Not only to rapidly and meticulously calculate the consequences of specific interventions, but also to measure
and control the way residents and visitors use the city,
how they move about in it or where they park their cars.
The term 'smart city' refers to this form of technological
innovation.

You could call 'smart city' a buzzword. Although
we have been working on smart cities for decades
(Remember the first automated traffic lights in the

1920s?), we have only now pinned all our hopes on increasingly smart information technologies for the solving of our problems.

As this seems rather a lot to ask, it would perhaps be better to distinguish various types of smart cities. Planner Boyd Cohen, a strategic consultant in this field, distinguishes smart cities on the basis of different stages in the application of technology.[90] First there is the Smart City 1.0, the city that is completely driven by technology. Take Songdo in South Korea, which is filled to the brim with technology that monitors its resident's use of roads, water, energy and waste disposal services. Or the Brazilian capital Rio de Janeiro, where the government watches over its populations from a central operations centre equipped with cameras. In such cases, technology is aimed at monitoring and efficiency.

The Smart City 2.0, the evolved version, uses technology as a means to improve and optimize city life. The information that is collected and applied is ultimately used to find solutions to urban problems such as air pollution or traffic congestion.

Copenhagen is such a Smart City 2.0. It uses technology to measure and work on the city. In 2016, for example, Copenhagen began to install smart traffic lights at busy intersections. Those traffic lights recognize and prioritize buses and cyclists. As a result, bus travel has become 5 to 20 per cent faster and cyclists now take 10 per cent less time to reach their destination.

Copenhagen also founded a so-called Street Lab, a collaboration between the government and enterprises such as network company Cisco and street lighting company Citelum. The test lab is located on H.C. Andersen Boulevard, the busiest street of the city, through which 60,000 cars rush every day. One of the main tasks of the lab is to use sensors and network technology to battle air pollution and traffic noise. They do this, for example, by using smart parking systems to reduce the time motorists spend looking for a parking space and by using smart litter bins that inform the centre when they are full to prevent garbage trucks from driving across the city to collect trash from empty litterbins.

Many designers are nevertheless sceptical about the smart city movement. Architect Rem Koolhaas, for example, warns that the ideas of technology companies and consultants must not come to dominate our thinking about the city as that would lead to a shift in the city's core values: from liberal ideas about freedom,

90
'The 3 Generations of Smart Cities', B. Cohen. At: *www.fastcoexist.com*, 8 October 2015.

fig. 7 — Real time maintenance of public facilities

91

'My Thoughts on the Smart City',
Rem Koolhaas at a meeting of the
High Level Group in Brussels,
24 September 2014.

92

*Smart Cities: Big Data, Civic Hackers
and the Quest for a New Utopia*,
A. Townsend, 2013.

equality and fraternity to ideas about comfort, safety
and sustainability.[91]

According to researcher Anthony Townsend, moreover, the city is not for everyone.[92] It is mostly white,
highly educated young men with sufficient knowledge
and money that will benefit from new technologies.
The question is what part ordinary people will end up
playing in the smart city. Are they reduced to pawns
bound to providing data to keep the system going?

The Boyd Cohen model may provide a response
to those warnings. For the last stage, the Smart City
3.ø, centres on collaboration with citizens. The Smart
City 3.ø not only uses technology to manage the city
efficiently, but it also allows the easy and effective
organization of communities.

Copenhagen is moving in that direction. It knows
that a smart city requires smart citizens. That is why
the Copenhagen Solutions Lab at the centre of the new
smart city projects in Copenhagen is keen to use the
knowledge and skills of its citizens. This starts with
information sharing. There is Copenhagen Open Data,
which comprises 200 data sets – ranging from demographic data to all the parking spaces in the city – that
everyone can access. The City Data Exchange is a market place where people can buy or sell data sets to each
other.

Citizens as the fourth power, side by side with to
the usual trio of government, industry and universities.
Perhaps this Quadruple Helix hides the greatest potential of the smart city. By sharing information, citizens
can bridge the knowledge gap that separates them from
governments and large companies. This will make it easier for them to claim the responsibility for the (co) development of their living environment.

fig. 8 — Wi-Fi points are installed
in public areas. These are coupled
to sensors for measuring the air
quality, among other things

What a combination of practical
measures and smart technologies
makes the city resilient

Where Copenhagen, Denmark

Design Copenhagen Solution Lab

Realized 2011 (ongoing)

Intervention various

Also good for renewable energy
(climate neutral city), healthy living
(more bicycles), sociocultural
connectivity (citizens get involved)

resilient infrastructure

Inner City Becomes Delta

More and more often, Eindhoven has to contend with floods after heavy rainfall. This is partly due to climate change. But more importantly, over the past two centuries the inner city of Eindhoven has changed from a closely knit natural catchment area into a canalized, brick drainage system. This design attempts to turn the tide by reintroducing a sophisticated urban catchment area. Water squares store the excess water and gradually drain it away.

To better understand the resilience of the greater Eindhoven water system, the designer has mapped it first. It turns out that between 1830 and today, many a meandering stream was either filled in or canalized. Banks have been paved and in some cases, the water flow has been redirected into pipes underneath the city, for example brooklet the Gender. The result of all of these rationalizations is that none of the water courses slow down or infiltrate anymore.

Next, the designer analysed where the functionality of the artificial water system and the sewer system were the most vulnerable and which places were the most likely to flood in future downpours. On that basis, she designed a catchment area for the centre of Eindhoven. Between buildings and roads, she found space to slow down the discharge of water and hence reduce the risk of flooding.

The process is illustrated by a profile of the Vestdijk, an Eindhoven city street. Large water squares are constructed between the tall buildings and the street, where the rainwater hits first. Once these are flooded, the water flows across the cycle path into the gutters on either side of the road and is drained away. The continuous sidewalks always stay above water.

fig. 9 — Continuous footpaths stay free of water

As the water level continues to rise, the character of the spaces that are slowly filling up with rainwater continue to change as well. This makes the public space a lot more interesting and encourages versatile use.

Designer Joyce Verstijnen
Academy Tilburg
Design Atelier Water Works
Where Eindhoven, the Netherlands
Lecturer/Teacher Jason Hilgefort, Marieke Kums

resilient infrastructure

Saline Culture for the Polder

Created around 1850, the Haarlemmer-meer polder solved several problems: it contained the 'Waterwolf', allowed food production and offered protection against invasions. The grand question today is: What can we do about the increasing salinization of the polder? One option is to take that salinization as a starting point, rather than fight it.

The construction of the Haarlemmermeer polder was part of a plan for the promotion of prosperity in the Netherlands; the land division pattern was dictated by military considerations.

The polder produced abundant crops for a century and a half, but currently the agricultural production is under pressure. During dry spells, the fresh water that is necessary to flush out the polder is increasingly scarce. Salt water seeping up from lower layers furthers salinization as well.

In today's agriculture, crop species are the starting point and the water system is adjusted accordingly. This means keeping the water level low and pumping a lot of water out of the polder.

Reversing the principle and adjusting the crop species to the water level would create a different kind of agriculture and horticulture in the Haarlemmermeer. The new crops thrive in wetlands and are salt resistant. A higher water level, even above surface level, means less pumping. During peak rainfall, the agricultural areas in the polder can contribute to the water storage capacity and thus help protect inhabited areas against flooding.

To ensure the proper functioning of the new water system, the old military dike through the heart of the polder is transformed into a military 'boezem' (bosom). This will increase the water storage capacity by 4 million m³ and also serve as a recreational route across the polder landscape.

Designers Ziega van den Berk
and Anne Nieuwenhuijs

Academy Amsterdam

Design Atelier SouthWest Works!

Where Metropolitan Region
Amsterdam, the Netherlands

Lecturers Marco Broekman,
Roel van Gerwen, Harm Veenenbos

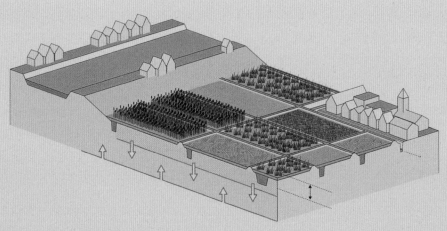

fig. 10 — The new water system

renewable energy

Klimakommune — Saerbeck (DE)

Renewable energy eats up a lot of space. If you add up all the space we need for wind turbines, rapeseed fields and solar farms you will find that they would not fit in the Netherlands. Smart combinations are prerequisite, especially if we also want to enhance biodiversity and the quality of the landscape.

The only indications that you are approaching the bio-energy park near Saerbeck are the seven wind turbines that tower over the greenery. The modern energy park merges perfectly with the century-old bocage landscape of the federal state North Rhine-Westphalia – known for its vast, tree-lined meadows.

And yet this is where some 126,000 megawatt hours of energy are produced from wind, sun and organic materials such as wood, corn, manure and bio-waste every year. That amounts to 2.5 times the energy requirement of the whole of Saerbeck. 93

The *Klimakommune Saerbeck* – the town has a population of 7,200 – wants to be energy neutral in 2030, but will not lose track of biodiversity and the quality of the landscape during its efforts. One third of the park's 90 hectares is even reserved for new nature.

This is not self-evident. Bioenergy or wind facilities are often at odds with their natural surroundings. The production of renewable energy from biomass, for example – the world's leading source of renewable energy – requires hundreds to thousands of times more space than the production of fossil energy in coal or gas plants. We run the risk of producing renewable energy at the expense of the food supply and habitat of plants and animals.[94]

Planner Guido Wallraven played a crucial part in the realization of the Klimakommune. In 2007 he and landscape architect Stefan Wallmann made a master plan for both the bioenergy farm and the town's climate goals. As a project manager, he is now closely involved in all of the 150 projects that the town initiated with an eye to its transition to renewable energy.

The ambitious climate goals necessitated far-reaching changes, Wallraven stresses, but took even more than

93

Values based on: *Energietransitie, op weg naar Circulaire Economie Duitsland – Nederland 5-1*, Lugies, J.H, 2014. Mobility is not included.

94

Power density. A Key to Understanding Energy Sources and Uses, V. Smil, 2015 and *Landschap en energie. Ontwerpen voor transitie*, D. Sijmons, 2014. Both use the term power density: energy per square metre. Both warn that power density is going to be a crucial parameter for the energy structure. Thus, the major challenge is not integration in the landscape, but rather the fundamental rearrangement of the landscape.

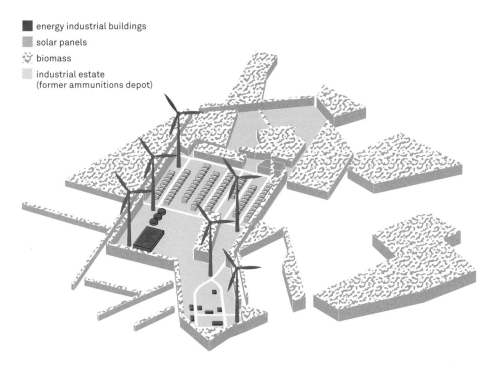

■ energy industrial buildings

solar panels

⁂ biomass

industrial estate
(former ammunitions depot)

fig. 11— Embedding
in the energy terrain

fig. 12— Production in
relation to requirement

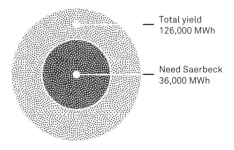

— Total yield
126,000 MWh

— Need Saerbeck
36,000 MWh

fig. 13— Following spread:
Former ammunition bunkers
now function as carriers for
new energy sources

that. 'The energy park likely creates most of its added value by housing educational, scientific and other social facilities.' The University of Munster established a research centre for energy crops and new forms of energy storage here, school children visit for classes about climate change and renewable energy, and there is also a sheltered workshop. The key to the success of the energy park, says Wallraven, was the decision not to present a watertight plan, but to paint a dot on the horizon. Set long-term goals, therefore, with room for spatial changes and growth. That is the only way to include the flexibility a project this large requires.

Take, for example, the stringent rules regarding nature
reserves. The northern part of the energy park is a protected nature reserve where rare moss species grow and
lots of amphibians and bats live. [95] To protect the ecological balance there are no wind turbines in this area,
which meant one of the planned eight wind turbines
had to be cancelled. A mix of renewable deciduous trees
had to further enhance biodiversity and the construction
of wetlands and moors helped attract new species.

The bioenergy park is the final step in a far-reaching
package of measures to make Saerbeck's energy supply
entirely sustainable.[96] In addition, the town provided
400 buildings with solar panels on their roofs and built
a local heating network connected to a heating plant
fired by pallets from a nearby sawmill. The result of all
these measures is that CO_2 emissions have almost been
halved: from 9.9 to 5.5 tons per capita per year.

Local residents had yet another good reason to go
along with the plans. For a maximum of 20,000 euros,
locals could become co-owners of the energy farm
and share in its proceeds. Four hundred people are
participating, which is 7 per cent of the town's total population. The cooperative owns the local energy network.
Designer Guido Wallraven: 'The bioenergy farm cost 70
million euros. It was entirely financed with local money,
without any external financiers. Citizens and local entrepreneurs financed it entirely and that makes it unique in
the world.' The power the locals do not need is exported
onto the national grid.

A number of local entrepreneurs that wanted to make
a larger investment own some of the wind turbines.
They united in a single company that shares the earnings
from the wind turbines equally. And that is important,
because to fit seven wind turbines onto the lot, they
are placed closer together than they usually are and the
blades are a little smaller as well. The advantage of this
type is that it is quiet as a mouse, its disadvantage is
that the turbines shelter each other from some of the
wind. Since all investors receive the same dividend, they
have reconciled themselves to a somewhat lower profit
percentage.

The genesis of the bio farm began in 2005, when the
German army announced it would shut down an ammunitions depot. This would cost the local community 80
jobs. The town had to find a new use for the site and the
mayor convinced the military to sell it to the town for
only 1 million euros. His argument was that the new

95

Like Orthotrichum rogeri
and Ptilidium ciliare: source:
Dipl.-Ing. (FH) Torben Fuchs,
Dr. Johannes Melter, Bio-
Energiepark Saerbeck, Spezielle
Artenschutzrechtliche Prüfung
(saP), 2010 and Landschafts-
ökologische Untersuchungen zum
Munitionsdepot/ Bio-Energiepark
Saerbeck, Bioconsult, 2009

96

An often-used instrument is the
measuring unit EROI, the *Energy
Return on Investment*. The EROI of
biomass is much lower than that
of hydro, wind and solar power
and much, much lower than that
of fossil fuels. In many cases
extracting energy from biomass
takes even more energy than it
produces, with an EROI below 1.
In comparison: solar power has
an EROI of 4 to 10, and gas of 100
to 1000 or even 2000. Smil, 2015.

fig. 14 — Energy park

owner would need to spend 200,000 euros to demolish each of the 90 bunkers on the site, a total of 18 million euros.

It was a clever find indeed, because as it turned out, the heavy bunkers with their slanting roofs provided the perfect place to install 24,000 solar panels. There are now plans to place batteries for the storage of energy inside the bunkers. The site already has room for energy storage, as well as a municipal recycle station consisting of two bio fermenters and a composting plant.

According to Wallraven, the history of Saerbeck makes it difficult to literally copy the process elsewhere. In addition, German legislation on the promotion of renewable energy is way ahead compared with other countries. The German energy grid prioritizes green energy and there are substantial subsidies available.

All the same, Saerbeck has invented a mix that combines a nature reserve and a bioenergy park. And that's a big step forward. Bioenergy parks that were built earlier just aimed to produce as much biofuel as possible. Take iconic parks like Nawaro in the German Güstrow, where 40 fermentation facilities distributed over 30 hectares extract biogas from crops including corn and wheat. Or Biopark Terneuzen in the Dutch Province of Zeeland, where biodiesel and biogas are extracted from

fig. 15 — Following spread: Biomass in the landscape

frying fat, manure and other residual products of local agriculture and industry. No matter how progressive they are, so far they are hardly integrated in the landscape at all.

Precisely therein lies the innovative nature of Saerbeck, says Wallraven. 'Here, we combine ambitions in the field of renewable energy with goals concerning landscape, ecology, education and sociocultural connectivity.' And that is a welcome solution to a pressing problem. On the one hand, 149 countries agreed to drastically reduce CO_2 emissions at the climate conference in Paris in November 2015; on the other, achieving those goals causes major problems.

Or, as Dirk Sijmons writes in his book *Landschap en energie*: 'The landscape is full of formal and informal claims that are unlikely to make room for major new additions without a struggle.'[97] In other words: given current legislation and technology, Europe simply does not have the space necessary to fully transition to renewable energy. By the smart combining of functions like in Saerbeck – an energy park with new nature and an attractive landscape – we can produce renewable energy in places where there is actually no room to do so.

fig. 16 — Energy park

97

Landschap en energie. Ontwerpen voor transitie, D. Sijmons, 2014.

What renewable energy production with an eye for biodiversity

Where Saerbeck, Germany

Design Stadt.Land.Fluss and Büro Stefan Wallmann

Realized 2008–2013

Intervention an energy park in combination with nature development and participation of citizens and social organizations

Also good for material cycle (fermentation and recycling), vital economy (local cooperatives keep money in the community), healthy living (biodiversity), sociocultural connectivity (education)

renewable energy

CO_2 Footprint as a Kick-Starter

Selwerd is a district in the north of the city of Groningen. It was built in the late 1950s. Its typical orthogonal structure is filled in with different blocks of housing and facilities. The designers follow this rational approach: each block has a different approach to energy efficiency and/or energy production. A cost-benefit analysis, finally, provides insight in the effectiveness of each intervention.

The orthogonal design of Selwerd is a product of the post-war reconstruction period: a rational district was expected to produce a rational society. The neighbourhood units consist of terraced houses at right angles and blocks of walk-up flats.

The design presents a lot of relevant information about the average inhabitant, the average household and average dwelling: demography, food consumption, mobility patterns and energy consumption. Combining the blocks and the data, it is possible to calculate exactly how energy transition measures will work out in Selwerd.

Until 2020, all investments will go towards the increased sustainability of the housing. Most of this is owned by housing associations, which will therefore pre-finance the investments. They calculate the most economical choice for each dwelling type taking into consideration the necessary investments, savings and payback periods. That's the low hanging fruit.

In the long term, each block gets to save energy in its own way. Because the CO_2 footprint of the locals – made up of the elements water, waste, energy, food – is known, the blocks can take one of these four components as a starting point. One block may want to focus on energy management and invests in other heat sources, more insulation and adding solar panels. Another may compost waste or reuse

fig. 17 — Renewable energy and water purification combined in a bathing facility

it as pigfeed. A third block may want to focus on the local production of food on rooftops and in the public space. And a fourth may want to store and reuse local rainwater. The plans for this last block are particularly striking: a disused courtyard is given new significance as a common laundry and bathing facility.

A numerical assessment per block will assess what measures have the greatest impact on the energy performance.

Designers Yerun Karabey and Mark Venema

Academy Groningen

Design Atelier Energietransitie Regio Groningen

Where Groningen, the Netherlands

Lecturers Alex van Spijk

renewable energy

Duckweed on Empty Lots

Europapark is an industrial area just outside the ring road around Groningen, in the southeast of the city. Its variety of businesses is considerable: industry, retail, car dealers and recently more and more quality offices. The designer demonstrates that it is possible to cultivate duckweed on the empty lots along the old Winschoterdiep Canal. This would allow the production of an efficient type of biofuel as well as increase the attractiveness of the area.

Europapark is under development. It is slowly transforming into a quality office environment and residential area. The monumental turbine hall of the Hunze power plant was converted into a Media Centre and the central railway station renewed. It is also the location of Football Club Groningen's Euroborg stadium.

The Winschoterdiep Canal dissects the area. In the past, an important settlement requirement of many businesses was access over water. Due to the increase in road transport, the water has lost its transport function. Empty lots are awaiting future development.

These lots can be used to cultivate duckweed in attractively designed basins. Duckweed, which grows rapidly, is an excellent raw material for biogas fermentation. Owing to its high protein content it can also be used as a vegetarian food or as an alternative to the imported soya that is used as animal feed.

The water flows into the basins from the Winschoterdiep Canal, which is purified by the cultivation of duckweed. Connecting the basins to an existing heating-cooling network will allow the residual heat of nearby industry to keep the basins at the desired temperature.

The culture landscape of the basins with duckweed thus adds value to the area in more ways than one. Now empty lots are reused for the production of energy, for the cultivation of raw materials for food and for the buffering of residual heat in the area. In addition, these activities create a park that invites use. Employees of neighbouring offices can go for a stroll during their lunch break and local residents can swim in the purified water from the canal.

Designer Douwe Drijfhout

Academy Groningen

Design Atelier Energietransitie
Regio Groningen

Where Groningen, the Netherlands

Lecturers Alex van Spijk

fig. 18 — Duck weed nursery park

material cycle

Urban Farming — The Hague (NL)

A Swiss company built the biggest urban farm in Europe in The Hague. The farm will provide hundreds of people from the surrounding area with fresh, locally grown vegetables and fish – and this in the middle of the city, on the roof of an empty office building.

On top of the roof, 30 m aboveground, sits a glass greenhouse; below lies The Hague's densely built-up Transvaalkwartier. Inside the greenhouse, various types of lettuce and tomatoes, cucumbers, aubergines, herbs and watercress grow. Bumblebees buzz around the flowers of the tomato and aubergine plants.

One level down, on the sixth floor, sit 30 tanks with tilapia. Once the pink fish are old enough they are given fatal electric shocks and immediately put into cold storage.[98] Stacks of orange crates await to quickly transport the fresh vegetables and fish. This urban farm covers a total of 1,900 m2, a third of a football field. And that in a former office building in the middle of the city, at about 3 km from the city centre.

Those who have read Carolyn Steel's book *Hungry City* know how big the impact of our changing eating habits on the city has been. Not only have we become more and more estranged from our food over the past decades, its production also became less and less visible in the city. Once upon a time, cattle walked from the countryside straight into the streets of each and every metropole, today, food from all over the world comes to us by plane and truck.[99] That is why agriculture on an inner-city location and for the local market, like in The Hague, presents an interesting trend break.

UF002-De Schilde is housed in De Schilde, an office building designed by architect Dirk Roosenburg for Philips in the late 1950s. For years, the building stood empty. It had a bad name, among other things because a number of fraudulent employment agencies had their offices here.

In 2012, the city went looking for a new destination. At that time, 13 per cent of all office buildings in the city were unoccupied.[100] Nation-wide, that percentage was even higher. A meeting attended by the alderman, representatives of Wagingen University – famous for its

98

'Greenhouse in the Sky: Inside Europe's Biggest Urban Farm', *The Guardian*, 27 April 2016.

99

Hungry City. How Food Shapes our Lives, C. Steel, 2008.

100

Investeringsprogramma Stedelijke Ontwikkeling 2013, City of The Hague, 2012.

fig. 19 — Revenue to
need households

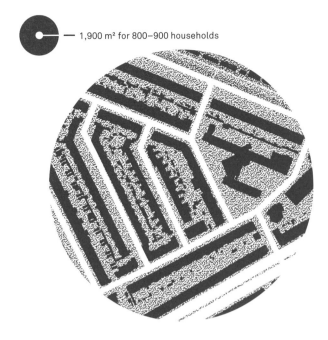

— 1,900 m² for 800–900 households

■ greenhouse
░ horticulture
▓ distribution and office
▒ fish breeding

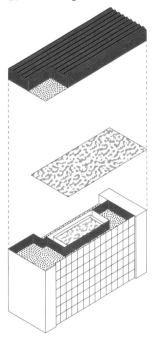

fig. 20 — Stacked urban typologie

fig. 21 — Following spread:
Section of the project

agricultural research – and the innovation department of accountancy firm Deloitte resulted in a plan to use the empty office buildings to experiment with urban agriculture. One and one is two, they thought in The Hague: the building gets a new destination and the city gets to produce food.

The city organized a competition and 70 offices from the Netherlands and abroad entered. That of Swiss urban agriculture company Urban Farmers AG (UFAG) came out on top. The project in The Hague was named UF002-De Schilde, because it is the second urban farm UFAG opened – with the Swiss Basel preceding The Hague. In Basel, UFAG manages a 250-m2 roof garden in collaboration with the Academy of Wädenswil. According to UFAG, the proceeds of its harvest cover its costs.

The urban farm in The Hague is almost eight times that size and wants to provide for 800 to 900 families and restaurants in the area. This involves 45 tons of vegetables per year. The fish-breeding tanks produce about 19 tonnes of fish per year. The investment was made jointly by a private investor, the city of The Hague and the European Regional Development Fund.

It seems quite the enterprise: greenhouses on the roof and water tanks on the sixth floor. But the conversion itself took less than six months, says Sascha Glasl, one of the founders of architecture office Space&Matter that

designed UF002. Between the signing of the collaboration contract in 2014 and the opening in May 2016, the
designers studied conditions: Which requirements does
a rooftop greenhouse have to meet, and what does that
imply to construction, safety and hygiene?

fig. 22 — View from the
greenhouse over The Hague

Before the construction could take off, the roof and
the floor underneath were stripped completely bare.
Calculations showed that the building would be carrying 150 tonnes of extra weight. And so the floors were
reinforced and the weight evenly distributed. The greenhouse had its corners reinforced to be able to withstand
the heavy winds at a 30 m height.

Rather than just make the design, the architects were
also involved in the concept behind the urban farm from
the very beginning. The office and the greenhouse on the
roof had to be one whole, says Glasl about his design, 'as
if they had always been just that'. UFAG also needed a
space to give information to residents, students and others that wanted to know more about urban agriculture.
To that end, the architects designed a connection to the
roof with a view of the greenhouses.

To facilitate agriculture in an office building, UFAG used a
sustainable and closed ecosystem with which it had first
experimented in Basel and which was further developed
and up-scaled in The Hague. The plants and the fish are

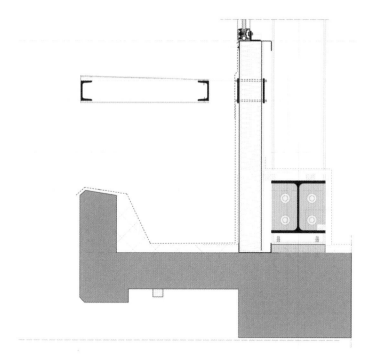

fig. 23 — Detail of the connection between the greenhouse and the office building

101

Using this method, the Japanese manage to grow some 10,000 heads of lettuce on about 2,400 m2 every day: 100 times that of conventional agriculture, using 40 per cent less power, producing 80 per cent less waste and using 99 per cent less water. See also: weburbanist.com.

fig. 24 — Following spread: View from the greenhouse to the offices

grown together in accordance with the so-called aquaponics method.

This works as follows. The fish tanks on the sixth floor are the heart of the ecosystem. Water is pumped around between the fish tanks and the greenhouses on the roof. Fish poop, which naturally contains ammonia, floats in the water from the fish tanks. Plants cannot absorb it. That is why the plants are grown in a layer of hydro granules rather than in garden soil. The bacteria that live among the plant roots consume the fish poop and convert the ammonia into nitrate. This is a valuable nutrient for plants, one that is also found in fertilizers. Once purified, clean water flows back into the fish tanks.

Fertilizers are superfluous and the system uses 70 per cent less water than conventional agriculture.[101]

A computer system controls the circulation of the water between the fish tanks and greenhouses. Temperatures remains constant between 25 and 28 degrees Celsius and ventilation and light incidence are closely monitored.

In this way UF002-De Schilde can grow and cultivate food in the immediate vicinity of hundreds of urbanites. As a commercial company, UFAG strives for standardization and scalability, aiming to make this technology applicable everywhere. Whether or not all of our food will soon be grown on rooftops remains to be seen. But thanks to UFAG, the wish to eat locally grown

food seems to have transcended the level of small-scale, bottom-up initiatives.

fig. 25 — Largest rooftop farm in Europe

What urban agriculture on the roof of an empty office building

Where The Hague, the Netherlands

Design Urban Farmers AG, Space&Matter

Realized 2016

Intervention a greenhouse on the roof with fish tanks on the floor underneath together form a sustainable and closed ecosystem

Also good for renewable energy (energy saving), vital economy (new activity in empty building), healthy living (organic vegetables), sociocultural connectivity (educational projects)

material cycle

Problem Neighbourhood Goes Eco

Today, district Tarwewijk in Rotterdam-Zuid is noted for its problems: unemployment, insecurity, decay. The implementation of municipal and private initiatives is meant to stop its downward spiral. The design describes an initiative that contributes to the closing of the district's water cycle. This will give Tarwewijk an autarkic water system – and more.

Autarkic eco districts are often suburban areas with mostly highly educated, white residents. The designer makes an attempt to introduce the principles of an eco-district in, say, well-off Culemborg or the Bedzed development in London, in an impoverished urban neighbourhood with a multicultural, mostly poorly educated population.

More specifically: the district is to have a covered biological water treatment plant. This looks like a greenhouse and functions as an educational community centre. Decisions about the scale and the location of the greenhouse result from a thorough analysis of the water balance in the area, of the course of the sewers and of urban and architectural elements. The water treatment greenhouse is located at the area's lowest point, in the heart of the district and close to other public services. This way, it is visibly a part of the network of facilities.

Allocating the greenhouse this location in the public infrastructure allows it to serve other purposes besides water treatment. It also functions as an educational space, for example, in which local residents can learn about the water system.

One of the products of the greenhouse is clean drinking water for the entire district, but there are others: the filtered sludge can be used as a fertilizer in the adjacent kitchen gardens. This allows the production of food in the district. The autarky has a non-material side as well: gradually, the locals may be able to take over the management of their everyday facilities. In any case, the greenhouse will become a community meeting space that contributes to the social cohesion in the area.

Designer Cécilia Miedema

Academy Rotterdam

Design Atelier De Grondstoffenfabriek (Tarwewater)

Where Rotterdam, the Netherlands

Lecturer Florian Boer

fig. 26 — Water treatment greenhouse in a multicultural neighbourhood

material cycle

New Earning Model for the Rotterdam Sewer

Replacing sewers is a costly affair. Are there any sustainable ways to manage the current network? Two scenarios examine the spatial implications of disconnecting large parts of the Rotterdam sewer.

Beneath Rotterdam lay some 2,300 km of sewer pipes. They need to be replaced every 60 years, which boils down to almost 40 km per year. This is an investment that weighs heavily on the municipal budget. Today, the sewer is still considered a costly system that transports worthless waste. But sewage water is actually a source of raw materials, for example for the production of energy and the fertilization of crops.

The first scenario focuses on the Rotterdam districts at the very ends of the sewer network. Their wastewater is no longer drained to the central water treatment plant, but to the countryside, for decentralized treatment. Excessive rainfall is collected in the countryside as well.

The sewer can now be used as a cable protection pipe for a new, decentralized and sustainable network. The space required for rainwater storage is adjacent to the ring road: the Fijnstofsingel. This green zone not only allows peak water storage, but also particle purification for the ring road and it creates a green connection between the city and the countryside.

The second scenario focuses on the excess capacity of the sewer that becomes available in central areas of the city. Now that the wastewater of the suburbs no longer runs through these pipes, they can be transformed into a single hybrid network for the transport of various raw materials (both waste water and biodegradable waste). The current water treatment plant in Sluisjesdijk becomes a

fig. 27 — A symbiosis of water, food, energy and waste in Polderdrecht

raw materials plant with a bio fermenter and a combustion plant. The wastewater system thus changes from a costly public facility into a source of income for the city of Rotterdam as a whole.

Designer Bram van Ooijen

Academy Rotterdam

Design Atelier De Grondstoffenfabriek

Where Rotterdam, the Netherlands

Lecturer Florian Boer

material cycle

Office Towers Purify Water

The wastewater that any one urbanite produces – some 120 l per day – drains away to treatment plants that are usually located outside the city. The plants consume a lot of energy and do little or nothing with the filtered raw materials. Decentralized, natural purification systems can be an alternative in the city, too.

Natural water treatment does not require energy. The nutrients and sediments are directly usable in food production and heat is generated as a by-product. But natural treatment requires a lot of space, which is scarce in densely built-up areas such as Rotterdam. Also, it takes height to add oxygen to the purification process. Vacant offices therefore offer a solution: they have a lot of square metres of floor space and the different levels create enough of a height difference to make the water flow. Such offices can accommodate 70 per cent of the treatment processes necessary for Rotterdam, with the other 30 per cent taking place in the surrounding countryside.

The designer lists the requirements such office buildings have to meet on the basis of the technology involved in the purification process. He then maps the Rotterdam sewer network. The Marconiplein towers turn out to be the best location. An entire building is used for purification purposes. Floors are lined with glass wool planted with helophytes. Water flows down the stairwell to absorb oxygen. Some lift shafts function as settling basins.

Partly purified, the water flows from the towers, cascading down through the surrounding cityscape to the port basins. This means the plants not only purify the water, but also the former industrial land around former gasholder Ferro Dome. The latter process takes some 10 to 15 years.

Other buildings in the area serve as a composting tank, a bio fermenter and a CHP plant. The sediment filtered from the water and the trimmings from the helophytes can be converted into nutrients for the growing of food or for the production of the electricity and heat necessary to power the purification.

Step by step, the area will grow cleaner, with more room for public facilities. In the long term, visitors will get to swim in local harbour basins and the soil will be clean enough for horticulture. During the purification process, spatial developments including housing are realized in phases to ensure that the investment of the municipality flows back to the city.

Designer Wander Hendriks
Academy Rotterdam
Design Atelier De Grondstoffenfabriek
Where Rotterdam, the Netherlands
Lecturer Florian Boer

fig. 28 — Reuse of office towers for water treatment

vital economy

Inhabited Industrial Area — Barcelona (ES)

A deteriorated industrial area in Barcelona received a major facelift. The district, now called 22@, became the city's technological and innovative hotspot, its companies surrounded by dwellings, shops, restaurants, museums and parks. But does the 22@ mix run the risk of becoming the victim of its own success?

Poblenou, which had a textile industry, used to be called 'the Manchester of Catalonia'. The Barcelona district was still one of the engines of the economy during the late nineteenth century, but the textile companies left in the 1960s. Industrial buildings fell into disrepair and the neighbourhood northeast of the centre became an unattractive place. Only a few artists and squatters would still live there. Poblenou became impoverished.

Things changed in the 1990s. A great many renovation projects were carried out in the run-up to the 1992 Olympic Games. The Waterfront, a section of the city bordering on the Mediterranean like Poblenou, received a makeover. An urban renewal plan for Poblenou emerged in 1996 and the district was renamed 22@ Barcelona.[102] The area was to again become the engine of the economy. The city made room for manufacturing, like in the old days, though this time in the form of 'knowledge-intensive activities' focusing on technology and it.

The scale of the plan the city council approved in 2000 is impressive: 200 ha of land, 4,000 new subsidized dwellings and the renovation of 4,600 existing homes, 114,000 m2 of public green spaces, a 180-million-euro investment in infrastructure and 130,000 new jobs. Good cycling and public transport connections ensured that the area became an integrated part of the city.

The transformation of 22@ focuses not only on economic development, but also on urban and social developments. People work in the area and live, are educated and spend their free time there. The three main principles are density, diversity and flexibility.

The 4,500 companies that have settled in 22@ since 2000 can be divided into five knowledge clusters:

102

22a is the Catalan classification for an industrial area, 22@ refers to knowledge-intensive activities.

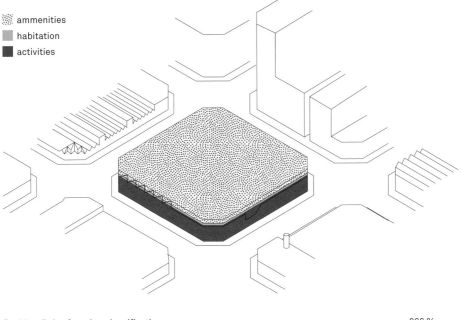

ammenities
habitation
activities

fig. 29 — Rules for urban densification

fig. 30 — Increase (percentage and total in 10 years)

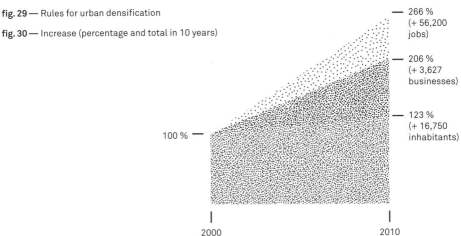

266 %
(+ 56,200 jobs)

206 %
(+ 3,627 businesses)

123 %
(+ 16,750 inhabitants)

100 %

2000   2010

media, IT, medical technology, design and energy. There are many small start-ups in the area, as well as public enterprises, university institutes and telecom giants. They deliberately choose each other's proximity, because clustering furthers knowledge exchange, productivity, growth and innovation.[103] Mutual contact is encouraged. The 22@ Network, a group of 90 affiliated companies, organizes monthly networking events and familiarizes new businesses with the area. In addition, there is plenty of opportunity to meet in public places, in restaurants and cafés, sports grounds and concert halls.

Under the new regime, real estate developers were allowed to mix residential and commercial functions in

103

'Can a Knowledge-Based Cluster be Created? The Case of the Barcelona 22@ District', E. Viladecans-Marsal, J.-M. Arauzo-Carod, 2011.

fig. 31 — Following spread: Mixing scale and functions

a single building and build higher than the usual three
floors. As a result, density rose from 2.2 to 3.[104]

The land of 22@ is in private hands, but the municipality was able to guide the plans. It earmarked some of
the development in exchange for building permits: 10 per
cent for subsidized housing, 10 per cent for green areas
and 10 per cent for so-called @activities.[105] These activities focus on innovation in numerous sectors, from IT to
graphic design, from media to medical equipment. The
city developed the rule that the maximum density could
be increased if the space was used for @activities.[106]

The most striking feature of @22 is perhaps the diversity of buildings: cutting-edge research labs, a renovated
factory chimney and brick buildings covered in graffiti
interspersed with new glass office towers, most notably
the Havana-cigar-shaped Torre Agbar. Old and new go
hand in hand here. The artists, squatters and craftsmen
who continued to live here fought for the preservation
of the old buildings. Their efforts ensured the development of urban craft workshops and various cultural
institutions, such as Hangar and La Escocesa.

There are shops, restaurants, sporting clubs, museums,
galleries, schools, concert halls and parks among the
houses and offices. This is now a genuine urban district
rather than an introverted industrial area. To keep the
skilled working class in the city, the latter has done just
about everything to create a lively and varied habitat.
It subsidized the construction of 4,000 new affordable
rental and owner-occupied apartments to ensure that
the area remains accessible to a mix of incomes.

Although the city had clear goals in mind, there is no
major master plan with a well-defined goal on the table.
The building blocks are developed one by one. The city
assesses listed buildings separately and then decides
whether or not they will be renovated and given a specific function. The area is largely privately owned, the
transformation follows the speed of private initiatives
and investments.

The rest of the area is subject to continuous change
as well. There is a lot of room for experimentation
in 22@. Companies can test innovations in urban planning, education and mobility in a pre-commercial stage,
in practice and under the colours of the 22@ Urban Lab.
These may include pilot projects for public lighting,
smart energy meters, electric cars and bicycle infrastructure. The 22@ district is thus in keeping with Barcelona's
smart city strategy.

104
Density is expressed in
Floor Area Ratio (FAR).

105
'City of Rents: The Limits to
the Barcelona Model of Urban
Competitiveness'. In: International
Journal of Urban and Regional
Research, G. Charnock, T.F. Purcell
and R. Ribera-Fumaz, 2013.

106
'22@ Barcelona Plan, A Programme
of Urban, Economic and Social
Transformation'. In: *Ajuntament de
Barcelona*, 2012.

fig. 32 — Battle in
the neighbourhood

107
'It is about developing productive
neighbourhoods with a human
pace in a hyper-connected and
emission-free city,' as Gert-Jan
Peek wrote in 'Radicale innovaties,
Gebiedsontwikkeling nieuwe
stijl en de Smart City'. In: *S+RO*,
2013/05, p. 14.

108
Charnock, Purcell and
Ribera-Fumaz, 2013.

Open innovation plays an important part.[107] The city has even adjusted its administrative organization to encourage smart city activities. Its super department Urban Habitat combines urban planning, infrastructure, environment, housing and ICT. More than 20 smart city programmes have been kick-started under the Urban Habitat umbrella.

Using incentives such as a higher density for @22 activities and relaxed building regulations, the municipality managed to guide private investment in the required direction for quite some time. The question is how long their success will continue. The success of 22@ has led to real estate speculation and rising house prices at the expense of the lively urban mix.[108] The older residents and artists that have lived here from the very beginning are being driven away, taking the bottom-up initiatives with them. Will @22 become the victim of its own success, or will it be able to realize its social, economic and sustainable ambitions in the long term?

fig. 33 — Development of a lot

What a modern industrial area in the middle of the city

Where Barcelona, Spain

Design 22 arroba bcn, s.a.u. (municipal organization)

Realized 2000 (ongoing)

Intervention complete transformation of an industrial area, with new offices spaces, dwellings and infrastructure

Also good for renewable energy (pilot projects), healthy living (bicycle connections with the city centre, mixed, compact neighbourhood), sociocultural connectivity (public space, dwellings, education and culture)

fig. 34 — Following spread:
Publicly accessible campus

fig. 35 — Following spread:
An iconic building marks the development of the neighbourhood

vital economy

Woodland Gets Its Own Underground Stop

Industrial area Riekerpolder appears to have secured the perfect location, midway between the Amsterdam city centre, Schiphol, Amsterdam-Zuidas and woodland the Amsterdamse Bos. On closer inspection, however, the area is sandwiched between, rather than accessed by, the large-scale motorway and railroad infrastructure. A new stop, Amsterdamse Bos, solves the problem.

Riekerpolder is located at the junction of motorway A4 and the A10 ring road. The railway line between Amsterdam and Schiphol runs along the central reservation. And yet Riekerpolder is only accessible by car. The large-scale infrastructure cuts the area off from the landscape on the other side – De Nieuwe Meer and the Amsterdamse Bos.

The monofunctional area comprises tall office buildings and a number of logistic halls, like that of IBM. Many buildings are unoccupied. The municipality has earmarked the location for redevelopment.

The designer sees opportunities for the area if the North/South Line from Amsterdam-Zuidas is extended to Schiphol. He creates an additional stop, Amsterdamse Bos, near Riekerpolder. Amsterdam-Zuidas and Schiphol now are both three-minute train rides away. Riekerpolder is reconnected to

the network of the knowledge economy. For it is precisely among the knowledge workers that will fill these buildings that car use is decreasing.

The area can transform from an environment dominated by cars to an attractive work environment with good routes for pedestrians and cyclists. The new station also reinforces the quality of the area, because it bridges the gap to the other side of the infrastructure.

This means Riekerpolder is connected to the high-quality recreational landscape of the Amsterdamse Bos, another feature that will help attract international knowledge workers. An additional advantage is that the Amsterdamse Bos becomes more accessible by public transport from the centre of Amsterdam. Adding facilities such as a hotel and a bicycle rental service creates a real entrance.

Designer Thomas Wolfs

Academy Amsterdam

Design Atelier SouthWest Works!

Where Metropolitan Region Amsterdam, the Netherlands

Lecturers Marco Broekman, Roel van Gerwen, Harm Veenenbos

vital economy

Algae Printer in Peatland Area

Traces of ancient manufacturing systems still mark the Zaandam area: peatland, windmills and industrial heritage. Living and working are closely connected with this landscape. The character of the Zaandam area offers starting points to renew its food industry. The designer combines waterways and algae growth with healthy food and new technologies like 3D printing, and foresees the emergence of an actual algae food campus.

The Zaandam area likes to present itself as the food campus of the Amsterdam Metropolitan Region. What are the concrete results of this renewed economic focus likely to be? Which manufacturing economy belongs to a food campus in the Zaandam area and what spatial interventions go with this transition? These are the questions the designer asked herself.

The peatlands in the Zaandam area are characteristic agricultural landscapes, but do not add any production capacity today. They could, though, even without disturbing the landscape experience: the waterways can be used for the cultivation of algae. They are partly converted into biogas, but more importantly, they can stimulate a new food industry in the Zaandam area. Algae are rich in protein and other nutrients. Once the algae are dried, 3D printers can turn them into food in any shape or form. This is currently only done on a small scale.

The designer establishes a food campus on the former location of the vanished industry. The campus focuses entirely on the processing of algae for food using 3D printers. Via a pipeline, the campus is directly connected to the algae growing in the peatlands. All parts of the algae food chain are gathered on campus: storage, processing, research, product design, marketing and retail. The campus also houses several schools.

Designer Willemijn van Manen
Academy Amsterdam
Design Atelier Zaans Next Economy
Where Zaanstad, the Netherlands
Lecturers Marco Broekman,
Dingeman Deijs, Rik de Visser

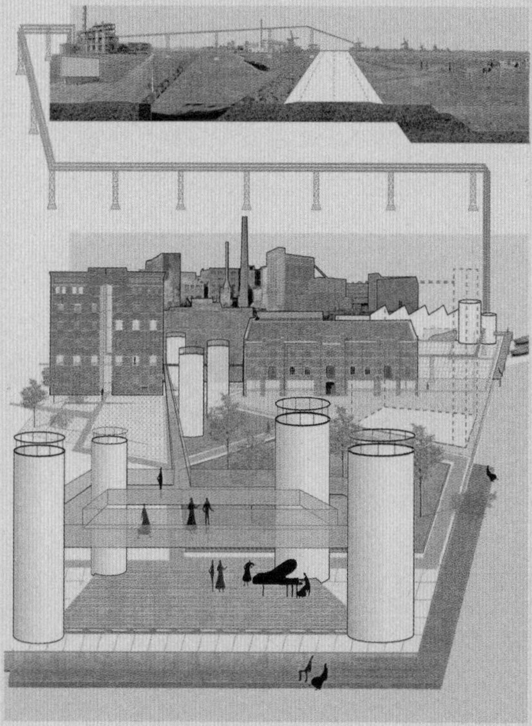

fig. 36 — The 3D printing chain

healthy living

A Place to Play — Enschede (NL)

Skimpy spatial standards and tight budgets for schoolyards force designers to be creative. In district Roombeek in Enschede, they have found smart ways to overcome the lack of space: by introducing shared playgrounds and converting a drop-off lane into a running track.

From above, it looks as if someone drew a human brain and a ruler on the aerial photo of Roombeek. The Enschede district that was largely wiped out during a fireworks disaster in 2000 has acquired an extraordinary new outdoor space in 2007. Between three primary schools, an apartment block for the elderly and a daycare centre lies the common playground of which the brain and the ruler are parts. It is publicly accessible, there are no fences.

The strikingly designed public space is a smart solution to a problem that all primary schools face: the skimpy standards for available outside (play) areas. Since 1997, a Dutch child is only entitled to 3 m² of outdoor space, with a minimum of 300 m² per school. The outside space may be completely paved. Compared to the US (8 m² per child) or the UK (40 m² per child), Dutch children get a raw deal. Moreover, the budget for the schools' outdoor spaces is alarmingly low. Result: too little space for physical activity and a healthy development. Dutch designers have to use their creativity to stretch these standards of space and budget into usable schoolyards.

The landscape architects of Buro Sant en Co designed the shared outdoor space in Roombeek. By combining separate play areas and by having classes take breaks one after another, it is possible to offer the children a lot more space. This does mean that the pupils of the different schools no longer meet during school hours, but that does not seem to be an objection.

There are six schoolyards, separated from the larger, communal playground by a solid privet hedge less than 1 m high.[109] The three primary schools and the day care centre each have their own play areas. The smallest children play in a sheltered area by a wall.

109
Initially there were four primary schools, a play group and a day care centre, hence the six schoolyards. One primary school has moved. The vacant building is now used by the largest of the remaining primary schools.

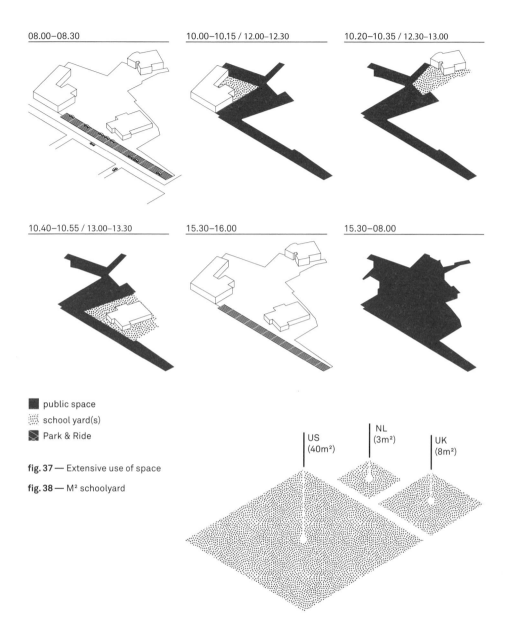

08.00–08.30

10.00–10.15 / 12.00–12.30

10.20–10.35 / 12.30–13.00

10.40–10.55 / 13.00–13.30

15.30–16.00

15.30–08.00

■ public space
▓ school yard(s)
◣ Park & Ride

fig. 37 — Extensive use of space

fig. 38 — M² schoolyard

US
(40m²)

NL
(3m²)

UK
(8m²)

110

Day care centre designers always face a contradiction between providing space for personal and independent development on the one hand and supervision and control on the other. See also: *Surveillir et punir*, Foucault, M., 1975.

fig. 39 — Following spread: Students take over the running track during recess

The areas are interlinked, creating an archipelago of play islands where children have the opportunity to run and play. For now, the only downside is that it is hard for teachers to keep an eye on everything. They cannot always see what is happening behind the hedges.[110] The outdoor space is not only popular with the primary school pupils, but also with local street kids who like to hang out in the public space after school. One of the lunch break supervisors says he often finds broken glass, empty weed baggies and broken playground equipment.

A further trick used to enlarge the play area was to give
the drop-off lane, which is empty at times when children
are not being brought by or picked up by car, a second
function as a running track. The schools combined their
drop-off lane budgets to pay for this design. The running
track is six lanes wide. Every 10 m is marked by large
numbers: 10, 20, 30 and so on. The track can be used to
hurdle race or do the 100 m sprint.

But the children do more than just run. During a visit
to one of the primary schools I saw a group of children
rushing outside during their break to place orange cones
on the intersections of lines to mark off a football field.
At the end of the break, one of the boys did a quick 20 m
sprint. A girl in group 7 tells us how she and her friends
take part in the relay race at the track each year. As is
often the case in schoolyard construction, sections and
lines encourage games and physical activity.111

111
See the guidelines for playground
design in the New York design
handbook for the promotion of
psychical activity: *Active Design
Guidelines, promoting physical activity
and health in design*, AIA et al., 2010.

The brain as seen on the aerial photo is located right in
front of the public primary school of which Truus Pleiter
is the director. It is a concrete area of approximately
1,500 m2, dark grey with white stones for the brain. 'It
looks great from above,' says Pleiter, 'but at eye level it's
mainly a dark area that moreover quickly gets hot in the
summer.' The play surface is low maintenance, but does
not challenge the children to engage in specific games
like the running track does, either.

Along the edges of the brain are coloured steel pipes,
like thick straws. Shortly after the completion there
were trees here, but they rotted away due to the high
groundwater level. 'A green schoolyard would have real
added value for children that live in a stone-dominated
environment,' thinks Pleiter. 'The big old chestnut that
used to stand in the schoolyard was particularly beautiful and also allowed children to play in the shade.' She
would also like to have had more space for a kitchen
garden in which children can grow their own vegetables. She does realize, though, that the construction and
especially the maintenance would make demands on the
school budget.

By half past two in the afternoon, the caretaker raises
the two barriers that close off the running track from
the street. The first cars crawl onto the site. When a
violent rainstorm erupts, parents and grandfathers and
grandmothers almost drive their cars inside the day
care centre to avoid getting wet. *Just push on* seems to
be their motto. It is a hectic coming and going of cars.
Half an hour later, peace returns to the otherwise sleepy
Roombeek streets and the barriers close again, until half

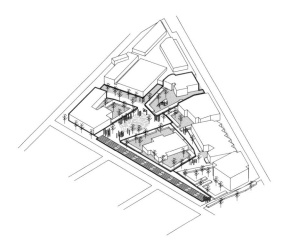

fig. 40 — Running track in context

past seven the next morning. Until that time, the running track, the brain and the space between the schools are the domain of local children. They can run around or play tag, football or badminton. And surreptitiously smoke a joint.

What combination of a drop-off lane
and a running track on a shared playground

Where Enschede, the Netherlands

Design Buro Sant en Co

Realized 2007

Intervention giving children more
space for sports and games around
school by combining outdoor spaces
and combining functions

Also good for sociocultural connectivity
(the shared schoolyard is open
to the neighbourhood)

healthy living

Post-War Reconstruction District for People and Animals

When residential areas are planned, the cost of green public space often goes towards balancing the budget. This is what happened in the post-war reconstruction district Presikhaaf, in the east of Arnhem. The blocks of walk-up flats and terraced housing are interspersed with plots of poorly maintained public greenery. They are being combined to provide the district with a green base that also functions as an ecological corridor between the Veluwe and the IJssel River.

fig. 41 — The passage functions as a connection between the Veluwe and the IJssel River

Presikhaaf is located to the east of Arnhem's city centre, sandwiched between railway lines to Nijmegen and Zutphen and the A12 motorway. The district takes its name from an estate where a family called Van Presichave lived in the fourteenth century.

The designers examined four models for the development of a high-quality landscape that provides room for both animals and people to live. The models each test a different spatial perspective.

One model focuses on a continuous green connection between the IJssel River and the Veluwe. To realize this, some buildings in the centre of the district will have to be demolished. The outskirts of the district allow densification in the vicinity of a new railway station. The access for motorists is adapted. An additional advantage is that a much-used shortcut is no longer available. Public facilities for education, recreation and sports are located at the edge of the green corridor, which also serves as a water

route and as storage for excess rainwater that flows from the Veluwe to the IJssel.

Another model empowers the green edges between the large-scale infrastructure and the district. Both residential blocks and infrastructure currently turn their backs on these strips of greenery. They are widened to at least 50 m, which allows all kinds of animals to move about in them undisturbed. This requires both the thinning out of a number of dwellings near the edges and densification in the heart of the district. This results in more diverse housing as well.

Designers Ludo van Dijken, Jeffrey Floor, Marcel van der Kroef, Renee Lugers, Frans Rubertus, Lean Sas, Lion Schreven, Youri Vijzelman, Lisa Wagemans

Academy Arnhem

Design Atelier The Ecological City

Where Arnhem, the Netherlands

Lecturers Bas Driessen, Thijs van Spaandonk

healthy living

Car-free Workers' District

The Arnhem district of Klarendal abuts the city centre. It is a typical working-class district from the early twentieth century: small, terraced houses separated by narrow streets. The latter have gradually been taken over by cars. Children can no longer play in the streets. Designers of public space sports facilities first have to rid them of cars.

Spacious expansion districts that date from the post-war reconstruction or subsequent periods always have plenty of playgrounds and sports fields in the public space. City centres and pre-war expansion districts have far less space for such things. When they were built, the car was a rare phenomenon and children just played in the streets.

The image analysis of the designers shows that cars dominate the Klarendal streets. They took recent black-and-white shots of local streets and coloured in the spaces reserved for cars to visualize how the right to have a car outside the front door trumps the right to a place to play.

Before they can even begin to make new designs to facilitate sports and games in the public space, they literally have to make room, by developing alternative parking facilities in the district. These facilities will never be as comfortable as parking space outside the front door and therefore the alternatives are equipped with new advantages for car owners. The designers name a few: charging stations for electric cars, shared bicycles, a pickup point for home delivery services. Some of the parking spaces, moreover, can be moved to the edge of the park in the middle of the district.

Street by street, space is cleared to build a network of slow traffic routes and play areas in the district, centring on park and playground De Leuke Linde. The design renditions show the benefits of replacing the cars in the narrow streets by, for example, a training circuit or a running track.

Designers Teun Leene and
Bas Rollerman

Academy Arnhem

Design Atelier Sports and physical
activity in the public space

Where Arnhem, the Netherlands

Lecturers Bas Driessen,
Thijs van Spaandonk

fig. 42 — Former parking lots provide space for sports and games

sociocultural connectivity
Baugruppe — Berlin (DE)

The Baugruppe is a popular building typology in Berlin. Architects say the trick is to create a design in which the building and the dwellings have room to grow with their inhabitant's development.

The Ritterstraße is just another wide, cobblestoned street in Kreuzberg, Berlin: a quiet street, flanked by parked cars and 1950s housing blocks hidden in the green. The building at number 50 looks both unobtrusive and modest, but was created in an unusual way. A recent result of a Baugruppe, Ritterstraße 50 (R50) provides a particularly high quality of living. When the city made the site available for new forms of housing, a group of six architects found its future residents themselves.[112] Candidates mostly came from among their friends and acquaintances. The group of 19 households comprises mostly designers, artists and journalists that managed to find the funding necessary for the construction of the apartment complex.[113]

The architects designed a compact block of seven floors with apartments and balconies on all sides and a large communal space on the ground floor. Unlike in regular new buildings, where residents only get to choose the bathroom tiles and kitchen cupboards, the residents of R50 had a lot of input. They could fill in the floorplan themselves, for example. None of the dwellings are the same and the building includes housing types that could not have been conceived beforehand. The substantive contribution of the residents had yet another important advantage: even before they moved, they felt really committed to their new environment.

Ifau architect Christoph Schmidt considers this the result of *Verhandlung*. This is more than a negotiation between architects and occupants; it involves continuous consultation and joint efforts to find solutions. 'This takes space and flexibility and that needs to be part of the design,' he says. According to Schmidt, designers play an investigative part in this process: they are initiators, architects, developers, estate agents as well as co-occupants. And they are dealing directly with the end-users from the start, never with intermediaries. That is why besides design talent, you also need inquisitive and social skills to work for Baugruppen.

112

Involved in the project were the ifau, the Institut für angewandte Urbanistik, led by Christoph Heinemann, Susanne Heiss and Christoph Schmidt, in collaboration with architects Jesko Fezer, Tim Heide and Verena von Beckerath. Ifau is a research office that has a lot of experience with participatory design processes.

113

In the Netherlands, banks are often reluctant to fund such forms of collective private commissionership (CPO). But the UmweltBank from Nürnberg, which calls itself 'Germany's green bank', put the individual mortgages in a joint financial package to ensure that all stages of the development were covered. The building was developed using private investments, without any government subsidy or support from a commercial developer.

communal spaces
private livingrooms
private bedrooms

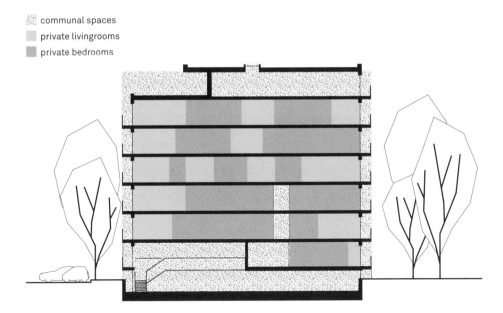

fig. 43 — Communal spaces
for shared use

fig. 44 — Advantage
in euros per m²

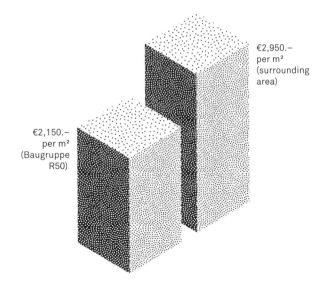

€2,950.–
per m²
(surrounding
area)

€2,150.–
per m²
(Baugruppe
R50)

fig. 45 — Following spread:
Shared use of continuous
balconies

Baugruppen have been popular in Berlin for quite some time. They are part of a long tradition of cooperative living arrangements such as the famous co-ops, communes and housing cooperatives, in which tenants co-own their residential complex. The Baugruppen surpass this, because the residents are also co-commissioners of their own building. This type of building initiative boomed around 2002. Owing to the economic crisis, hardly any houses were built at all. As land was cheap, architects went looking for commissioners themselves and made their own plans. This way, they

developed a new market for collective private commissionership: the Baugruppe.[114]

The influence of the residents on the design results
in a wide variety of dwellings. And because there is no
intermediating market party that wants to make money
by selling off the apartments, the Baugruppe results in
affordable housing as well. This is not unimportant in a
city like Berlin, where rents have skyrocketed in recent
years because of the city's growing popularity. The influx
of major foreign investors does the rest: the prices of
private properties have gone through the roof. Hipster
Heaven Kreuzberg, the location of R50, is no exception
in that respect.

Baugruppen create a counterbalance: when R50
was completed in 2013 the apartments cost 2,150 euros
per m² compared to a district average of 2,950 euros
per m².[115] Prices have risen considerably since.

Yet financial feasibility is not all that counts. Even
though the fact that they can live relatively affordably is
undoubtedly a pleasant side effect to the residents of R50,
they chose to live here because of the communality, one
of the main features of this Baugruppe. Whereas private
spaces in regular housing developments are growing
ever bigger at the expense of the communal space, this
Baugruppe decided to make room for this communality.
There are shared balconies that encircle the floors and
there is also a shared garden and a communal room on
the ground floor. Its shared spaces are the strength of
this Baugruppe.

The communal areas allow flexible use. The balconies,
for example, must remain available as an escape route,
but can be used and decorated in consultation with the
neighbours. The design did not include a garden plan,
partly because it did not appear there would be a budget
for it once the building was completed. But the fact that
there is no fence around the garden is not the result of
a lack of money: it was a deliberate decision that allows
the neighbourhood children to play there as well. Now
that some money has been saved up, new initiatives for
the garden are emerging.

Since the design includes opportunities for flexible
use, the negotiating process and the balancing of individual and communal interests is ongoing. This also
happens when residents move and new people take their
place. Because there was no fixed plan in advance, the
Baugruppe can absorb new residents and their changing
needs. That is perhaps best illustrated by the communal

114

The book *Self-Made City: Self-Initiated Urban Living and Architectural Inventions* (2013) claims that a very innovative type of housing production with new dwelling typologies, more spacious accesses and more communal spaces has emerged in Berlin.

115

Figures CBRE, 2013.

fig. 46 — Communal spaces in the building

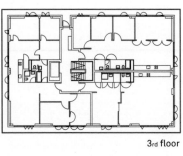

3rd floor

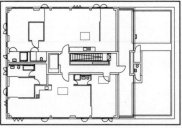

attic

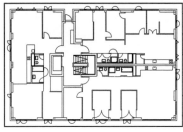

2nd floor

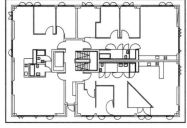

6th floor

1st floor

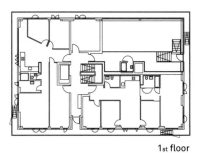

5th floor

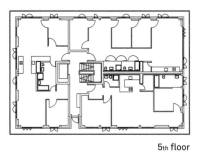

basement

4th floor

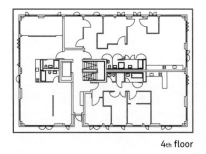

fig. 47 — Floor plans

fig. 48 — Ritterstraße 50, Berlin

space on the ground floor, the function of which has changed in the course of time.

The initial design included a communal area on each floor, but the residents decided to combine these into one large area next to the entrance of the building. It is a nice open space with high windows, sparsely furnished with an eclectic collection of furniture, a piano and Ping-Pong table. On the mezzanine floor is a guest room for visitors and there is a large kitchen for shared use. After three years, it turned out that the residents hardly used it, except for some music lessons and the odd residents' meeting.

In late 2015, the residents offered the space as a temporary accommodation for a family of 13 refugees. The open space may not have provided the family with the privacy it wanted, but the kitchen finally did see some proper use. The residents regularly ate with the family. Lending out their space temporarily enhanced the group's sense of community.

fig. 49 — Shared dining in a commual space

What an apartment complex with plenty of communal space and committed residents

Where Berlin, Germany

Design ifau, Jesko Fezer, Heide & von Beckerath

Realized 2013

Intervention architects approached prospective residents themselves and in consultation created a flexible design and filled in the details

Also good for healthy living (cooking and gardening together)

sociocultural connectivity

Raw Materials Bank in Miner's Colony

Vrieheide is a miner's district – a colony – located in the municipality of Heerlen in the Dutch Province of Limburg. Built in the 1950s, it is now completely run down. The district is provided with a new perspective. The creativity and initiative of its residents are encouraged, permanent and temporary use combined and connections between the district and the countryside created. The strategy includes a crucial role for a raw materials bank.

The miner's colony Vrieheide, established in 1959, was designed by famous post-war reconstruction architect Peter Sigmond. The modern white houses in the rolling green countryside immediately bring Le Corbusier to mind. After the mines closed, the district gradually deteriorated.

In the 1990s, the rental dwellings were sold to the occupants. They have subsequently systematically adapted the dwellings and expanded them using accidentally available materials and improvised constructions. The mostly unemployed residents are increasingly unable to afford the upkeep of their homes. The public green areas, too, show serious neglect.

The design deliberately chooses not to protect or restore the modernist architecture, but embraces the do-it-yourself history of the area. The badly insulated houses are equipped with a double, openable façade. To finance this costly investment, the locals will do a lot of work themselves. The demolition waste is not removed (which would cost a lot of money), but stored in a 'raw materials bank'.

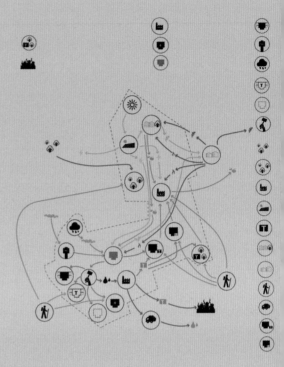

fig. 50 — Flows strategy in Vrieheide

The residents can subsequently use the materials in that bank to build recreational modules for temporary habitation. These will be located strategically in the district and in the surrounding countryside. They can be used both by residents themselves and rented to day-trippers and tourists. The modules are eye-catchers as well as an export product that the district can use for festivals, campings and art routes.

Designer Nadine Nievergeld
Academy Maastricht
Design Atelier Design Lab Vrieheide
Where Heerlen, the Netherlands
Lecturers Jules Beckers, Marco Broekman, Niek Bisscheroux

sociocultural connectivity

German Students Cross the Border

Shrinkage and vacancy are major challenges for the cities in Parkstad Limburg. But where Heerlen struggles with empty buildings, Aachen faces an acute shortage of student housing. Heerlen can fulfil a need by constructing a fast public transport link. This will allow the beautiful parkland in the east of Heerlen to draw international students.

On the east side of Heerlen's city centre, more and more large buildings are being abandoned. The former users of the buildings often decided to move to other places in or outside the city. The buildings were once designed for a specific type of use, which means reuse or redevelopment are hardly ever feasible. In addition, the population of the region will continue to decrease in the coming years, with the number of vacancies only increasing.

In contrast Aachen, on the other side of the border, faces a shortage of housing for its population of 40,000 students. Is it possible to transform an area with many vacancies, such as Heerlen-Oost, into an attractive proposition for international students from Aachen? And what would such an area look like?

The countryside forms the basis of the intervention. It is drawn into the city to create a new ground level to replace the current infrastructure of roads, parking spaces and paved sidewalks. As a result, the buildings will be situated in a park. The façade of the abandoned 1985 Grand Hotel will be stripped, leaving the characteristic concrete skeleton to form a magnificent vessel for a combination of varied student housing and student facilities at different levels.

fig. 51 — An abandoned hotel is transformed into student housing

Designer Roel Raeven

Academy Maastricht

Design Atelier Connected in Parkstad

Where Heerlen, the Netherlands

Lecturers Peter Defesche, Franz Ziegler

Part 2 -- How

Research by design is a great tool for understanding
urban systems and identifying opportunities to
improve them. And perhaps more importantly:
it brings parties together and makes them collaborate.
This part addresses how research by design works.

The first chapter examines the new context in which
designers operate. Urban regions face so-called wicked
problems, interlocking clusters of problems that
have neither head nor tail. Unsurprisingly, designers
are offered fewer and fewer clearly defined spatial
commissions.
    Instead, they are asked to improve the performance
of the urban system as a whole. Designers are asked
to clarify the question themselves. And that is where
research by design – or more broadly formulated,
design thinking – comes into play.
    The type of outcome research by design can gener-
ate is dependent on, among other things, the challenge,
stage and scale. It can be a building, a street profile or a
model, but also a point of view or a concept. Or even a
new, more targeted research question for the follow-up.

Next, we will discuss the three models the research
group Future Urban Regions tested in practice.
The c3 Cube helps us to define the problem and
position it based on its scale, the actors involved
and the urban challenge.
    The DTP Diagram explains the stages the design
process goes through, which actors are involved
and what these expect at each stage.

The ICCI Model, finally, divides the research by design into four tangible steps. The process diverges in the first two steps and then it converges. This model is repeated several times during the research by design.

Designers can play an important part in solving wicked problems. However, these problems are not solved easily, quickly or solitarily. They require multidisciplinary collaboration, patience, reflection and perseverance.

Wicked problems and the Art of Design Thinking

It sounds so easy: 'Work on healthy urbanity.' But the reality is rather less manageable, notably because it involves dealing with so-called 'wicked problems'. Professor of design theory Horst Rittel invented the term in the late 1960s to refer to complex social problems that are difficult or even impossible to solve.

Unlike problems with heads and tails, wicked problems are clusters of problems that can each be seen as a symptom of yet another problem. Unhealthy eating habits, for example, can be related to poverty, poor education and single-parent families, phenomena that are in turn entangled with social, economic, cultural and spatial divides.

In contrast to 'tame' problems that are scientifically verifiable and manageable, wicked problems lack an associated, generally applicable methodical approach. Their mutual entanglement makes it difficult and perhaps even impossible to measure whether chosen solutions meet with success. There is therefore not much point in trying to identify 'true' and 'false' solutions, though it is possible to assess whether solutions improve or worsen the situation. However, this in turn means that the perspective of the person that defines the problem plays an important part.

Of old policymakers – whether they represent central government, knowledge institutes or public-private parties – are responsible for the tackling of wicked problems. Partly on the basis of the needs and desires of citizens and businesses, they set the spatial agenda or at least ask well-informed questions to arrive at a definition of the challenges designers are asked to meet. But this division of responsibilities is now rapidly disappearing. More and more often, designers are presented with abstract ambitions and they are gradually learning the skills required to define the challenges that lie behind the ambitions.

According to Horst Rittel, wicked problems share ten characteristics, the latter of which may well be the most striking: people that tackle a problem do not have the right to be wrong, in other words, they are

responsible for the consequences of their interventions.[116] Any
designer willing to accept such a challenge is hereby forewarned, after
all, it is not possible to test solutions in advance: every step taken
changes the problem and will thus result in another question.

Widening the Challenge

Traditionally architects, urban planners and landscape architects are
focused on space; it is the framework they use to define both problems
and their possible solutions. That is why it makes sense to call them
spatial designers. However, as Part 1 of this book demonstrates, the
framework space provides is too limited: the flows that traverse the city
are equally important. It is precisely this metabolic outlook – and the
associated flow analysis – that allows designers to come to grips with
the coherence behind wicked urban problems.

Flows furthermore allow the accentuation of the goals of interventions. Urban development can no longer exclusively focus on securing
morphological coherence, filling in empty spaces in the urban fabric
and unrolling real estate green fields, but will explicitly have to concern
itself with the improvement of the metabolism and the performance of
the city.

Both the physical and the social performance of the city as a whole
require improvement: energy management, food production, water
management and biodiversity as well as economic vitality, health and
sociocultural connectivity.

In other words, the focus is shifting from location to performance.
This does not (always) require a spatial intervention or grand gesture.
Or, as Rem Koolhaas recently put it: 'In the future,
architecture may well be valued most for its non-
architectural features.'[117]

In recent years, such major changes have not only
been taking place in spatial design, shifts are occurring
throughout the design world. There is a striking demand
for new products: not only for tangible objects but also
for experiences, services, innovations, transformations
and perceptions. Hypotheses, scenarios and accentuated
questions are also increasingly the (intermediate) product of designers' investigative efforts.

In addition, designers work together more and
more: the individual effort is replaced by the collective
approach and not only where the input of experts from
other disciplines is concerned: end users are made part
of design teams as well (inclusivity-based co-creation).

Due to these changes in the design process, traditional design tools no longer suffice. Besides sketches,
drawings, prototypes and models, designers use new
tools, such as animations, narratives and performances.

116

Rittel developed the notion of
wicked problems together with
urban planner Melvin Webber in
Dilemmas in a General Theory
of Planning, 1973.

117

During the AIA Convention
2016 Rem Koolhaas said:
'Architecture and the language of
architecture—platform, blueprint,
structure—were just about the
favourite language to describe
many phenomena that come to
us from Silicon Valley. They took
over our metaphors and that made
me think that regardless of our
pace, which is too slow for Silicon
Valley, we perhaps should not think
about the modern world in terms
of buildings, but rather in terms of
knowledge or organization and of
the structure we can offer society.'

Design Thinking
Wicked problems require an alternative way of working, a method
that is supportive and investigative rather than targeted and solution-
oriented, that departs from an open, inquiring attitude rather than from
omniscient expertise. Research by design is such a method.

Designers and scientists look at problems in fundamentally different
ways. Whereas scientists are used to looking back, as they relate to the
present by analysing and interpreting results from that past, designers can afford a more speculative approach. Using imaginative research,
they can extrapolate the present to explore future prospects.

Designers can use reversed engineering, or back casting, to create an
understanding of the steps that must be taken today to realize a projected future. This can make clear, for example, what knowledge has
to be amassed to be able to determine whether a proposal is feasible.
In other words, a design is a hypothesis that can be confirmed or dis-
proved by an examination of the present.

Though 'research by design' is the popular term for the use of design
as a research tool, professional literature is teeming with combinations
of the words 'research' and 'design'. Broadly speaking, three kinds can
be distinguished: research into design, research for design and research
by design. FUR is mainly concerned with the latter.

At the risk of adding to the confusion, FUR also speaks of
'design thinking' in cases where design actions and
thinking coincide.[118] In this context, thinking is conceived of as a mental process involving the creation of an
image or representation of something, or an idea, understanding, insight or plan that is formed or even actively
implemented.[119] 'Design thinking' refers to the attitude
with which designers approach problems.

A variation is the term 'design-oriented thinking',
used by Charlotte Geldof and Nel Janssens of Flemish
art academy LUCA. They refer to the utopian character of
both architecture and urban planning, which always
focus on intervening in the present with the idea that
the future holds a better spatial and social context.[120]

Designers do not have a monopoly on research by
design, it is a way of thinking that people have used for
thousands of years.[121] However, through endless exercises, designers did greatly refine this common human
talent and therein lies their added value.

To sum up: here, research by design is understood as
the exploration of lines of reasoning to solve possible
challenges that can come up either today or in the future.
These challenges aim to improve both the performance
of the existing city and its underlying system, as well as
add new quality.

118
According to German architect
and architecture historian Ungers,
designing is the representative
process of thought.

119
'Ontwerpen aan mogelijkheden',
J. Visschers (SAUD) and W. Lofvers
(FUR) in: HUIG-Academie
Rotterdam, 2015.

120
'Van ontwerpmatig denken naar
onderzoek' in: *Casus Mare Meum:
een oefening op de zee*, Vlaams
Architectuur Instituut, 2007.

121
'We humans have a long history of
design thinking, as the works of
art of ancient civilizations demonstrate, and the unbroken tradition
of local design and traditional
craftsmanship ... Designing comes
naturally to people and "design"
has not always been considered
something that takes extraordinary
skills.' *Designerly Ways of Knowing*,
N. Cross, 2007.

Three Models
FUR used three models for its research into healthy urbanity:

1. The C3 Cube (Complete City Cube)
   – the definition and positioning of the challenge.

2. The DTP Diagram (Design Thinking Process Diagram)
   – the development of the design process
   and of the attitude of the actors involved.

3. The ICCI Model (Inform, Combine, Choose, Implement)
   – the research by design process in four steps.

As we shall see, these models partly overlap and are furthermore part of
an iterative process: their outcomes often lead to new cycles of research
and design. They share this entanglement with the wicked problems
they address.

Using these models, students of the Dutch Academies of Architecture carried out research. Each of a total of 18 topical challenges
formulated was examined in a design atelier.[122] This not only resulted
in concrete design proposals for the investigated situations, but also
allowed the students to experience research by design as a method:
How does one translate an initial idea into a challenge and then into
a specific commission during a process?[123]

The complexity of the challenges – involving networks with multiple actors rather than a linear, single-commission situation; anticipating
existing conditions rather than starting from pictures of the future –
required a flexible attitude, good reflective and communication skills
and the ability to use a large arsenal of tools, in short,
the ability to learn by doing.

But not only the students developed: their input and
experiences helped the research group to transform
the tacit knowledge involved in the approach of spatial
problems into explicit knowledge. In the course of the
research group, the models were refined and focused.
Together they form a, not strictly scientific, theoretical
model of the research by design carried out at the
Dutch Academies of Architecture.

The C3 Cube
As we have seen, it is extremely difficult to pin down the
challenges involved in wicked problems and that of
healthy urbanity is certainly no exception to the rule.
The C3 Cube was developed as a tool for the positioning
of challenges.[124] The model uses three perspectives.

122
See appendix 1 for an overview of
all ateliers →p. 296.

123
A total of 33 design proposals are
included in this book, in each case
following the Practical Examples.

124
The *Complete City Cube* (C3) was
conceived by Fabric, the office of
Eric Frijters, for the study 'Gezonde
verstedelijking' commissioned by
the Ministry of Infrastructure and
the Environment (2012) and further
developed for 'A New Metabolism
for Rotterdam' commissioned
jointly by the municipality of
Rotterdam, the Port of Rotterdam
and the IABR 2014.

1. The themes the challenge deals with:
   economy, sociocultural connectivity and ecology.

2. The actors involved in the challenge:
   governments, market parties, citizens.

3. The scale at which the spatial challenge manifests:
   region, city, street and block. National strategies not only
   have spatial consequences at the regional level, but also at
   lower scale levels, and vice versa.

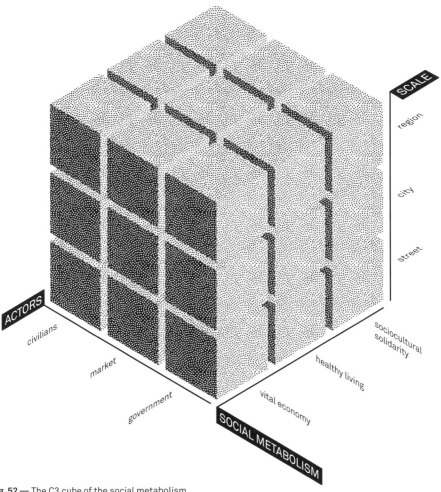

fig. 52 — The C3 cube of the social metabolism

The c3 Cube can be used to check for errors such as overlooking perspectives, actors or scales and to bundle challenges and qualities. It can inspire a coalition that has a sociocultural plan at the level of the street, for example, to ask itself questions such as: What does the plan mean to the city or the region? Can the plan be connected to other themes? Are there other actors who would be willing to help?

Research by design into healthy urbanity evolves: actors can drop out and new actors can join in; the scale of the work can change and in the course of time even the substantive themes can change. Advancing understanding can lead to a shift of focus inside the wider domain of healthy urbanity. The positioning of the problem is therefore not static: any challenge can change position within the three dimensions of the cube. Thus, the c3 Cube is also a tool to illustrate the progress of a research by design process.

As mentioned above, new actors can join in and themes and scales can be added, but the overall trend is that the c3 Cube becomes smaller as the process runs its course. Of the initial 27 blocks ($3 \times 3 \times 3$), an increasingly smaller number is left. The cyclic refining of the design challenge makes it increasingly specific, until it finally results in a regular project with a clear theme at a specific scale level and involving well-described actors.

To the deliberate monitoring and direction of this progress, the following diagram is better suited.

The DTP Diagram

What stage of the process is this? Has an external party asked a question or did a designer come up with the initial problem? Which parties are claiming a role in the process and to what extent are they committed? What steps are now necessary to involve new actors or satisfy existing ones? These are questions the Design Thinking Process Diagram (DTP Diagram) can clarify.

The research by design process evolves from abstract to specific, it converges from wide to narrow. In the beginning, when everything is still open and there is not yet a specific challenge or commissioner, the process centres on development of a strategy. In the end, it is all about design and about the implementation and monitoring of the project. The following representation of the model distinguishes seven stages – strategy, idea, concept, project, design, product, monitoring – which can of course be further specified if necessary.

Each stage is a consolidation point. The transitions between two stages are diamond-shaped to indicate that each stage is always initially followed by a search for new information. This is then combined with older information (a divergent process). Next, the best version is selected and implemented (a convergent process). The following ICCI Model represents ways to deal with the process inside the diamond shape.

The diamond shapes grow smaller in the course of the process, because the bandwidth of the research narrows as the entire diagram converges towards a solution, or rather, towards a refined question.

Research by design plays a part during the entire process, but its part gradually transforms from 'research by design' to 'research for design'. The first stage – from strategy to project – is primarily concerned with 'research by design', while 'research for design' is more dominant during the final stage – from project to product.

FUR focuses on the first stage, that is: the stage from strategy to project. In this context, a project is always defined as an activity that is limited in terms of time and resources and has a specific creative goal. It differs from a programme or process by its singular nature.

The DTP Diagram can not only be used to monitor the stages of the research by design process itself, it also shows, as a parallel development, that the practical applicability of the design increases and that the commitment of the actors grows.[125]

When the diagram is used in practice, it is about a strategy in the beginning of the process. At this stage, the design only has to be conceivable. In the course of the process the design becomes more realistic: it must first prove to be tenable, then feasible, then practicable and finally it has to be actually useful. That means the question is progressively refined in the course of the process until finally everything falls into place.

The diagram is also about the attitudes and expectations of the actors. At first, they are neutral about the idea that is presented to them. After all, they have not heard of it before, they are only beginning to imagine that it is possible in principle. In the course of the process the idea is refined and information is added, so that the actors can assess whether the idea will eventually be useful to them.

The goal of research by design is thus to guide a group of actors and stakeholders from a strategy to a product, by changing their attitudes towards the idea: from neutral, to interested, to committed, to invested until they are finally willing to realize it. This process is supposed to run parallel to the development of the design itself; the researching designers provide the actors with information on the basis of which they can and will want to adjust their attitudes.

Once a new stage begins, it remains important to sharply delineate the way stakeholders relate to the issue. Next, the researching designers guide the various actors to the next stage. Not all players go through the process in the same way: some will drop out and new ones will join in. This subject is addressed in Part 3.

The DTP Diagram helps to keep an eye on the design process (from vision to monitoring) as well as on the actors (who are involved, what is their attitude and what

125
Management van processen, T. Bekkering and J. Walter, 2001.

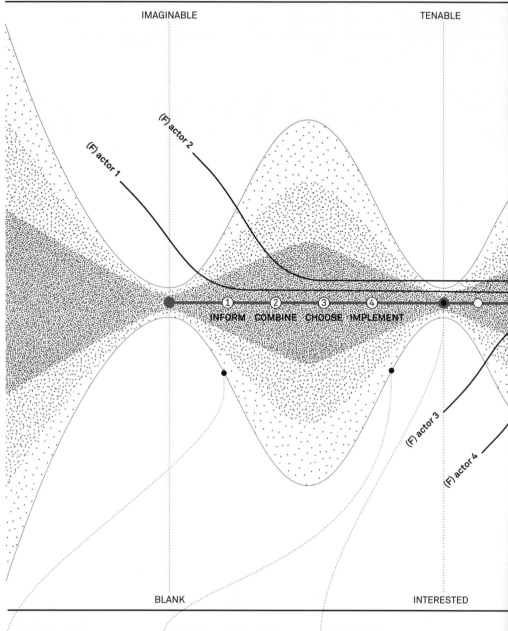

IMAGINABLE   TENABLE

(F) actor 1

(F) actor 2

① ② ③ ④
INFORM   COMBINE   CHOOSE   IMPLEMENT

(F) actor 3

(F) actor 4

BLANK   INTERESTED

diverge: INFORM + COMBINE	converge: CHOOSE + IMPLEMENT	consolidate: C3 CUBE
– add facts, take position, formulating arguments	– focus on new reality	– determine and capture a new representation of the idea
– brainstorm, philosophize, take position, formulate arguments	– summarize, narrow down, negotiate concessions, choose, come to agreement	– new facts, opinions, relations and relevant stakeholders
– the idea is subject to deformation and development	– The idea becomes shaper and more mature	– the idea becomes tangible through a new comprehensible representation

fig. 53 — The DTP Diagram

FACTORS/FEASABILITY

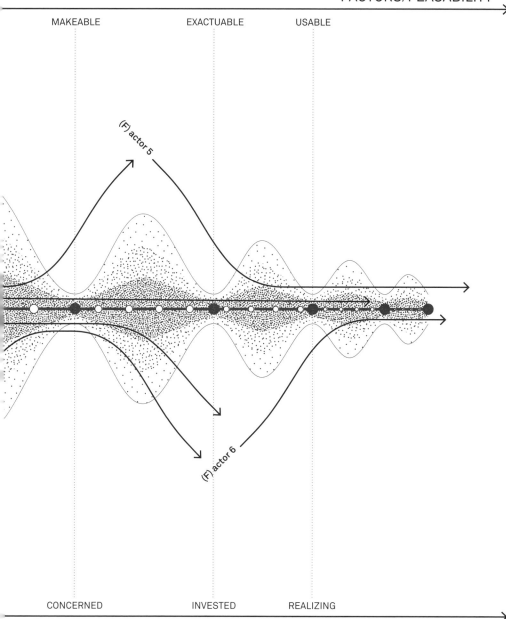

MAKEABLE   EXACTUABLE   USABLE

(F) actor 5

(F) actor 6

CONCERNED   INVESTED   REALIZING

ACTORS/SUPPORT

do they need). Or put more formally: the DTP Diagram is a tool that increases the synthesizing capacity of design thinking and that focuses on providing alliances of actors with a joint perspective related to a spatial challenge.

The ICCI Model

To give designers control over the process inside the diamond, FUR has developed its own model, the ICCI Model. This model structuralizes the data gathering process, the translation of data into information and subsequently into knowledge and wisdom, and is used for the development of plans, designs and activities. The model structuralizes design thinking in the narrow sense of the term and ensures its usefulness in practice.[126]

Any research by design undergoes many ICCI cycles. The outcome depends on the stage the process is in: it can be a building, a street profile or a model, but also a vision or concept, like the DTP Diagram already indicated, or a newer, more refined research question for the follow-up.

The ICCI Model distinguishes four activities:

I Inform – study the challenge from different angles and gather information using geographical and statistical analysis, exploratory fieldwork, literature studies and so on. The aim is to picture both the spatial expression and the underlying system and their organizational coherence.

C Combine – gather the flows of information from the first stage together in a new context by establishing relationships between past, present and future, between hard and soft values and between explicit and tacit knowledge.[127] This process is never straightforward and unambiguous, it develops in cycles of back casting. Because the challenges are multidisciplinary and cross borders and scales, collaboration with areas of expertise outside the discipline is required. This step results in the identification of a number of scenarios.

C Choose – further develop the proposed scenarios from the previous stage so they can be judged on their usefulness and the action perspectives they offer. Complement existing design tools by new ones such as scenario planning and storytelling at this stage.[128]

126

The ICCI Model was developed in the course of the research group and only used in all of the design ateliers in 2016. It is derived from John Boyd's OODA Model, which divides processes into four development stages: observe, orient, decide, act. The ICCI Model differs fundamentally from the OODA Model, because it is not focused on training and internalizing routines, but rather provokes intuitive reactions to standard situations.

127

This is essentially what distinguishes research by design from scientific research. Whereas scientists are looking for explanations for events that have already taken place, designers can create non-existent futures. In this stage, the role of design is to introduce an intellectual approach that is emphatically and culturally informed. In combination with a more methodical and investigative attitude that alternatively has deductive, inductive and certainly also abductive dimensions, design thinking is injected into the process.

128

On 19 and 20 March 2015, FUR held a masterclass Scenario Planning in Groningen led by Christian Salewski (ETH Zurich).

Finally, test the selected scenarios on the community of actors and select a preferred scenario.

I Implement – develop the preferred scenario in collaboration with the actors. This results in a design, plan or action, or in a new, more focused research question. This inclusive approach requires an open, reflective design attitude and the communicative style of the designer must be in keeping with that of the target group. The ownership of the problem is reaffirmed during the framing and further refining of the chosen scenario: Who feels responsible for the revised challenge?

The ICCI Model makes a process explicit that we often use subconsciously in our everyday life: we observe, consider alternatives, make a choice and act accordingly.

Focusing on research by design, what stands out is that the emphasis is on research during the first two steps (informing and combining): the subject is examined from all sides and prototypes are developed. This is a divergent stage, the information and ideas fan out in all directions, the wider the better.

The last two steps (selecting and implementing) are more centred on the design: refining the obtained information, making choices by weighing pros and cons and drawing, and creating a focal point.

This diverging and converging scissor movement characterizes the research by design process: it develops new knowledge by generating prototypes. These are then evaluated by comparing them with the original hypothesis. Below, both the divergence and the convergence are described in detail.

The Diverging DOCA Approach

The six themes of the city of tomorrow described in Part 1 presuppose a complementary, alternative reading of the city. They not only address the spatial expression of the city, but also its underlying system.

Designers tend to overlook this rather less visible forcefield of urban metabolism. FUR developed an additional tool, the so-called DOCA Approach, to prevent this and to encourage a divergent, inquisitive attitude.

DOCA stands for *Data* (hard, explicit knowledge), *Opportunities* (possibilities for the future), *Challenges* (the challenge of the here and now) and *Anecdotes* (soft, implicit knowledge), and provides a framework for the gathering and organizing of various types of input. Each goal has been coupled with a specific method: Mapping, Simulating, Modelling and Fieldwork.[129]

129
The Future Cities Laboratory that the ETH Zurich developed together with Singapore distinguishes comparable techniques: fieldwork, mapping, modelling, lab-work.

D Data / Mapping
  Question: What is actually happening?
  Action: Gather factual information by desk research

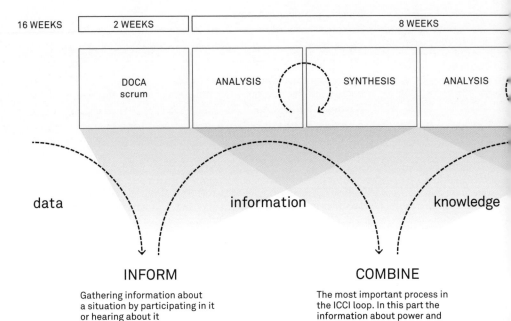

INFORM

Gathering information about
a situation by participating in it
or hearing about it

COMBINE

The most important process in
the ICCI loop. In this part the
information about power and
infrastructure is confronted
with spatial opportunities
and challenges. It is collected,
ordered and projected (blue cards)
on three scale levels. Back-casting
makes clear what needs to be done
to realize the future vision

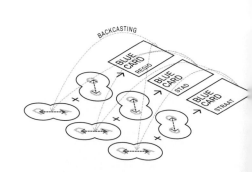

DOCA consultation

— economy and mobility

— waste & food

— water & soil

— energy

Dialogue themes

— data versus anecdotes

— challenges versus opportunities

— matters of fact versus
matters of concern

— connecting to scales;
region, city, street

fig. 54 — The ICCI Model

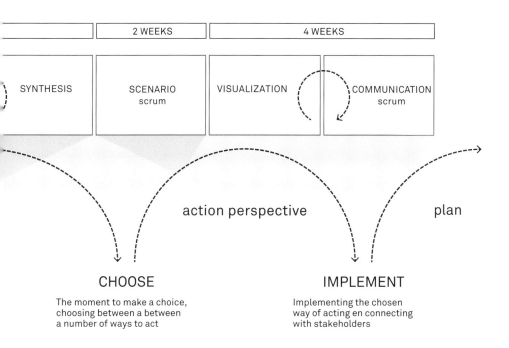

	2 WEEKS	4 WEEKS
SYNTHESIS	SCENARIO scrum	VISUALIZATION	COMMUNICATION scrum

action perspective

plan

CHOOSE

The moment to make a choice, choosing between a between a number of ways to act

IMPLEMENT

Implementing the chosen way of acting en connecting with stakeholders

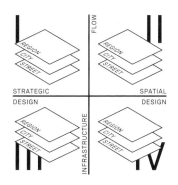

Scenario development

— four ways of flow design

— four thinking arenas

— four life cycle analyzes

— four intervention scenarios

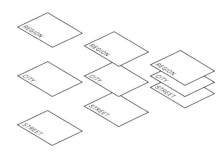

Stakeholder identification

— Fathom the meaning of metabolism and circulair purposes in a spacial context

– identifying possible stake/shareholders

(reports, data bases, statistics and maps) and distil
patterns from them.
Technique: Mapping by means of statistics, charts,
diagrams, data sets and maps.[130]

O Opportunities / Simulating
Questions: What are the opportunities? Where do
they occur? And who is involved in them?
Action: Visualize possible spatial developments
to fathom, understand and test scenarios.
Technique: Simulating in the form of drawings,
diagrams, maps, infographics and videos.

C Challenges / Modelling
Questions: What are the challenges? When do they
occur? And if they occur, who is going to put which
things in motion and where?
Action: Spatially translate challenges at the level of
buildings, streets, cities and regions.
Technique: Modelling through visualizations, models,
drawings, diagrams, maps, infographics and videos.

A Anecdotes / Fieldwork
Questions: Are there any small, subcutaneous
harbingers of change? Meaningful details that are
beyond a statistical approach, but that connect
the research to reality, in what Jane Jacobs called
'non-average clues'?[131]
Action: Gathering information and capturing it
through – observational – fieldwork, interviewing
experts and users, and consulting media sources.
Techniques: Carrying out fieldwork through excur-
sions, spatial explorations, interactive work sessions
and interviews.[132]

The diverging phase thus primarily focuses on the examination of the situation. In this stage, the role of design
is speculative and helps to frame research questions. The
aim is to map urban elements and structures, as well
as the qualities of the urban system and the key actors.
With regard to the main issues, there are actually two
questions. What is happening and where is it happening?
   Answering the question of what is happening
requires a continuous dialogue between explicit knowledge about these underlying processes (data) and the
more implicit knowledge of users and experts (anecdotes). This means data and anecdotes are compared. As
the research by design process progresses, the overlap

130

On 1 and 2 April 2016, FUR
organized a mapping masterclass
in Maastricht led by Catalogtree.

131

In the final chapter of her book
*The Death and Life of Great American
Cities* (1960), Jacobs addresses 'the
type of problem that a big city is'.
Her advice – in addition to: look for
non-average clues – is to think in
terms of processes and to take an
inductive approach, that is, reason
from the particular to the general
rather than the other way around.
The similarities to the methods of
research by design are striking.

132

The *Seven Walks* developed by
Raoul Bunschoten – *walk towards,
walk across, walk along, walk into,
walk out, walk through, walk about*
– are an example of a structured
field exploration. See *Urban
Flotsam: Stirring the City* (2001).

MAPPING

– statistics
– graphs
– diagrams
– datasets
– maps

DATA

– desk
  research
– reports
– database
– monitoring

SIMULATION

– visualizations
– models
– drawings
– graphs
– maps
– infographics
– videos

OPPOR-
TUNITIES

– design
  research
– workshops
– reports
– plans
– visions

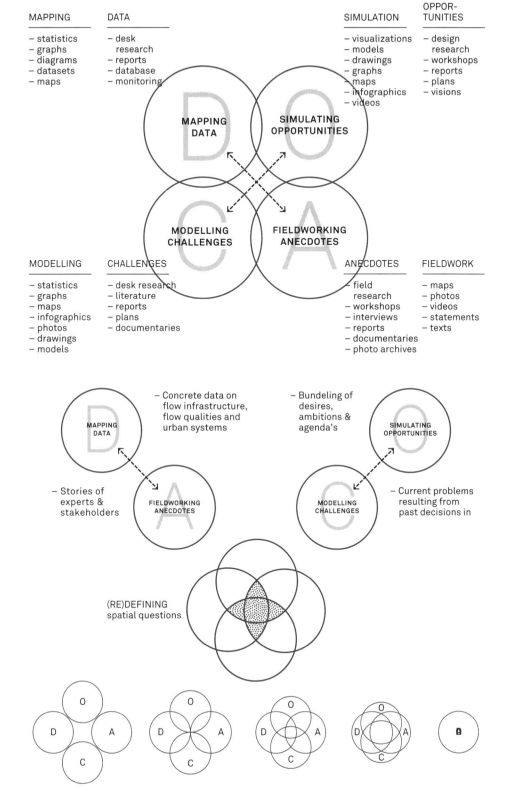

MAPPING
DATA

SIMULATING
OPPORTUNITIES

MODELLING
CHALLENGES

FIELDWORKING
ANECDOTES

MODELLING

– statistics
– graphs
– maps
– infographics
– photos
– drawings
– models

CHALLENGES

– desk research
– literature
– reports
– plans
– documentaries

ANECDOTES

– field
  research
– workshops
– interviews
– reports
– documentaries
– photo archives

FIELDWORK

– maps
– photos
– videos
– statements
– texts

MAPPING
DATA

– Concrete data on
  flow infrastructure,
  flow qualities and
  urban systems

– Bundeling of
  desires,
  ambitions &
  agenda's

SIMULATING
OPPORTUNITIES

FIELDWORKING
ANECDOTES

– Stories of
  experts &
  stakeholders

MODELLING
CHALLENGES

– Current problems
  resulting from
  past decisions in

(RE)DEFINING
spatial questions

D   O   A
    C

D   O   A
    C

D   O   A
    C

D   O   A
    C

fig. 55 — The DOCA Approach

between data and anecdotes will grow. In other words: the information will become more and more realistic.

The question of where things are happening is a spatial one. It has to become clear in what area problems (challenges) arise and how they can be answered in the future, so they can become chances (opportunities). Therefore the overlap in the interaction between challenges and opportunities will grow in the course of the process as well. Thus, the rings of the model move towards each other to cover a growing common domain.

On the Role of Scenarios

Exploring the future is pre-eminently the domain of the design discipline. But how is it done? There are five basic ways of imagining the future: by oracle, by prophesy, by utopia, by prognosis and by scenario. The latter is especially interesting to designers.

The Dutch planning tradition has quite the track record where scenario thinking is concerned, says Swiss architect and urban planner Christian Salewski.[133] He distinguishes six scenario functions: it is a planning tool, a generator of options, a prediction tool, an analysis tool and a means of communication, but certainly also a romantic tool. In this respect, he follows philosopher Richard Rorty, who wrote: 'At the heart of Romanticism is the thesis of the priority of imagination over reason – the claim that reason can only follow paths that the imagination has broken.'[134]

This is precisely the part design plays in the divergent stage of the ICCI Model. After all, this is where scenarios for the future are developed: 'If you do not produce any new options or new knowledge, your attempt to write a scenario is futile.'[135]

The heart of every scenario is a hypothesis about the future. It is important to realize that what we think about the future is highly dependent on what we think about today. After all, both the future and the past are constructions of our minds. It is therefore imperative that the uncertainties and assumptions that underlie the scenarios are made explicit. Working in multidisciplinary teams ensures the availability of necessary knowledge that is external to the spatial design domain.

The converging stage of the ICCI Model is focused on the further development and testing of scenarios. Here, the emphasis shifts from research to design. A balanced combination of imagination and reason, the design is a narrative figure that aims to increase its feasibility.

The cognitive value of any scenario is related to its research question, used models and associated data. Here, too, the balance between imagination and reason is crucial. Scenarios are tested by simulating the transformation involved using tentative master plans and by visualizing new urban models. If possible, the performance of the design is evaluated empirically as well.

133

In *Dutch New Worlds: Scenarios in Physical Planning and Design in the Netherlands 1970-2000*, Christian Salewsky adds scenarios to Georges Minois' enumeration of ideas of the future in *Geschichte der Zukunft: Orakel, Prophezeiungen, Utopien, Prognosen* (1998).

134

'Pragmatism and Romanticism', R. Rorty. In: *Philosophy as Cultural Politics: Philosophical Papers*, Vol. 4.

135

Ten Lessons for Scenario Makers, Ch. Salewski, 2012.

Time plays an important part: Does the scenario take place in the here and now, or in an open-ended future? What is the scope of the scenario, is it a forecast or a thought experiment? What scale levels, physical developments and values are taken into account? Are the process, the product and the political context transparent and predictable?

The aim is to create, together with the stakeholders, a single scenario that includes a strategic framework, a set of rules, phasing proposals and key projects for achieving the goal. Such a scenario is a narrative that can mobilize people, facilitate communication between key actors and that invites participation because it appeals to the imagination.

resilient infrastructure

Rebuild by Design — New York (US)

Hurricane Sandy forced New York to carry out fundamental research into the weakness of its coastline: rather than repair the damage and move on, the city decided it first wanted to fully understand what had gone wrong. Its starting point was a design competition.

The images of hurricane Sandy ravaging New York in October 2012 went global. The hurricane wreaked havoc. The rivers flooded and the sewers could not cope with the water. Debris was swept into subway tunnels. From the air, an ink-black blot could be seen to divide Manhattan in two: in a power-failed south and a lamp-lit north. For the first time since 1888, even the New York Stock Exchange on Wall Street closed, in fear of flooding. The damage in and around New York City ran into tens of billions of dollars.

One thing was clear: never again. The usual reaction of the American government in such cases – clear away the debris, help the victims and repair the damage – was no longer enough. Transforming New York City into a resilient city able to cope with extreme climate conditions was going to take extensive measures.

A coalition formed, supported by President Barack Obama and with two designers at the helm. They were Shaun Donovan, the head of the Hurricane Sandy Rebuilding Taskforce, and Dutch key official and Water Envoy Henk Ovink, who was hired by the Ministry of Infrastructure and the Environment. Partly thanks to the financial support of private organizations such as the Rockefeller Foundation and Deutsche Bank, 1 billion dollars was made available for a design competition. Tellingly, it was named *Rebuild by Design*.[136] Reconstruction by means of design: How does that work in practice?

136
The project is excellently documented, see www.rebuildbydesign.org.

From 148 entries, ten teams were selected that jointly set up their research, starting with a broad-based investigation of the area's weak points in which the designers used economic, social, administrative, financial and ecological data, among other things. Residents, entrepreneurs and local politicians were also an important

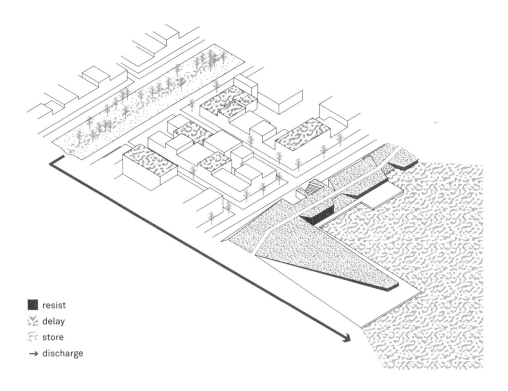

resist
delay
store
→ discharge

fig. 56 — Spatial resilience measures

fig. 57 — Winning Proposal Allocations to City and States

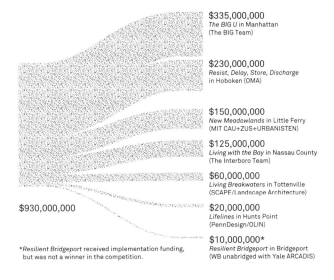

$335,000,000
The BIG U in Manhattan
(The BIG Team)

$230,000,000
Resist, Delay, Store, Discharge
in Hoboken (OMA)

$150,000,000
New Meadowlands in Little Ferry
(MIT CAU+ZUS+URBANISTEN)

$125,000,000
Living with the Bay in Nassau County
(The Interboro Team)

$60,000,000
Living Breakwaters in Tottenville
(SCAPE/Landscape Architecture)

$930,000,000

$20,000,000
Lifelines in Hunts Point
(PennDesign/OLIN)

*Resilient Bridgeport received implementation funding,
but was not a winner in the competition.

$10,000,000*
Resilient Bridgeport in Bridgeport
(WB unabridged with Yale ARCADIS)

fig. 58 — Following spread:
Blackout in a large part
of Manhattan

source of information: they provided the anecdotal information about the region that Excel sheets cannot provide.

This resulted in new insights about the New York coastline. The built-up banks of Manhattan may be world famous, but the state of New Jersey has more faces. It includes spacious suburbs as well as compact

urban districts, industry but also nature reserves and recreational areas.

This preliminary investigation resulted in over 40 design proposals that covered all of those areas. It became clear how interconnected the different problems are. Take economic inequality. The areas that run the greatest risk of flooding are often the areas where the largest numbers of poor people live. And these are also the areas where people find it difficult to get away in case of emergency and that have heavy industry or storage spaces for hazardous substances nearby. Residents here run huge risks and do not have the money to take measures against flooding.

fig. 59 — Destroyed streets after hurricane Sandy

Sandy affected few places as severely as Hoboken. This low-lying and densely populated suburb is separated from Manhattan by the Hudson River. Immediately after the flood the National Guard had to turn out to evacuate thousands of residents. So much water flooded into the city that in some places, it took a month to pump it all out.

Building a wall around the river is of course not a solution. Not only because no one wants to take people's view of the river away from them, but also because ultimately the battle against the rising sea level will be lost anyway. Hoboken's Achilles heel turned out to be its sewers. The water had nowhere to go and flooded the city from the overburdened sewer system.

The solution came from Rem Koolhaas's Dutch Office for Metropolitan Architecture (OMA). The office developed a 'large-scale flood strategy' based on thorough research and on the Dutch experience with flooding.[137] Sea water levels are rising, precipitation is intensifying. This led the Netherlands to conclude that though it is impossible to stop the water once and for all, it is possible to let some in some of the time and subsequently steer it in the right direction and prevent flooding.

In the case of Hoboken, OMA suggested complementing dikes and other infrastructural interventions to stop the sea water by a 'green infrastructure' comprising parks and other vegetation at strategic points along the river to help to drain the water. A system of water pumps and basins prevent the overloading of the discharge system. Some 230 million dollars was made available for the project.

The OMA study provided a comprehensive insight into the region's water management. The designers identified the weak spots and the ways they were connected to

137
The used term was *comprehensive urban water theory*, also see: *Store Discharge: A Comprehensive Urban Water Strategy*, OMA, 2014.

other risk areas. This resulted in concrete proposals to make the city, including Hoboken, more climate resilient, and in general suggestions for policy and funding.

Take, for example, the proposal to cleverly cluster the walls that protect fire stations, power plants and other critical infrastructure from high water, rather than protect each location separately. This way, a single intervention serves multiple purposes, which is cheaper and allows a more effective organization of defence systems. It also meant that the law that stipulated that every critical infrastructure was required to have its own walls had to be changed, though.

The design process was also a way to reach out to residents and other people that had to deal with the interventions directly. A coalition formed around the project in an early stage. The researchers processed the feedback from surveys and organized meetings to give explanations about the costs and benefits of the proposed measures. In addition to a technological project plan, OMA wrote a pamphlet about the risks of flooding to make sure that laymen could join in the conversation, too.

OMA's approach is similar to the DOCA Model, which combines hard data and anecdotes to address the vulnerability of systems.[138] OMA devised different scenarios, including a strategy to protect JFK Airport and an arithmetic method that calculates the flood risk in urban development investments.

Research by design, then, is a way to map a complex problem and find a concrete solution. This large-scale research by design project into the effects of extreme climate conditions in New York and ways to deal with them resulted in the selection of six projects. One was OMA's plan for Hoboken.

138
For more information about DOCA, see →p. 131.

What a design competition to make the city resilient against extreme climate conditions

Where New York City, United States

Design Hurricane Sandy Rebuilding Taskforce

Realized 2014

Intervention research by design coupled the construction of coastal defences to other urban challenges

Also good for healthy living (more green in the city), sociocultural connectivity (investing in social resilience)

fig. 60 — Following spread:
Climate-proof measures
stimulute the use of public space

resilient infrastructure

Algae Procution in Canal

The Eindhoven Canal lost its infrastructure function some decades ago. Could it be turned into a cultivation pond for algae? Large-scale algae production is a good alternative to biofuels. Adapting the production methods to the local setting creates unique urban, residential and rural areas.

Algae represent a new raw material for such products as cosmetics, paint and medicine, but above all they are a new energy source. Production takes up a lot less space than biofuels like palm oil, elephant grass, linseed or corn, which compete with food production and nature. With diagrams and references the designer explains how the algae production works. And she shows how production actually takes place: in tanks, tubes or bags.

Next, the Eindhoven Canal is carefully analysed. Maps show functions and intersections with roads and railways, and the areas the canal flows through: an urban industrial park, residential neighbourhoods and a rural zone. This shows, among other things, that the production of algae can be combined with the waste streams of adjacent companies.

The designer investigates not only how algae might be produced, but also what the canal and its surroundings will look like. Each different production method gets its own spot along the canal. The plan includes proposals for the various settings, depicted in a strategy map and section designs.

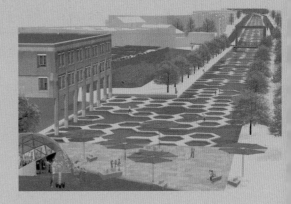

fig. 61 — Floating tanks for the production of algae

At the head of the canal will be floating hexagonal tanks; the rims of the tanks form a network of walkways above the water. In the residential areas along the canal, a pipe system for algae also separates the gardens, and vertical elements will be added to the public space. Further away from the city, in the rural area, algae are cultivated in artificial pools and ponds with adjacent recreational routes.

Designer Jessica Stoop
Academy Tilburg
Design Atelier Water Works
Where Eindhoven, the Netherlands
Lecturers Jason Hilgefort,
Marieke Kums

resilient infrastructure

Fresh water for Saline Polder

The Haarlemmermeer is intensively used for food production, infrastructure and urban development. However, the climate resistance of the polder is threatened by salinization. It must therefore be reconfigured, for example with a water battery.

The Haarlemmermeer was created through peat extraction and expanded due to sea surges and a lack of dikes. The 'Waterwolf' devoured the land and threatened Amsterdam. After drainage and land reclamation between 1849 and 1852, the polder was used as farmland and later for Schiphol Airport and the development of residential areas like Hoofddorp and Nieuw-Vennep.

The Haarlemmermeer seemed safe, but a new problem with the water has now emerged: salinization. To combat this the polder is regularly flushed with fresh water, but climate change is choking off the supply of fresh water during the summer months.

Increased water storage capacity in the area will make seasonal storage possible. In periods of heavy rainfall the water levels at the edges of the Haarlemmermeer are increased. In dry periods this water can be used to flush the polder. At the same time, these retention basins can serve as a water battery, where renewable energy from windmills can be stored. Slowly draining the basins creates electricity using generators. The site of the water battery is connected to the line of high-tension electricity pylons and windmills.

In addition to water and energy storage, the basins can also serve as a recreational area. There could be ice skating in winter, and the outflowing water could be used in the summer as an artificial wave, allowing people to windsurf or water ski.

Designer Roeland Meek

Academy Amsterdam

Design Studio SouthWest Works!

Where Amsterdam Metropolitan Area, the Netherlands

Lecturers Marco Broekman, Roel van Gerwen, Harm Veenenbos

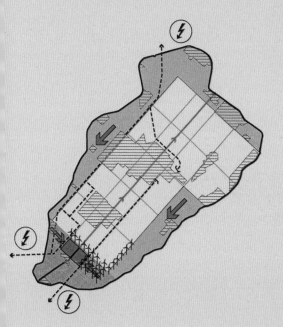

fig. 62 — Energy landscape

renewable energy

'What if'-scenarios — Leiden (NL)

The city of Leiden wanted to make the entire municipal energy supply renewable and to that end called a meeting of neighbouring municipalities and designers. Research by design and what-if scenarios helped to concretize and refine the suggested solutions.

Leiden struggled with two complex problems. First, 20 per cent of the municipal energy supply needed to be renewable by 2020 – the city even wants to be completely energy neutral by 2050. By June 2016, it had realized 3 per cent renewable energy, so there was still a lot of work to be done.[139] A parallel development is one that all municipalities in the Netherlands face: central government requires them to draw up environmental strategies from 2018. The strategies serve to promote a better coordination of municipalities' plans for spatial development, nature and the environment.

Writing an environmental strategy is not an easy thing to do. Previously, such documents were based on classic themes such as house-building or the accessibility of the city, but now they also involve slippery themes like biodiversity, waste recycling and robotization. Leiden's environmental strategy prioritized the energy transition.[140] Research by design helped the city to concretize this complex and abstract challenge.

The city of Leiden immediately invited nine of its neighbouring municipalities to participate, because a city cannot make society more sustainable by itself.[141] Representatives of network manager Alliander, Delft University of Technology, circular economy adviser Evolv and Buck Consultants were also approached. Together they formed an ad hoc coalition that went to work on the energy challenge for the benefit of the regional environmental strategy 'Hart van Holland'. In addition, the city engaged Posad and Fabric, two offices involved in research by design for complex, spatial problems. Their task: sort out the chaos. They identified the most important questions and wrote scenarios to concretize the consequences of the plans: they were not expected to come up with a single ready-made solution.

'With every party involved at the table, we could start to think about long-term consequences,' says Fred Goedbloed of the city of Leiden. 'Rather than just talk

139
Klimaatmonitor, accessed in June 2016.

140
Rotmans defines the energy transition as a gradual and continuous transformation process of energy management that intervenes at a fundamental level in the nature of a society. J. Rotmans, R. Kemp, M. van Asselt, 'More Evolution than Revolution: Transition Management'. In: *Foresight*, Vol. 3, 1, 2001.

141
They are Kaag en Braassem, Katwijk, Leiderdorp, Noordwijk, Oegstgeest, Teylingen, Voorschoten, Wassenaar and Zoeterwoude.

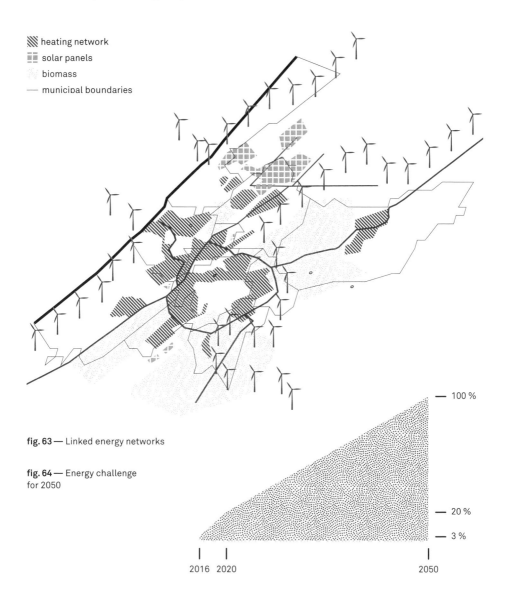

heating network
solar panels
biomass
municipal boundaries

fig. 63 — Linked energy networks

fig. 64 — Energy challenge
for 2050

— 100 %

— 20 %
— 3 %

2016 2020   2050

about cables and power plants, we asked ourselves what
spatial implications decisions would have both now and
in 25 years.'

When the parties met for the first time, no one in the
region had clear ideas about the energy supply of the
future. The city of Leiden wanted to pursue a radically
green course. But nobody actually knew how. This is
not unusual. The territory is uncharted and the effects
of measures are likely to be comparable to those of the
post-war reclamation of Flevoland or the large-scale
land consolidation that radically overhauled the Dutch
countryside in the twentieth century.

fig. 65 — Following spread:
Mix of renewable energy sources

The research by design helped to concretize this far-reaching challenge. In Leiden, this was done in three steps. Step one was taking stock of problems and possible solutions. Talking about the approach Olv Klijn, the Fabric researching designer involved in the Leiden study, says: 'We wanted to know what an energy transition actually was, how far-reaching it would be as well as what contribution the parties involved could make.'

This is how the idea arose to connect to the so-called heat roundabout that is being developed in Zuid-Holland. This is an exchange system for residual heat and geothermal heat. In addition, the roundabout couples supply and demand. The residual heat from a factory, for example, can be used to heat dwellings or a farm's greenhouses. Especially the residual heat from ports and industry offers opportunities.

Previously, Fabric estimated that the Port of Rotterdam alone may waste 67 Petajoules of residual heat annually – that is as much energy as the entire Province of Friesland, with 650,000 inhabitants, uses annually. But what infrastructure is needed to connect the city of Leiden to the heat roundabout?[142]

In the second stage of the research, the collected ideas were further developed using 'what-if' scenarios, a kind of thought experiments.[143] Take, for example, the scenario for a 'triple regional ring' of wind turbines on the fringes of the Dutch Green Heart. What if the region were to fully commit to wind power: How many wind turbines would that take and what would that do to the landscape? What was found was that wind power can at best provide up to 22 per cent of the energy required. Wind power alone is therefore not enough.

In the third and final stage, the ideas were developed into applicable proposals. This led to plans for solar panels in the dunes, on floating islands or bulb fields. Or for green beaches of olivine, a mineral that extracts CO_2 from water. 'What we could develop, we made directly imaginable. That way, everyone knew what we were talking about,' says Klijn. Take the solar panels in the dunes. Nobody thought that was a good idea, until a drawing illustrated what it would actually look like.

Research by design not only feeds the dialogue. Posad's urban planner Boris Hoks adds that a researching designer can sometimes come up with unorthodox solutions by combining different disciplines. 'We wanted to give people the feeling that you can combine things. That there are more ways to generate biogas, for example, than the industrial way.'

142

Urban Metabolism: Sustainable Development of Rotterdam, a project in the context of the International Architecture Biennale Rotterdam 2014, by Fabric, JCFO and TNO, 2015.

143

'Beyond the Visual Dimension: Using Ideal Type Narratives to Analyse People's Assessments of Landscape Scenarios'. In: *Land Use Policy*, R. Soliva and M. Hunziker, 2009.

fig. 66 — Following spread: Solar panels in dune landscape

fig. 67 — Central grid

fig. 68 — Decentral grid

The helicopter perspective thus created is crucial to abstract problems such as the transformation of the entire regional energy supply. 'If you cut the story up, people lose sight of the necessity,' says Fred Goedbloed. 'Then you get criticism: Why coloured foil in a bulb field or a roundabout of wind turbines? In such a complex task, it is important that you tell people what's what from the start.'

Incidentally, the researchers themselves learn by doing as well, Hoks observes. In a similar project, he developed a new computer model to calculate more quickly what the maximum energy yield of a region can be. 'At first, we did that manually and it took us months. Using a computer, it now takes us 40 minutes to calculate the energy costs of a new housing estate.'

The study found that Leiden and its surroundings need a mix of renewable energy sources. Take solar panels on the roofs: even the most optimistic scenario shows that they only cover up to 7 per cent of the energy needed. Energy extracted from biomass can only provide 2 per cent and local geothermal heat up to 13 per cent. This is not going to work without wind power or a regional heat network. And it's clear that everyone will also have to be on their best energy-saving behaviour.

These are not good tidings, but they do make everyone face the facts: there is no time to lose. Research by design speeds up the process, as Leiden has shown. It lays bare the urgency by confronting the parties involved with the right questions and by testing solutions put forward by scenarios.

What research by design helps focus the future of regional energy supply

Where Leiden, the Netherlands

Design Fabric, Posad

Realized 2016

Intervention 'What-if' scenarios

Also good for vital economy (development of new technology and manufacturing industry) and sociocultural connectivity (collaboration with neighbouring municipalities)

renewable energy

Canal Becomes Water Battery

The Eindhoven Canal (1846) has always played a part in the production and transport of energy. Coal was shipped to Eindhoven on the canal; a gas plant and gas holder were built in the harbour. This all ended in 1974, however: the canal was closed to shipping. In this design, the canal regains its economic role with renewable energy storage.

The Netherlands is nowhere near meeting its objectives for generating renewable energy, and storage is one of the main headaches. With graphs, the designer shows how unpredictable energy production from renewable sources is. Solar energy is produced when the sun shines and wind turbines generate electricity when the wind blows, but power is also needed when it is cloudy and there is no wind. One option for storing energy is a water battery.

A water battery is a reservoir that is filled with water when the demand for energy is low. The moment it is needed, small-scale turbines generate electricity by draining the water from the canal.

With practical examples and an eye for technology, investment and shared use, the designer shows why this is a great way to repurpose the canal, which can contribute to the resilience of Eindhoven's energy production. The proposal calls for eleven dams in the canal, the design is basically ready to implement.

The choice of the specific type of dam is made by comparing various pumps and techniques and then projecting those onto the site. The type's yield determines the effect of the intervention. In the end, it comes down to how many households can run on the water battery.

Apart from that, the construction of the dams could also lead to programmes that enrich their direct surroundings, such as recreational shared use.

Designer Li Gubai
Academy Tilburg
Design Atelier Water Works
Where Eindhoven, the Netherlands
Lecturers Jason Hilgefort,
Marieke Kums

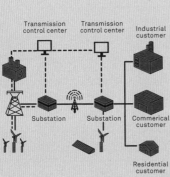

fig. 69 — Canal becomes water battery

renewable energy
Redevelopment of Parking Places

Car sharing is becoming more and more popular. This means fewer cars on the road and fewer parking places in our cities. A module is being developed for parking spaces that are no longer being used that will create public space out of the now relatively boring spaces.

In the Netherlands, the average car is driven one hour a day. And when it is used – especially for business purposes – it is usually only by one person. In most post-war neighbourhoods, parking places take up the majority of the available public space.

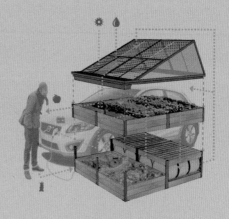

fig. 70 — Vegetable production on parking lot

The status of owning a car is slowly making way for the ease of mobility as a service. Not only are car-sharing concepts like Greenwheels and Car2Go becoming more popular, people are also sharing their own cars (ZipCar, SnappCar) or rides (BlaBlaCar) more often. If these trends continue, car ownership will decline, and the need for parking space along with it.

The parking places that become available can contribute to the activation of the public space in several different ways. This project consists of a modular system that can be applied to any parking place. A presentation folder is already available for interested residents. The modules should be available at DIY stores. The system offers a variety of choices: from solar panels to generate electricity for electric cars, the cultivation of vegetables, breeding fish and keeping chickens, to a work area or a water purification system. Repurposing parking places also offers social options, like a space for playing children and seating areas for neighbourhood residents. All of these functions can either be installed as individual modules or connected to each other. The dimensions of the module are based on the standard dimensions of a parking place. Step by step, the dreariest spots in residential areas will be transformed into productive public space.

Designer Nina Schouwman

Academy Groningen

Design Atelier
Energietransitie
Regio Groningen

Where Groningen,
the Netherlands

Lecturers Alex van Spijk,
Sjoerd Betten

renewable energy
Energy Bridges a Gap

The ecological residential district of
Drielanden was ahead of the curve in
the 1990s, but that is now a thing of the
past. An energy bridge that generates
and stores electricity will put it back on
the map and unite its residents.

A private initiative at the end of the 1980s
led to the ecological residential district
known as Drielanden, on the outskirts
of Groningen. Several ecological principles were applied: the district has little traffic (cars are discouraged); it has a
separated sewer system, waste water is
treated using a helophyte filter; and the
houses were built with ecological materials. Many of the features of the district that were unique at the time have
now become commonplace. In spatial
and functional terms, the district is also
hardly distinctive: it was laid out based
on standard parking norms and there are
few amenities.

After 20 years, the energy services of
Drielanden need a new impulse. This presents opportunities to again make the district a leading example for others. Rather
than tackle each house individually, a
new element is to be added to the district: an energy bridge that generates and
stores renewable energy. The top of the
bridge will be lined with solar panels and
the generated electricity will be stored in
batteries in used containers (e-units). The
solar panels on the roofs of the houses
will also be connected to the energy
bridge. Furthermore, the bridge will have
charging points for electric bikes and
(shared) cars.

The bridge is not restricted to energy:
it also provides space for neighbourhood
services. Fruit trees and greenhouses
for vegetables will supply healthy food
cultivated with fertilizers from the area.
There will also be workshops and a daycare centre. The walking route across the

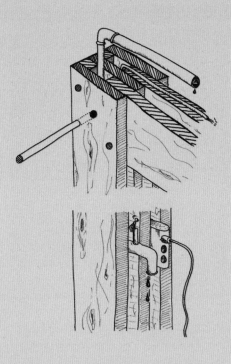

fig. 71 — Energy charging point

bridge allows the residents of Drielanden
to experience all these different elements,
making the energy transition a literal
experience.

Designer Lamia Towalski

Academy Groningen

Design Atelier Energietransitie
Regio Groningen

Where Groningen, the Netherlands

Lecturers Alex van Spijk,
Sjoerd Betten

material cycle

Blue Economy — Rotterdam (NL)

Tropicana, a tropical swimming paradise gone bankrupt, now houses a laboratory comprising businesses that are largely operated on each other's residual flows. Initiator BlueCity010 is developing a single ecosystem in the building. And if there is any malt waste, they will set up a bakery, too.

A lesson in circular economy in Rotterdam: Spireaux is a company that cultivates spirulina – nutritious, blue-green algae – in water tanks. The algae grow beneath LED lights. This creates residual heat. Once the company starts to grow and the water tanks are situated beside the heating system, the lighting will be able to contribute to the heating of the rest of the building.

In addition to light, the algae also need CO_2. Spireaux found it at fellow business RotterZwam, which cultivates oyster mushrooms: this gives off CO_2. The mushrooms, in turn, are grown on coffee grounds collected at cafés and restaurants that previously threw them into the bin. Coffee grounds make a rich food source for mushrooms. The first testing installation for the introduction of CO_2 into the water in which the algae grow has already been constructed.

Like quite a number of other enterprises, Spireaux and RotterZwam are located in Rotterdam's former swimming paradise Tropicana. The building is still under development but they are already putting 'the blue economy' into practice by reusing all of their waste – or rather: residual flows.[144] How are they managing to develop such a circular economy among the old slides and former pools and saunas?

The city of Rotterdam commissioned Center Parcs to build the pool in the 1980s. The temperature inside was always 30 degrees Celsius. Palm trees and Greek columns completed the tropical experience. But as the years went by the pool fell into disrepair. The place looked dirty, was ill maintained, people were harassed. In late 2010 Tropicana went bankrupt and closed its doors.

All sorts of new plans for the pool emerged. It was to be demolished to make way for luxury apartments for seniors or it was to be converted into a hotel or

fig. 72 — Coffee grounds are used for growing oyster mushrooms

144

Based on *Blauwe economie*, G. Pauli, 2004.

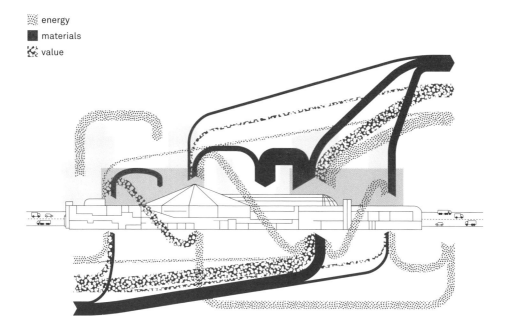

energy
materials
value

fig. 73 — Dynamic of streams

entertainment venue. Others just wanted to turn it back into a pool. In the meantime, business owners were allowed to use the property. When it became known that the property was going to be auctioned in the autumn of 2015 to pay off the mortgage debt, those same entrepreneurs saw an opportunity.

They united under the name BlueCity010 and were joined by several other local entrepreneurs. They found an investor and put a well-worked-out business plan and 1.7 million euros on the table. Though they were not the highest bidder, they got to buy the property because their plans were so convincing.

The companies want to turn the property into a single ecosystem. To that end, as many residual flows will be short-circuited as possible. This is even more far-reaching than the 'circular economy' many companies pursue, says Floris Schiferli, urban planner at architecture office Superuse Studios, one of the founders of BlueCity010. 'Companies often say they want to close their cycles to prevent creating waste. What we want is an open structure: our thinking starts from the collective of businesses united in this building and we explore the ways they are alike and can benefit from each other.'

There were a lot of brewers that wanted to participate, for example, and therefore BlueCity010 is now looking for a baker. For the two would complement each other,

says Schiferli. Brewing beer from grain leaves a residual product called bagasse, malt waste, which a baker can use to bake bread. 'Based on the size of the spaces and the production possible in them we have calculated that we can provide a bakery with as much as 20 per cent of the ingredients its needs to bake bread. Just imagine how much that will save on purchasing costs.'

One business's waste is the key to another's business model. Schiferli considers this constant exchange of residual flows as the metabolism of the property. 'You could call the building a means of production,' he says. 'We are building an ecosystem here and so we prioritize gathering sufficient knowledge about the building and the way it works. It is a complex and dynamic system and we want to monitor it well.'

To gain insight in the residual flows produced by each business, they introduced a so-called flow inventory. To sustain it, each business accurately documents its used and residual materials. 'That way, what is still missing becomes clear,' says Schiferli.

The designer will make the exchange of residual flows in BlueCity010 possible. What does each business do, how much space does it need and what businesses can best be put together so that they can make the most use of each other's residual products? But also: Which parts of the building receive visitors? Much of the property is in fact open to the public. The rapids and the open-to-air part of the pool, for example, now house a popular bar and restaurant.

The characteristics of the building also control the way businesses are going to use it. The pool had various spaces for all kinds of entertainment. The former sauna, for example, was designed for a different climate than the beauty salon in the cellar. This determines where the various companies get to settle.

Interventions on and around the property also prioritize reuse. Schiferli: 'We do not look at what needs to be built first, and then at what materials we need to do so. We work the other way around: What materials do we have and what can we do with them?'

The new users of the former discotheque asked the same question when they began to renovate it shortly after they had bought it. The discotheque is a separate building next to the swimming paradise. They decided to convert it into meeting and office spaces that benefit from the light coming in through the large windows. Here, too, the residual products of others formed the starting point. A demolition contractor supplied 300

fig. 74 — Hall in BlueCity010

fig. 75 — Following spread: Final vision of BlueCity010

145
Through the online market place www.oogstkaart.nl that Superuse Studios helped to develop. For residual materials from bricks to washing machine parts and even buildings.

used Red Cedar window frames; someone else supplied a load of scrap iron.**145** Schiferli: 'Only then did we start to look at ways to convert the building, using those materials.'

It is important for a designer to be flexible, whether you are renovating a house or suddenly need to adapt to a change in the ecosystem of a building 'The work is never done, really. Just imagine what will happen if the brewery that provides the bakery with bagasse goes out of business. You want to be able to respond quickly, because now the baker suddenly has to buy more expensive ingredients. As an architect, you're not done when the construction plan is finished. You're actively involved after that as well. You have to continue to monitor waste flows and make adjustments to the building when a new company joins. And this always centres on the ecosystem we are building here.'

What a group of business owners converts a former swimming pool into an ecosystem of businesses that reuse each other's residual flows

Where Rotterdam, the Netherlands

Design Superuse Studios, BlueCity010

Realized 2015 (ongoing)

Intervention each intervention in the building begins with a thorough analysis of the residual flows and the available space

Also good for renewable energy (waste prevention), vital economy (residual flows turn into a business case), sociocultural connectivity (involving local companies, providing information)

fig. 76 — Meeting and office units in a former disco

material cycle
Raw Materials Square in Poor Part of Town

The per capita income of the residents of Rotterdam-Zuid is half that of the average Dutch citizen. This is largely spent on food and other consumer items that generate waste. In addition, an annual waste tax is levied. The city then pays to have its rubbish incinerated. If trash was treated as a source of valuable raw materials, however, it could generate money instead. The design places the facilities needed for the circular economy in the public space.

An analysis of the economics of rubbish shows that AVR, the former municipal waste disposal agency, makes money twice in processing trash. It collects waste tax and it then sells the energy generated by incinerating the waste.

The designers want to use the waste tax to invest in research on how to obtain usable raw materials from the household waste of Rotterdam-Zuid. These investments form the basis of a new economic model whereby all the household waste in the area is turned into things like biogas and biodiesel, heat, compost and reusable paper and plastics. This will profit the residents of Rotterdam-Zuid both financially and materially.

The designers have developed a generic model for the installations and facilities needed to implement the cycle. In this they identify waste sources (homes, schools, shops), collection points, locations and methods for processing (bio fermentation units, heat hubs, small bioplastics factories), workshops and sales outlets.

An analysis of the area then identifies which locations are suitable for this generic, decentralized waste processing model as 'raw materials squares'. In this design atelier, the Afrikaanderplein in the Tarwewijk and the Nachtegaalplein in Charlois were selected. Two raw materials squares were elaborated in greater detail.

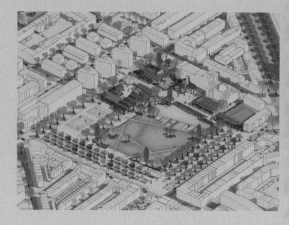

fig. 77 — Isometric drawing of raw materials square on the Afrikaanderplein

Designers Wander Hendriks and Ruud van Leeuwen

Academy Rotterdam

Design Atelier Afval als bron

Where Rotterdam, the Netherlands

Lecturers Dirk van Peijpe, Floris Schiferli

material cycle

Slaughterhouse near Food Cluster

The food industry is organized into global chains that operate out of sight. This is also true in the Spaanse Polder industrial and commercial estate, where the Food Cluster consists of a loose collection of businesses in the food industry. A slaughterhouse on site could significantly shorten the food chain, as well as produce raw materials for other businesses.

Spaanse Polder is one of the first true industrial and commercial estates in the Netherlands; in its current form it was constructed soon after the Second World War. It spans about 200 hectares and hosts about 700 businesses.

Part of Spaanse Polder is the Food Cluster, which accommodates both wholesale markets as well as food-processing multinationals. These are links in worldwide food chains, which means the gap between food production and food consumption is enormous, physically as well as experientially.

Analysis of the Food Cluster shows which points along the chain the businesses occupy and what input and output of products they have to deal with. This forms the basis for the designer's proposal: adding a slaughterhouse in order to shorten the chains. This will turn the Food Cluster into a physical and functional link between the cows in the pastures of Midden-Delfland and the steak on the plates of Rotterdammers.

The slaughterhouse works with the meat trade and the meat-processing industry in Spaanse Polder, so that it can obtain local, fresh meat. The waste-product streams from the slaughterhouse can serve as raw materials for the production of paint, medicine, soap, sweets and energy, so that the slaughterhouse contributes to the closing of material streams in the area. The stream schematics of the current and project situations effectively illustrate the effect of the slaughterhouse.

A cooking studio and restaurant for locally bred, raised and processed food can drag the industrial-looking Food Cluster out of its anonymity and become part of the agricultural route that flows into Rotterdam from Midden-Delfland via the Schie Canal.

Designer Barend Mense

Academy Rotterdam

Design Atelier Food Hub Spaanse Polder

Where Rotterdam, the Netherlands

Lecturers Thijs van Bijsterveldt, Willemijn Lofvers

Examples of the benefits of a short chain

The use of an appointed cattle farmer for a reliable delivery of gelatine. Gelatine is used to add shine to the film roles

fig. 78 — Local chain for reliable and quility delivery (reference KODAK)

vital economy

High Streets — London (UK)

'Do the drawings and win' is one of the lessons of architect Mark Brearley, Greater London's former head of Design. His team mapped the 600 streets of London and discovered the importance of length and depth.

According to architect Mark Brearley, the High Streets (city streets) of London are a major driving force in the city. The 600 streets have a combined length of more than 500 km. They accommodate hairdressers, dentists, schools, stations, banks, libraries, cinemas, offices, pubs and of course shops and dwellings.

The mixed activities are oriented towards the streets, as opposed to the work done in closed skyscrapers and on industrial estates. Brearley found that, though less visibly than a financial centre such as the City of London, these streets are of great importance to the city. 'But they are so ordinary and commonplace that we easily overlook how special they are.'

Commissioned by the then mayor of London, Ken Livingstone, Brearley and his Design for London team literally and figuratively began putting the city streets on the map in 2006.[146] Their research provided an insight into how the streets function and showed their importance to the economic and social development of London. The maps and analyses zoom in on the level of the building, the block, the street and the neighbourhood and show city streets that are highly diverse, complex, lively and attractive.

Outside the centre, Brearley shows, half the jobs are found on city streets and two-thirds of all Londoners lives within a five-minute walking distance of such a street. What is special about these streets is that they are physically connected, that they offer a wide variety of services and goods, and that they are an important part of social life.

The Design for London study was an experiment in urban development. Its aim was to develop a strategy for the revitalization of the city. Rather than intervene directly in the urban fabric, the researchers first made maps of the current situation to show where the strengths of these economic areas lie. This allows adjustments rather than major and costly redevelopments.

146

Brearley worked with various architects such as Gort Scott and institutes like the University College London. Mayor Boris Johnson discontinued Design for London in 2013.

■ new businesses
▨ street walls (width/height)
▦ plots (depth)

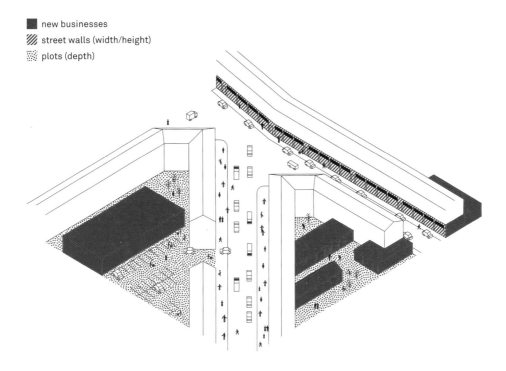

fig. 79 — Plot of related
economic developments

50%
of the jobs is
located on
a high street

2/3
of Londoners live
within 5 minutes
of a high street

fig. 80 — Outside central London

147

Learning from London's High Streets,
Mayor of London, 2014.

Once the researchers were familiar with the areas in
which (small) changes were needed, they could perform
bespoke interventions. Livingstone's successor, mayor
Boris Johnson, commissioned a *High Street London Report*
(2010) and founded the Outer London Fund and the
Mayor's Regeneration Fund. Between 2010 and 2014, he
invested £175 million/€ 218 million in the city streets.
The money was used to restore store fronts, address
vacancy and improve public space.[147]

A concrete example is the revitalization project 'High
Street 2012', which not coincidentally coincided with the
Olympic Games that took place in London that year. The
6-km-long city street connects the City with the Queen
Elizabeth Olympic Park in Stratford. Historical (retail)
buildings were renovated, the green areas along this
street extended and improved and the area is now safer
and more agreeable to cyclists and pedestrians. There is
also more public space now, with places to sit, talk or
play for a while.

But Mark Brearley also showed that many city streets
are struggling to survive. They suffer rising rents and
the competition of both huge shopping malls outside
the city and web shops. This threatens to make the
streets more monotonous as well. Says Brearley: 'A good
city would want to embrace a diverse and productive

fig. 81 — Growth

fig. 82 — High Streets, London

fig. 83 — The different
burroughs of London

fig. 84 — Well connected

social life. Its urban fabric would support a mix of functions and accommodate an extroverted economy. But
London is eating itself from the inside out.'

To revitalize the city streets, it is especially necessary to look at the city in a different way, he argues. He
reckons London planners and policymakers are used
to thinking in central locations, whereas they ought to
think in connecting roads. Of old, the focus is on the
redevelopment of major locations (dots) such as the City
of London, Canary Wharf, Chiswick Business Park and
Granary Square. These are the areas that attract large
companies and knowledge institutes: their economic
importance is clearly visible.

The importance of city streets (lines), however, was
overlooked. Yet they are an important and connecting
part of the economy. The research of the Design for London team introduced a new perspective on the urban
economy: from dots to lines.

Two other important aspects of the High Streets study
are length and depth. Length refers to a route of activities across different neighbourhoods and areas. City
streets form important social and economic connecting roads. Such a through route is, for example, clearly
visible between Clapham High Street and Balham High
Road. The activity is hardly interrupted, with the exception of a couple of introverted post-war buildings. The
type of activity does change, for example near underground stations or because the type of residents and
entrepreneurs vary from area to area.

However, most of the added value of the city streets
came from depth rather than length. The building blocks
accommodate a broad network of support activities in
their back rooms and walled gardens and in the surrounding streets and alleyways. At the ground floor level
there are mostly shops, restaurants, cafés, hairdressers
and other local amenities. One floor up are the dentists,
lawyers and accountancy firms. Semi-detached blocks in
turn offer space for bakeries, printers and garages.

It is this ecosystem of different, interconnected spaces
that makes city streets so attractive to small businesses
and start-ups. The variation in type of space also means
that many different types of businesses can settle close
together.

The Design for London study has yielded extraordinary
data that have had a major impact on the development
of the city. The design team was able to exert influence
because it had the support of the mayor. At its very

height, the design team consisted of 25 employees that developed a large number of design visions and master plans.

They developed a broad network, collaborated with various partners, organized exhibitions and discussions and established a feedback group for the mayor, the Mayor's Design Advisory Panel. Mark Brearley: 'It was about the development of ideas, narratives, policy and guidelines as well as about creating enthusiasm.'

Nevertheless, the Design for London project was discontinued in 2013; the research into city streets abandoned. During mayor Johnson's second term (2012-2016), the political focus shifted to community building and addressing vacancy in the shopping streets and this was at the expense of research. And so people still looked at dots rather than lines after all.

Mark Brearley now shares his knowledge of and enthusiasm for city streets and his research methods with designers, researchers and policymakers in other European cities such as Brussels, Rotterdam and Hamburg. These new locations help Brearley to better understand the applicability of the city street concept outside of London.

What detailed maps (mapping) of London city streets (High Streets)

Where London, United Kingdom

Design Design for London, Mark Brearley

Realized 2006-2013

Intervention detailed analyses and maps of the ways city streets are used allowed the targeted improvement of buildings, green and public spaces

Also good for healthy living (mixed neighbourhoods encourage walking and cycling) and sociocultural solidarity (city streets encourage mutual proximity of businesses)

vital economy
Biobased Furniture Factory

The Zaanstreek has long been one of the most important working areas in the vicinity of Amsterdam. Globalization and digitalization demand a revitalization of the area's economic foundations. Using historical spatial features creates an attractive residential and employment environment that dovetails seamlessly with the new economy.

The character of the Zaanstreek has continually been determined by the economy throughout the centuries. This is where the first marshes were drained to reclaim land; windmills were used to process lumber and more recently the area was a crucial link for the Amsterdam region's seaport. Its current, monofunctional industrial estates testify to this history.

The circular economy presents opportunities for the Zaanstreek. The historical spatial configuration of this urbanized area, completely marbled with waterways, forms a perfect basis. New forms of clean manufacturing can find a place here. The combination of large and small buildings makes a mix of housing and employment possible.

Based on historical research, the designer has chosen to zoom in on the area she dubs the Zaanfront, the present Hembrug area. The metro is to be extended to this point from Station Sloterdijk, so as to create a direct connection to Amsterdam's city centre. The Bruynzeel furniture factory, located on the Hembrug area sinds 1920, will become the epicentre of the circular economy.

Bruynzeel will concentrate entirely on producing bio-based furniture and interiors. The flax produced in the hinterland will go to a factory located alongside, where semi-finished goods will be made of bio-composites, processed by Bruynzeel. This manufacture is non-polluting, which means a pleasant residential setting

fig. 85 — Biobased factory and flax field

can be created on the Zaanfront – using construction materials from Bruynzeel.

Area housing will become more dense, with a mix of sturdy apartment buildings that allude to the first steam-powered factories and contemporary interpretations of the typical houses of the area, the *Zaanse huisjes*.

Designer Brigitta van Weeren in collaboration with Frank Vonk

Academy Amsterdam

Design Atelier Zaans Next Economy

Where Zaanstad, the Netherlands

Lecturers Marco Broekman, Dingeman Deijs, Rik de Visser

vital economy

Agricultural Hotspot

Little by little, the farmland in the Haarlemmermeer is being transformed into low-density residential areas. On its northern edge there is a patch of polder that is losing its agricultural function due to the relocation of the A9 motorway and the future expansion of Schiphol Airport. It is precisely that agricultural character, the international accessibility and the proximity of the capital in the Zuidas business district that make this little polder ideal for an Agricultural Innovation Campus.

The Haarlemmermeer is an area of constant transformation. Around 1850 it was the first polder to be drained using steam power. The Netherlands earned its worldwide reputation as a food exporter in part thanks to the efficient production in the Haarlemmermeer. This economic model is now under threat, because profit margins on large-scale food production are steadily decreasing. The Netherlands is increasingly turning to innovation and the export of knowledge and know-how.

Its location between Schiphol Airport and the Zuidas business district lends itself ideally to a campus that unites knowledge, capital and experimental agricultural production and that couples international accessibility with high-level agriculture – the comparison to Aalsmeer, the international hotspot for the flower trade, is self-evident.

The leftover farmland that still exists here is being increasingly eaten away by the growth of Badhoevedorp and Schiphol. An innovation campus would benefit from just such an area of transition. Scenic connections with the Amsterdamse Bos nature area, the polder and the water network of the Ringvaart canal and the River Schinkel can be made easily. With the metro the campus is connected to the regional public transport network and via attractive slow-traffic routes to the recreational facilities in the environs and the residential areas of Badhoevedorp.

The campus is composed of various zones that – viewed from Schiphol towards the polders and Badhoevedorp – go from enclosed and private to increasingly open and public. It therefore resolutely opens up to its surroundings, allowing everyone to experience the innovations integrated into the landscape design.

Designer Paul Plambeck

Academy Amsterdam

Design Atelier SouthWest Works!

Where Amsterdam Metropolitan Area, the Netherlands

Lecturers Marco Broekman, Roel van Gerwen, Harm Veenenbos

healthy living

Serious Game — Oosterwold (NL)

A new way of area development is in the making in Oosterwold, a 4,300-hectare polder area east of Almere. Here, residents and businesses rather than governments determine what the urban agricultural area is going to look like. It all started in 2011, with a game called Play Oosterwold.

The Netherlands has a rich planning tradition. The Dutch are accustomed to governments that decide on land use, down to the last centimetre. But the time of unquestioned top-down planning seems to be over. Central government has designated Oosterwold, a polder area east of Almere, as a pilot area for experiments with area development. It thus anticipates the new environmental laws that, from 2019, are expected to make spatial planning easier as they comprise less and simpler rules.

Oosterwold is an initiative of the municipalities of Almere and Zeewolde, the Central Government Real Estate Agency, the district water board of Zuiderzeeland and the Province of Flevoland. The experiments in this urban agricultural area surpass, for example, those of the self-build plots in Almere-Poort. In Oosterwold, there are no demarcated plots. The future residents get to define, design, build and plant their own plots.

The responsibility for the area development, too, is left to the residents, businesses and institutions. That means central government will not provide any road network, lighting, sewer system, electricity network

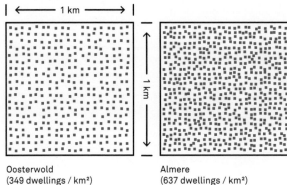

Oosterwold
(349 dwellings / km²)

Almere
(637 dwellings / km²)

fig. 86 — Building density

■ housing
⚘ food production
■ energy
▦ infrastructure
⠄ polder

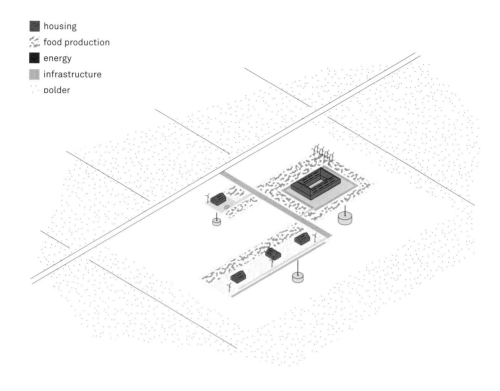

fig. 87 — Self-sufficient and
self-organizing

or waste collection. The investors are also responsible for this. This makes the land, with a building density of 3.5 dwellings per hectare (15,000 dwellings per 4,300 hectares), a lot cheaper. Expectations are that the investors will find the most economical way of developing and therefore work more efficiently and cheaper than any government.

When Almere's councillor for spatial matters, Henk Mulder, addressed the first group of investors in January 2016 he told them that Oosterwold was all about 'do-it-yourself planning'. This does not mean that the government is absent altogether. The two municipalities involved have outlined a structural strategy. There are a legal framework for the licensing and a municipal area director to establish contacts between initiators and landowners, for the sale of plots as well as for collaborations in the field of energy. The area director furthermore monitors whether rules are observed and assesses all plans.

Current initiators range from idealists who want to build their ecological dream home to groups of fifty-somethings that want to realize a communal residential environment and entrepreneurs looking to

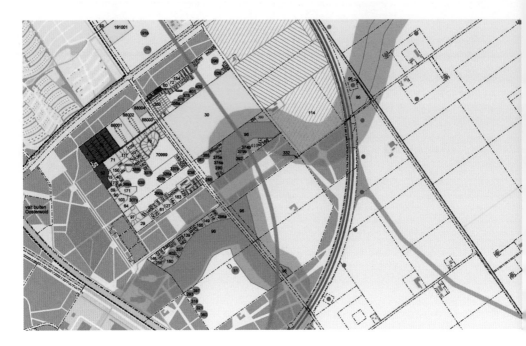

develop a care farm with a tea pavilion. They are not
completely free to realize any plan they want, they have
to adhere to the ten rules of a game developed by architecture firm MVRDV. Project architect Jeroen Zuidgeest:
'This means they cannot simply build a house with a garden, but also have to build part of the infrastructure, of
the energy network, and so on. The most important rule
is that though they have more freedom, they also have
more responsibility for the development of Oosterwold.'

The rules of the game have been taken from a serious
game: in this case an urban planning game for which the
parties involved sit down at the table together and play
at developing the area. First introduced in 2011, the Play
Oosterwold game has repeatedly been played since.[148]

This is how it works: players can buy an agricultural
plot, a landscape plot or a generic plot and, over several rounds, build roads, cultivate the plot, choose an
energy source and create green areas and water courses.
Individually or jointly. The simulation game is used to
further refine the ten leading principles for building,
water management, green areas and infrastructure.

The first principle is that it is the people that make Oosterwold. They can be residents, businesses, institutions
or project developers and either individuals or groups.
They have to work together, even if only to get the collective facilities off the ground. The second principle is
that investors can freely choose the size and location of

fig. 88 — Plots in the
polder area of Oosterwold

148
See: bit.ly/2aqDjRb.

fig. 89 — Play Oosterwold

their plots. The content is largely fixed, however (third principle): 20 per cent buildings, 50 per cent agriculture and the remaining 30 per cent for pavement, green areas and water. Owners can depart from this rule in favour of greener plots or plots with more buildings (fourth principle). More green or more buildings must be compensated on other plots, so the overall composition of Oosterwold remains the same.

Green is leading in Oosterwold: two-thirds of the urban agricultural area has to remain green (fifth principle), in the form of kitchen gardens, ornamental gardens, meadows, fields, woods or parks. The idea is to make the former polder area more ecologically varied. Thanks to the urban agriculture, the district will produce most of its own food. That means consumption takes place close to the source, resulting in less transport and lower CO_2 emissions.

In addition, the buildings are surrounded by greenery (sixth principle) to preserve the green character of Oosterwold. The Floor Air Ratio (FAR) for buildings is 0.5: a single-floor building is allowed to cover 50 per cent of the surface suitable for building, two floors 25 per cent, and so on. More compact buildings are also allowed, for example with a FAR of 1.0. However, this also has to be compensated elsewhere, for example by adding extra (public) green areas.

The seventh principle states that the investors are co-responsible for the local road network. Owners must construct a road along their plot and connect it to the road along the next plot. A road network will naturally ensue. Central government remains responsible for the national and provincial road network.

Investors themselves are responsible for the water management, wastewater treatment and energy supply (eighth principle). The municipality will not construct sewers, collect waste or provide district heating. Utility companies will only install cables and provide a low-capacity drinking water supply. Residents must produce their own energy using solar panels or wood stoves and use thermal storage. They are also responsible for the discharge of water, while the water quality and groundwater level may not deteriorate. The new residents will be doing a lot of discovering and coordinating and the suppliers will probably be doing a lot of finetuning.

Principles nine and ten state that plots are financially self-sufficient and thus built without any subsidies. Government investments follow public money, rather than the other way around. Only when enough people have come to the area will the government make money

fig. 90 — Following spread: Redevelopment of the Flevopolder near Oosterwold

available for public services and the widening of existing roads.

fig. 91 — Meeting of future Oosterwold residents

The first residents moved into Oosterwold in the summer of 2016. Expectations are high, but it will take several years before we know what this new way of area development will yield in terms of buildings, infrastructure, energy and food production, and biodiversity.

Initially, area development new-style is cheap for municipalities, because the land is sold without the usual planning, accessing and site preparation costs. However, whether municipalities will make a profit in the end remains to be seen. Concluding the many agreements with individuals that are necessary will probably take more administrative time and therefore be more expensive than concluding similar agreements with a small number of big developers.

On the other hand, the approach can result in an individually formed and multifaceted low-density living environment and a high-quality green environment. One risk is that private parties may drop out because of the large number of agreements involved. This could result in the replacement of individual plans by more traditional project development with large numbers of similar houses and leased agricultural land.

The municipality can intervene if things threaten to go wrong, but for now Oosterwold promises to be an ideal living environment entirely created by hands-on

149

In *Arcadia for All: The Legacy of a Makeshift Landscape* (D. Hardy and C. Ward, 1984) the *plotlands* on the eastern outskirts of London in the 1920s and 1930s have been extensively studied—a spacious world of allotments in which everyone could afford a detached home.

150

Stefan Cozzolino, an Italian scientist that works at the Politecnico Milano, is writing a dissertation about Oosterwold.

citizens. Who would not want to live on an oversized allotment?[149] There is also foreign interest in this experiment that, with limited government intervention, is headed towards a new, healthy and socially engaged kind of urban development.[150]

What an urban agricultural area created by residents and businesses

Where Almere, the Netherlands

Design MVRDV

Realized under development, first residents in 2016

Intervention central government backs away from area development no blueprints and subdivisions, but rules based on a simulation game

Also good for resilient infrastructure (plenty of green, not much surfacing), renewable energy (home energy production), material cycle (no sewer system, home waste processing) and sociocultural connectivity (joint developing)

healthy living

Olympic Rowing Course in River Bed

The elite Dutch sport centre Papendal lies in the woods near Arnhem and is of little value to the general public. This gave rise to the idea of establishing a satellite location in the floodplains of the Rhine, in the middle of the city, in the form of a rowing course. Gradually the rowing course grew from a light-hearted idea to a feasible design.

In an inner bend of the Rhine, between Arnhem-Noord and Arnhem-Zuid, lie floodplains that include the Meinerswijk nature area. Here is where the designers have conceived Papendal's satellite location – more specifically an Olympic rowing course. The location is highly visible and accessible from the bridges that connect the two parts of the city.

At first glance the design is primarily a funny idea. The design was created step by step, discussed with stakeholders, improved and resubmitted to new stakeholders and experts.

Members of the local rowing club provided the designers with information on the dimensions of an Olympic rowing course. An expert from Rijkswaterstaat, the Dutch government's Directorate-General for Public Works and Water Management, responsible for water safety on the river, provided insights into the performance of the floodplain area at various water levels.

When the Rhine has to discharge extremely high amounts of water, it can cut off its bend and flow through Meinerswijk. The rowing course will be positioned to become a component of this water management. The design takes the landmark elements in the area and the existing infrastructure into account: the course can easily be accessed from the existing roadways and cycle paths.

fig. 92 — Rowing course with soft banks

The city's ecologist also furnished input, with the result that the course is to have soft banks and ecological water steps can be created.

This is how the idea grew into a presentable plan, a feasible intervention and finally even an implementable design. The only obstacle in its way, according to the designers: the Netherlands already has an Olympic rowing course, the Bosbaan in Amsterdam. Whether there is room for two courses of this size is debatable.

Designers Jasper van den Bogaard and Joris Dijke

Academy Arnhem

Design Atelier Sport en bewegen in de openbare ruimte

Where Arnhem, the Netherlands

Lecturers Bas Driessen, Thijs van Spaandonk

healthy living

Fast Cycle Route
– The Last Mile

A high-speed cycle path was recently laid between Arnhem and Nijmegen. The clear route in the rural area becomes confused as it enters Arnhem, to the detriment of the experience of the cyclist. Various interventions are proposed to optimize the potential of the high-speed cycle route, interventions that make the use of the route more appealing and more comfortable.

The high-speed cycle path between Arnhem and Nijmegen is identifiable in the rural area by its clean lines, its unity of materials and its futuristic light posts. When one enters the built-up area of Arnhem, however, that identifiability is lost. The road surface and contours continually change in character and the position of the cyclist in relation to the other road users constantly changes as well; often the cyclist no longer has the right of way. To put it succinctly, the route is fragmented. This does not contribute to comfort and convenience and it makes using the high-speed path less appealing.

The designers painstakingly drew the entire route in order to identify all bottlenecks. In addition they inventoried potential users as well as their starting points and destinations.

They elaborated an improvement to the cycle route on three levels. The profile of the cycle path is addressed in order to create an identifiable route in the built-up area as well. One minimal intervention is the installation of the same light posts along the entire route. In addition, the landscape experience is also reinforced. The route goes past the Rhine floodplains, but the position of the cycle path in relation to the roadway currently makes that difficult if not impossible to notice. Finally, the high-speed cycle path

fig. 93 — Fast Cycle Route

is supplemented with a few new facilities to make the journey more pleasant for the cyclist. This includes covered places at intersections, where schoolchildren can wait for their cycling buddies protected from the elements, but where one can also pump up a tyre, for example.

Designers Taco Bijleveld
and Wim Spijker

Academy Arnhem

Design Atelier Sport en bewegen II
[Sport and Exercise II]

Where Arnhem, the Netherlands

Lecturers Bas Driessen,
Thijs van Spaandonk

sociocultural connectivity

High Line — New York (USA)

It is perhaps the most famous city park of the twenty-first century: the High Line in New York. Yet this railway viaduct was nearly demolished. After residents had discovered the abandoned railway in the middle of the city, a well-known photographer pushed this hidden world into the limelight, which helped to swing public opinion.

The High Line is a 2.4-km-long and 9-m-high abandoned railway viaduct across Manhattan's Meatpacking District. The area was out of bounds for years. Weeds covered the viaduct and only one or two local residents ventured upon it by climbing out of their bedroom windows and crossing a foot plank. Since 2009, however, the viaduct is a public promenade that attracts 5 million visitors every year. The High Line is currently one of the city's most-photographed icons.

The story of the High Line started like a children's book. Two young professionals, Joshua David and Robert Hammond, met in 1999 during a neighbourhood meeting in the Meatpacking District. The city, under pressure of major real estate owners, wanted to tear down the High Line. David and Hammond climbed onto the overgrown railway and were fascinated by the idea of a public promenade. They founded Friends of the High Line and recruited members and funds with a compelling story about the preservation of cultural heritage and of a local park. Several major financiers introduced the men to a network of real estate owners and influential politicians.

fig. 94 — Initiators Joshua David and Robert Hammond

The initiative only really took off after a new mayor was elected. Until 2001, Rudy Giuliani was the mayor of New York: a successful crime fighter who was sensitive to the real estate lobby. He did not like the plan to preserve the High Line. When his successor Michael Bloomberg, a data-driven mayor, took over, this marked a turning point. The rear-guard fight turned into a broad-based initiative that could count on political and financial support.

One of the first major sponsors of Friends of the High Line was a real estate owner that had several buildings

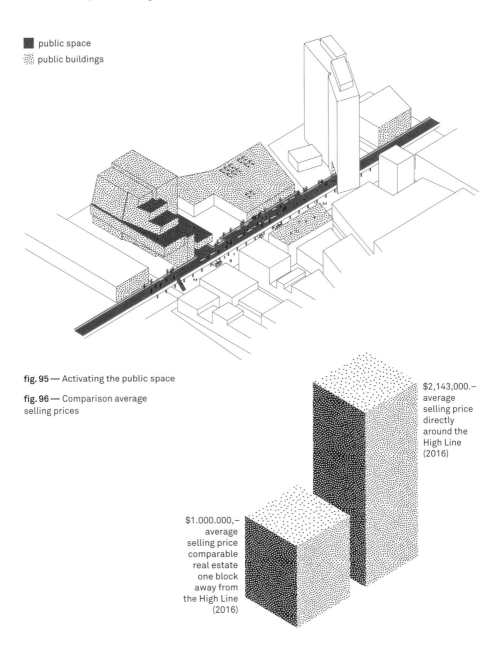

public space
public buildings

fig. 95 — Activating the public space

fig. 96 — Comparison average
selling prices

$2,143,000.–
average
selling price
directly
around the
High Line
(2016)

$1.000.000,–
average
selling price
comparable
real estate
one block
away from
the High Line
(2016)

151

*Analyzing the Economic Feasibility
of the High Line,* HR&A, 2002.

fig. 97 — Following spread:
High Line – View of New Jersey

nearby. He commissioned an economic feasibility study
that showed that redevelopment would significantly
increase the value of real estate around the High Line.[151]
The city would also benefit, by revenues from real estate
taxes. Bloomberg's staff was convinced by this economic
analysis, which proved to be an important step in the
research by design.

But for the general public, it all started with the
pictures. Few New Yorkers knew what the closed-off

viaduct looked like from above. At the invitation of David and Hammond, photographer Joel Sternfeld photographed the four seasons from 2000 to 2001. His poetic images of a weed-covered railway in the middle of Manhattan were a hit. The photos showed the exceptional nature of the urban greenery and provided a whole new perspective of New York's skyline. The photo project instantly put the High Line on the map as a hidden and exciting part of the city. The creation of that

fig. 98 — Street entrance to the High Line

fig. 99 — Park annex
pedestrian boulevard

image was the most important element in the research by design.

In 2002, the chances of preservation had increased significantly thanks to Bloomberg's support and Sternfeld's photo project and an international design competition was held. It was emphatically meant to generate redevelopment ideas, rather than a design to be carried out in full. As a result, designers mainly submitted their entries to generate publicity. Partly thanks to the prominence of the jury, there were 720 entries from 36 countries.

The competition managed to attract a lot of international attention by also exhibiting the entries at New York's Grand Central Station. The winning plan, a kilometre-long pool, was unachievable but did portend that the High Line could radically change people's view of the city. The ideas competition proved a successful publicity stunt that further contributed to the High Line's image.

In 2004, a design team was selected to construct a park on the High Line viaduct. Together with the Friends, the team went on a field trip to Paris to explore the Promenade Plantée, which was completed in 1993. The fact that another elevated park on top of a railway viaduct already existed reinforced the credibility of the plan for the High Line.

In addition, the trip allowed the designers to compare their plans with an example. What they saw in Paris, however, was a neatly styled garden, the opposite of what they had in mind. They wanted to preserve the viaduct, its weeds and its tranquillity. 'Keep it simple, keep it slow, keep it quiet, keep it wild': such were the starting points for the High Line and they still stand proudly at the entrance in big block letters. Architect Ricardo Scofidio made a statement that became quite famous, saying: 'Our job is to defend the High Line from architecture.'

Friends of the High Line was awarded 150 million dollars from public and private funds for the first two development stages. The third and final stage required another 125 million dollars. The Friends currently collect 98 per cent of the annual budget by themselves, for example by organizing fundraising events and charity evenings such as the annual High Line Spring Benefit and their Summer Party.

Anno 2016, Friends is still led by co-founder Robert Hammond. In interviews, he explains how it was clear from the beginning that the design would not be the sum of many consultation rounds, though designers did have to keep on giving presentations to interested residents to ensure that their designs would stay close to the starting points. The question remains, therefore, to what extent residents have actually had a say in matters such as the starting points and the design.

James Corner Field Operation (JCFO) designer Richard Kennedy clarifies the difference between a 'democratic design process' and an 'inclusive design process'. In the context of the first, the designer presents variants and design choices are made on the basis of the majority vote. This is a consensus-driven process that leads to a lot of compromise. In an inclusive process, stakeholders respond to the development of the design. Is the story still consistent? Are the proper interests promoted? In the case of the High Line this approach worked, because the starting points of the design principles were based on the initial situation and widely embraced.

There is no doubt that the High Line has become a symbol of a project for and by the community. It is the pride of the neighbourhood and the entire city. The park has also made the Meatpacking District world famous and has attracted plenty of investments. But is it, with 5 million visitors a year, still a neighbourhood park? The visitors of the High Line are mostly tourists. The success also had a downside: gentrification. Property prices have

fig. 100 — Pedestrian boulevard on the High Line

risen so fast that some residents were forced to leave
and the community is falling apart. Friends of the High
Line, an organization that now has members all over the
world, is aware of this trend and tries to actively involve
less affluent residents in the High Line and create jobs
for them.

What a park on a railway viaduct in the
middle of Manhattan, realized thanks
to the imagination of local residents

Where New York, United States

Design James Corner Field Operations,
Diller Scofidio + Renfro, Piet Oudolf

Realized 2009

Intervention thanks to Joel Sternfeld's
photographs, everyone got to see
the potential of the railway viaduct as
a park and demolition was prevented

Also good for healthy living
(walking in the park)

sociocultural connectivity

Parkstad Connects

The spatial development of the area around Heerlen goes back to settlement patterns in Roman times. Over the course of two millennia, a patchwork of pieces of city developed. To connect these, the authorities spent decades investing in building roadways. Result: an overcapacity in infrastructure that works not as a connection between districts, neighbourhoods and communities, but as a barrier.

The A76 motorway and the N281 provincial road run pretty much parallel past Heerlen. The N281, because of its profile and speed limits, also functions as a motorway. One road would suffice for the traffic capacity.

This surfeit of roadways is a legacy of the spatial evolution of Heerlen and Parkstad. First there were the Roman settlements, which eventually more or less joined together to form ribbon villages along roadways. When mining necessitated housing tens of thousands of miners and their families, mining colonies were established on parcels of land belonging to the mining concessions. This created an intricate, extensive network of communities. In such a spatial structure, the car proved the most apt form of transport.

To reduce dependency on the car, the route of the N281 is transformed. A monorail is to be constructed that will finally provide a proper connection between Heerlen and Aachen, Germany, so that these cities can truly become a common area. The profile of the roadway is also addressed, allowing for crosslinks. The 11-km route is divided into smaller sections, each of which will be able to

fig. 101 — Analysis chart based on interviews

have its own character, depending on its context. There are all kinds of opportunities to give these sections a public function using specific programmes of activities – for example a skate park, a campground, an art route or a science park.

Designers Mick Dubois,
Channah Mourmans and Leon Nypels

Academy Maastricht

Design Atelier Parkstad verbindt
[Parkstad Connects]

Where Heerlen, the Netherlands

Lecturers Christian Uwer, Franz Ziegler

Part 3 – Who

Never mind that the challenge is urgent and the design brilliant, when it does not catch on, all efforts have been wasted. Research by design is not a solitary, linear activity that allows the designer to pass the buck by creating brilliant finds, but an interactive process that involves many stakeholders, all of them necessary to take the design to the next level.

Part 3 begins with a brief discussion of coalition building and of why it is important to – rather than only talk about problems – also talk about the opportunities healthy urbanity creates. Not only is it hard to catch flies with vinegar, a one-sided emphasis on problems does not do justice to the potential of research by design, either.

Coalitions vary depending on the challenge, its ambition and its scale, but especially on the stage the process is in. The role of design and designers varies accordingly. To clarify this, the coalitions of three examples are mapped in detail below: Who were part of the coalitions? How did parties get involved? How did their roles develop? How did coalitions jointly define the question and the most appropriate approach?

The analysis of 2050 – An Energetic Odyssey, the wind power plan presented during the IABR 2016, centres on the ideas and strategies stages.

The development of Buiksloterham, a district in Amsterdam-Noord, focuses on the concept stage – a living lab for circular urban development – though there appear to be some parallel processes.

Finally, there is a detailed description of the water square in Rotterdam that is at first glance nothing but a project for a lowered playground serving as water storage in times of heavy rains, but on closer inspection involves all the stages of research by design.

In a concluding reflection the FUR researchers address the optimal scale level for research by design.

Coalition Building

Typically, research by design into wicked problems does not involve a classic client – designer relationship. Research by design centres on coalitions of different kinds of actors that jointly encircle the problem and find a way to address it.

The composition of a coalition not only depends on the challenge – the construction of resilient coastal defences requires other partners than the reactivation of the manufacturing industry in a disadvantaged neighbourhood – but coalitions change during the process as well. Parties can drop out halfway because they have made their contribution and there are no further steps for them to take, or may do so because they have lost faith.

New parties may join that have an open mind about the problem initially and that can gradually, if all goes well, step into their predecessors' shoes. Such parties will not be standing in line: their recruitment will take active searching and convincing, using ideas that initially need only be conceivable, to then become more concrete and realistic over time. The DTP Diagram introduced in Part 2 is a useful tool to determine which partners a coalition requires →p. 128.

Part 2 mainly focused on the question of how to get from one stage to the next, that is, on the diamond: first diverge and then converge. This Part zooms in on the stages themselves, that is: the points at which the research by design process consolidates temporarily.

The first stages of the diagram are the most interesting because more to the right, the diagram represents classic designing that involves a clearly defined commission that 'simply' requires a good design.

The initial stage – when even a strategy has not yet been developed – is the most diffuse: nobody is responsible yet, there is no framework for testing, there is really nothing but a problem. And a problem is like a hot potato that people prefer to pass on as quickly as they can: 'Very important, but let someone else worry about it.' As it turns out, it is essential to translate problems into opportunities, first. At least potentially, there must be a way out, otherwise all that is left is doom and gloom.

Research by design can play an important part in devising such a 'way out'. When the European Commission presented the Roadmap for Renewable Energy in early 2007, all the Dutch experts looked at the North Sea. The Stichting Natuur & Milieu took the lead and its former head of communications came up with the idea to ask Rem Koolhaas to visualize the ambition. Energy company Eneco, the ASN Bank and Stichting Doen were willing to act as sponsors.

Koolhaas came up with Zeekracht (Sea Power), a plan for a super ring of wind turbines covering the entire North Sea and producing as much renewable energy as the countries around the Persian Gulf produced in terms of oil at the time.[152] 'A hugely powerful image, we made the opening of the NOS news with it, featuring our director explaining things from the beach,' says current head of communications Talitha Koek. Koolhaas's ring released a lot of energy, the Balkenende IV cabinet designated 14 wind farms all located along the ring and granted the licences. Unfortunately, no extra money was made available so only three of the farms were actually built.

'The production of wind power at sea is best realized according to a plan, as this will make it cheaper and spatial planning issues can be included,' says Koek and with Koolhaas's plan in hand. Natuur & Milieu together with NGO's from other European countries and grid operators such as Tennet went looking for ways to create a renewable grid at sea. Though in the end it turned out that a ring was not a smart solution at all – a spider web is much more logical, as the next chapter will show – 'the grid idea survived'.

It is impossible to identify the direct impact of the Zeekracht project. Good ideas are born in many places once the time is right and success has many fathers, but it is certain that Zeekracht has accelerated the plans for the North Sea by literally making the strategy conceivable. Koek: 'We used Zeekracht for nearly ten years, because the idea is so visionary. Now it has served its purpose, the plan Hajer and Sijmons presented at the IABR this year is much more realistic and even more comprehensive.' The following chapter presents the IABR plan at length.

The example of Zeekracht makes something else clear as well, namely that especially the early stages of research by design do not have to lead to a follow-up commission. A design can be a stone in the pond, an impulse that sets other parties in motion, without any commissions ensuing. Koolhaas was awarded the credit and the publicity, but even this is not always the case. The design image is protected by copyright, but strategies and ideas themselves are not protected, anyone can do with them what they want. That is a blessing of our open society and a driving force behind innovation, but it can be a bitter pill for a designer to swallow if in a further stage they suddenly find themselves outside the coalition.

An Alliance on The North Sea

The heart of the International Architecture Biennale 2016 was undoubtedly the Energetic Odyssey that head curator Maarten Hajer and Dirk Sijmons, the éminence grise of Dutch landscape architecture, undertook.[153]

152
See:
www.oma.eu/projects/zeekracht.

153
The project '2050 – An Energetic Odyssey. The Vital Role of the North Sea in the Energy Transition' is an initiative by Maarten Hajer, professor in Urban Futures at the University of Utrecht. The design was made by Dirk Sijmons, who preceded Maarten Hajer in 2014 as curator of the Biennale. As Government Advisor for the Landscape, Sijmons published an advisory report on wind energy in 2007, he wrote the Kleine Energieatlas in 2008 and the book Landscape and Energy in 2015.

On a huge screen, a 12-minute animation shows how from 2050, we could produce the unimaginable amount of 5,500 terawatt-hour per year.[154] Watching it, you slowly see a sustainable network of 25,000 wind turbines emerge.

The bar was set high from the beginning: an energy transition on the scale of the North Sea. For Maarten Hajer's analysis is as simple as it is grim: bottom-up initiatives alone cannot provide sufficient renewable energy. They are obviously sympathetic, important and indispensable, but they are focused on energy generation by households, local communities and local players. Together, these can only take on 15 per cent of the total demand. Projects of a very large size are therefore necessary to successfully complete the transition, which is why the project was given the somewhat provocative working title Big is Beautiful.

The choice of scale level partly determined the composition of the coalition. Large parties were necessary, parties with money moreover, because the entire project had to be financed externally.[155] In approaching the right players, the prestige of the IABR and the large network of Hajer and Sijmons came in handy.

The first parties that joined the public-private partnership were the Port of Rotterdam, network operator Tennet and offshore company Van Oord. Gradually, other parties came on board, including the Ministries of Economic Affairs and of Infrastructure and the Environment, energy giant Shell, the European Climate Foundation, energy company RWE, real estate giant The Crown Estate, Stichting Natuur & Milieu and the port authorities of Zeeland and Amsterdam.

These parties have very different interests and tasks. How were they convinced to undertake a joint search on the basis of a shared sense of urgency? According to Sijmons it is essential to have parties participate actively. 'You cannot simply ask them to sponsor a project, you have to interest them in the problem that you put on the table and then in the way you want to solve it. That is the only way to prevent a noncommittal attitude. The coalition examines the entire process, using design to demonstrate that something can be done. More and more companies and institutions then join in the course of the manufacturing process, it's a snowball effect.'

154

That is nearly double the energy consumption of the 28 countries of the European Union in 2015, see: www.bit.ly/2akTIa8.

155

Sub-studies, incidentally, can choose a different point of departure and therefore have a different coalition composition. Coalitions are emphatically not static.

Crucial to the involvement of parties was a screen of more than 7 × 5 m lying flat on the floor on which the plan was projected from above. 'By standing around it, people realized they had to think on a different scale level, they started to relate to the sheer size and impact of the plan. Many environmental organizations, for example, were accustomed to focusing on the environmental impact assessments for individual wind farms or limited-sized offshore installations. This installation instantly demonstrated that this is the wrong way to view the situation.'

During the IABR, Sijmons organized a conference of marine ecologists from all of the North Sea countries: 'Literally looking at an area of 52,000 km² – 13 times the size of the Netherlands – makes the opportunities of the ecological system visible. The organization of fishery-free zones will allow the North Sea system to catch its breath – currently, the entire seabed is broken up by fishery equipment three times a year.'[156] The design therefore generates a shared perception of the spatial content, not only in terms of the energy transition itself, but also in terms of fishery and nature.

A second important decision was to not present a static end result, which would give the impression of accomplished facts, but to introduce an animation in which the design gradually develops. Stakeholders see the network gradually build on that which already exists.

This 'organic growth' is not only a matter of presentation technique, it also embodies an essential feature of the design in question. Rem Koolhaas's Zeekracht plan presupposed an increase in scale: the plan only works if the complete ring is built. The IABR-design grows gradually and around 2040, the network is so close-knit that it is fairly simply to turn it into a grid by using conduits and allowing countries to collaborate with each other. Without any pre-investment of capital, the system takes leaps forward. Sijmons: 'In reality things are developed in small steps, that was the fatal flaw in Zeekracht.'

The IABR plan also includes a forward leap, incidentally, namely the construction of an island roughly in the middle of the North Sea where alternating current is converted into direct current. This is the only way to transport electricity over long distances without too much loss.

In early June, just before the end of the IABR 2016, network operator Tennet presented a sketch for such an island on Doggersbank. Sijmons exercises restraint: 'The location of the island still needs to be carefully considered. This is the domain of Natura 2000 and therefore you want to handle the nature people with care, before you know it you've shattered the consensus. You could perhaps call Tennet the Rijkswaterstaat of the North Sea, but it's the Rijkswaterstaat of the 1960s, wanting a quick fix. We have offered our help.'

But even without an existing island, parties can gradually build links that foreshadow the total structure. And this creates short-term prospects for action for both the coalition partners and external parties. Maike Boggeman, team member on behalf of Shell: 'Designers use scenarios in a totally different way than we do. We use scenarios to map uncertainties as comprehensively as possible. Designers on the other hand select a single future and show that it is a possible future. That makes it a great tool to reduce uncertainty.' You can create ownership and connectivity this way.

Of course, the Energetic Odyssey of the IABR does not stand alone, there have been similar plans before and others are likely to follow. Sijmons: 'This is what Richard Dawkins calls 'mimetic' plans: plans that buzz around in professional circles for quite some time and that take

156
Sijmons writes about the ways wind farms can contribute to the creation of a fishery-free marine nature reserve on the North Sea as early as in 1998 in his book =Landschap.

on different shapes.' He compares this plan to the Zuiderzee Works. 'Lely had already made seven plans for the Afsluitdijk and the Zuiderzee polders before the definitive plan was adopted in 1916.'

Although design and designers play important parts, the process described above is not design-driven. Sijmons: 'Design has a role in the imagination and in politics. By designing you can articulate ideals; they can absorb part of the political decision making.'

That makes research by design an antidote to the bureaucratization of a political arena that is increasingly dominated by files and spreadsheets. Design coalitions can gradually telescope the domains of politics and design: 'This is more than good collaboration alone. It changes the playing field, alters the stage.'

During the European summit, the whole installation was moved to Amsterdam a couple of times: at the headquarters of Shell the Directors General of all EU countries familiarized themselves with it and later, during a session at The Grand Hotel, so did the Ministers of Economic Affairs.

On 6 June 2016, the nine North Sea countries signed the Political Declaration on Energy Cooperation between the North Seas Countries. A direct reference to The Energetic Odyssey of the IABR is missing, but in the press release the Ministry of Economic Affairs wrote: 'It is conceivable that in the future wind farms that are close together in different neighbouring countries are connected, for example, from sea to land by a single power cable, rather than using a separate cable per country.' And that is precisely the essence of the IABR plan.

How this will continue is of course unknown: Sijmons: 'The North Sea plan is ambitious, it requires Chinese building speeds. But it is possible. The partners are now convinced that it is feasible and that it can be realized.' The CEO's of the participating companies, in any case, have voiced their intention to persist. Shell, for example, has taken the initiative to put the subject on the agenda of the next cabinet formation and wants to use the animation in that context. Perhaps it will also help that the king, on his own initiative, has already been round to look at the Energetic Odyssey.

Alternative Area Development

The northern IJ banks are hip and happening, with residential towers and hotels shooting up like mushrooms. Just before the summer of 2016, the Amsterdam Tower on Overhoeks opened its doors. The former Shell Tower now houses a mix of dance-related businesses, two clubs and a hotel. The rotating, 80-m-high platform offers breath-taking views of the city.

Success attracts success, but what a difference a decade makes. Ten years ago, the city of Amsterdam wanted to build 9,000 dwellings in Amsterdam-Noord, but the crisis threw a spanner in the works. Developers and investors backed away. Especially Buiksloterham, a polluted harbour and industrial area between Overhoeks and the NDSM area where at least 3,000 dwellings were projected, was considered just the place to get your fingers burnt. Even the collectives of private commissioners (CPO's), for which large plots had been reserved, abandoned the area.

To break the impasse, the city of Amsterdam decided to organize a competition for De Ceuvel, a fiercely polluted shipyard immediately behind Overhoeks. The winner would get to use the land free of charge for ten years. The best plan was submitted by a temporary collaboration of three agencies: Space&Matter, Metabolic and Delva wanted to turn De Ceuvel into a breeding ground for circular experiments.

They dragged old houseboats onto the shore, ready for creative businesses to move into, while plants purified the contaminated soil underneath. Wastewater was treated on-site with the aid of dry compost toilets and helophyte filters: struvite, which is used in aquaponic food production as a substitute for artificial fertilizer, was extracted from the urine of the café customers.[157]

De Ceuvel became the placemaker of Buiksloterham: together with the project Schoonschip it acted as a driving force for sustainable local initiatives. Because meanwhile, other private initiatives were being introduced, for example by Frank Alsema who had already left his mark on the NDSM shipyard. He founded Citylab Buiksloterham, a flexible collaboration of initiatives in the field of sustainability.

The concrete translation of sustainability goals into attractive spatial images convinced more and more people of Buiksloterham's potential. Individuals as well as collectives, developers and corporations seized their opportunities. The low land prices were a leg up: they left some money to invest and experiment. This created space for plans that were not only conceivable and sustainable, but also feasible and practicable.

In 2014 a large number of parties signed the Manifesto Circular Buiksloterham, expressing their ambition to transform Buiksloterham into a living lab for circular urban development. The plans and experiments drew a stream of researchers to Buiksloterham to broaden the existing coalition. Wageningen University and Delft University of Technology, for example, used their own funds for a study into the spatial and systemic translation of sustainability concepts and the way in which governance played a role in the increasingly complex organization of initiators, designers, consultants, government agencies and academic institutions. Amsterdam's third university, the Amsterdam Institute for Advanced Metropolitan Solutions (AMS), joined as well.

With the financial support of, among others, the city of Amsterdam and the Creative Industries Fund NL, design offices could expand their activities by researching circular techniques and their spatial impact.

The individual initiatives continued to develop as well. Frank Alsema's Citylab, One Architecture and Mobile City formed a new initiative together: Hackable City. Goal: to find out how technological means can help convince individuals and collectives to become involved in city making.

This was also the background against which Cityplot emerged, an initiative by De Alliantie. This housing

157
See Practical Example 'Urban Farming – The Hague' →p. 76 for more information about aquaponics.

association, which ventured to buy land in Buiksloterham at an early stage, now wanted to examine how the lessons learned from the existing small-scale initiatives could be upscaled to the level of a more traditional area development. The goal was to realize at least 500 dwellings and 4,000 m² of work units and hospitality spaces.

Cityplot was mainly a strategy or a working model, certainly not a master plan. It built on the knowledge gained in the circular experiments in De Ceuvel and on the learning process that individuals like Frank Alsema underwent. Cityplot accommodates various pioneering forms of city making.

Gradually and spontaneously, an innovative environment for circular processes developed at Buiksloterham. The initiators formed an organism together, always seeking each other out voluntarily and synchronizing their activities whenever possible and desirable. This is an open process without central coordination: Buiksloterham is a concept rather than a real platform and it represents a spirit of creativity and innovation. This also means, however, that its results are rather diffuse.

To achieve some degree of coordination, Citylab Buiksloterham started regular consultations between all the aforementioned parties, to facilitate a more effective search for coherence. These new forms of collaboration also provided new methods and tools. For the Schoonschip project, Metabolic devised a sustainability master plan that developed architectural starting points and process guidelines for architects. This master plan answered various questions. Which cycles should be closed? What technologies and processes can be used to achieve those goals and what will be the layout of the system? What investments need to be made and what is their cost recovery period?

The new tool was thus mainly focused on the system and helped new collectives to realize their goals. It was therefore complementary to, for example, an urban master plan that describes the spatial framework.

Now that Buiksloterham is slowly entering the realization phase it is also becoming clear that not every stakeholder is equally interested in the experiment. Perhaps the individual initiators that operate at the level of the plot will manage to maintain their high level of ambition, but initiatives on a larger scale level, such as Cityplot, are lagging behind.

In Buiksloterham, individuals get to experiment with sustainable measures to their heart's content: the sun is used in some 20 different ways here. But innovating on a privately owned plot is easy and if the costs disappoint, idealism makes it bearable. It is more complicated for Cityplot, which wants to upscale such strategies. On the one hand joint initiatives collide with the public interest, on the other it is difficult for residents to recognize the fruits of collective investments in the higher appreciation of their individual properties.

The design of the public space provides an example of the first issue. The moment the residents of Cityplot and the designers together decide to dispose of rainwater across the ground level, this produces problems for the type of management carried out by the city of Amsterdam. The residents are perfectly willing to take on that management themselves, but if they do, they want the costs to be deducted from their compulsory contribution to the municipal management.

This is a frequently occurring problem in this kind of area development. The transition from the private to the public domain produces situations in which it is unclear who is responsible for what and where the costs and benefits of the investment belong. This applies, for example, to waste and to drinking water. If individuals invest in sustainability they still have to pay taxes and cannot recover their investments. A possible solution would be the type of balancing that is used for sustainably produced energy. If a resident were to engage in sustainable composting on their balcony, the municipality would then reinvest the waste tax that resident pays in their specific living area or, alternatively, that resident would only have to pay per disposed garbage bag.

The second problem concerns the question of who benefits from public investments. If individual homeowners equip their roofs with solar panels they can calculate exactly when they have recovered their investments. It gets much more complicated when they invest in a bio digester with a long cost recovery period together with their neighbours, because not only they themselves benefit, but so do others.

Another problem with upscaling like that in Cityplot is that end users are not involved in decisions about investments. Buyers are only involved once the plan is already in an advanced stage. The probability is therefore high that they are less ambitious in terms of sustainability or at least that they are not all that willing to bear the extra costs that entails.

Many developers are sympathetic towards sustainability, but mainly when investments are easy to recover and buy additional comfort. Energy neutral dwellings are therefore popular, but circular experiments not so much and they furthermore require development time as well.

In the wording of the DTP Diagram (→p. 128) early private initiators invest and in part they even realize the plans. Their position is to the right of the diagram, because they have been involved in the formulation of objectives and the making of design from the very beginning. But the new residents of Cityplot, who joined only after the developer and the designers formulated the objectives and preconditions, are simply not ready. They are at best attentive or interested, but not willing to invest yet. With regard to the collaboration and planning involving these newcomers, rather than on feasibility and practicality, the research by design first and foremost focuses on convincing them that changes are necessary and conceivable.

A Metabolic Square

Rotterdam is densely built-up, like many other cities. It has a lot of buildings and even more pavement. The inner city in particular has very little water storage capacity, such as canals. At the same time rains are becoming heavier and, therefore, the danger of flooding is increasing. That is why in 2004, a plan was conceived to create a water square.

When the weather is dry, a water square is a nice place to play basketball and skate. In heavy rains, its basins can collect the rainwater that pours down on the square and the surrounding rooftops, about 1.7 million litres of water altogether. This water no longer needs to drain directly into a sewer, which is therefore less likely to flood. The heart of the approach is very local, but since it is a node in a larger network, the water square impacts a much larger area.

The square looks as clear and bright as its construction was complicated. The whole process took over eight years and many players came and went. The designer was the only constant factor in the process. The municipality was a major player all along, but its role changed from commissioner to partner and then back to commissioner again. Internally, the process was passed by the Urban Planning and Housing Department (ds+v) to the engineering office of the Public Works Department. Other stakeholders were various district water boards.

The entire thing almost went wrong. It seemed a mere formality: citizen's participation. But the inhabitants of the area in which the square was projected could do very well without a water square, thank you, and the plan went to waste. But owing to the tenacity of the designers and the faith a couple of Public Works officials had in the problem-solving powers of the water square, the process began again in a different location.

At this stage citizens and social organizations were no longer seen as difficult hurdles that needed to be taken, but were given a more active role. This changed the focus of the challenge from resilience – water management as part of the climate challenge – to a combination of resilience and sociocultural connectivity. The inclusion of the social agenda also helped to make the plan more financially feasible.

The process involved a lot of learning by doing, because no one had ever realized anything like this before. The attitude and role of the designers also changed during the process. Initially the team consisted of inward-focused professionals who proceeded dogmatically and purposefully: we are making a water square. After the restart things were different: using a graphic novel, a dedicated team and a large group of stakeholders launched an open planning process.

Chronological Overview

The whole process starts in 2004, when the municipality of Rotterdam puts the water issue on the agenda for a policy document called Rotterdam Water 2035. From that moment on, people work on a long-term exploration of the water challenge Rotterdam faces. Three offices are commissioned to examine the way the city deals with its water: vhp takes on the past, h+n+s focuses on the present and –scape and Urban Affairs design for the future.

Under the heading Experience & Enjoy the duo –scape and Urban Affairs formulates five thematic visions for the watery city of Rotterdam: dikes (the later dike programme), climate challenge (the water squares), river banks (the tidal park), various residential typologies (living on the water) and transport by water.

These five strategies for the waters of Rotterdam are developed in the context of the IABR 2005, themed *The Flood*. Led by Lodewijk van Nieuwenhuijze of H+N+S, the involved parties work closely together as a team for three months. The outcome is prominently displayed at the IABR.

The Public Works Department is excited about the idea of a water square and begins to work on it together with –scape and Urban Affairs. The idea is explored in an open process of workshops with officials. The work concept leads to the first models of the water square.

The faith the Public Works Department has in this work concept is crucial to its future development. Officials John Jacobs and Pieter de Greef create a municipal platform for the further development of the water square and thus manage to put it on the local political agenda.

In 2007 the municipality devotes a separate chapter to the water square in its Waterplan. The water square is officially acknowledged as potentially a different way to deal with flooding and simultaneously improve the quality of the public space.

Subsequently, five versions are developed for five locations in Rotterdam, including a square in Spangen, one in Bloemhof and a street in Crooswijk. This eventually results in an overview of all site interventions and a model explaining the water square principle designed by artist Jeroen Bodewits and commissioned by the Public Works Department. The model, presented at the third IABR, explains the water square to a wider audience.

Next, the project is further developed for the Bloemhof area in Rotterdam-Zuid. Bloemhofplein is located in the middle of the neighbourhood, several streets in the immediate area still need to be redeveloped and it has good drainage, so everything falls into place. Unfortunately, the initiators overlooked the fact that the square had been redeveloped only two years earlier in close consultation with local residents. Understandably those residents, having little or no experience with water, are adamantly against the water square.

The Public Works Department and the designers have underestimated the sociocultural conditions; and, at that very moment, the district council is in the process of replacing the portfolio holder in question. The traditional method – create an internal proposal first and subsequently submit it to residents in a formal communication and participation process – has failed.

The project seems irretrievably lost, but Florian Boer does not resign to that. He has been involved in the water square from the beginning, first at –scape, later as a partner at VHP. Meanwhile, Boer has established his own firm, De Urbanisten, and to ensure the ideas and knowledge concerning the water square will not be lost, he initiates the production of a graphic novel called *De Urbanisten en het Wondere Waterplein*. Nai010 publishes the book in early 2010 with the support of the Creative Industries Fund NL.

The city, too, is forging ahead, with a plan bij ds+v for a water square on the Bellamyplein in Spangen. This water square is part of a green, larger city square and the entire neighbourhood will get a makeover. Meanwhile De Urbanisten exerts all its influence to get back on board as an expert.

A location scan by ds+v and De Urbanisten leads to a broader commission: the water square is no longer only a solution to a problem (flooding), but now has a social function as well. Other additional parameters are the funding and the question of whose challenge this actually is. The city of Rotterdam also comes up with a new location, Benthemplein, directly behind Central Station.

The broadened approach requires the involvement of more parties in the plan. Businesses, institutions and residents of the square join in because this is about their square, the Public Health Authority because it is responsible for water quality and health in the city and ds+v once again joins in because the square is in the urban public space. The water boards of course continue to be partners as well: to them, the square is and will always be an emergency measure for the mitigation of cases of extreme flooding.

The graphic novel is used as a tool to communicate the principles behind the water square. During four workshops all of the stakeholders collaborate on a widely supported design proposal. De Urbanisten develops the design, the Public Works Department adds the details and then De Urbanisten examines it once more.

Every previously formulated water square principle is used to redevelop Benthemplein. The sewers are adjusted to optimize its operation. The rain pipes of the buildings around the square are disconnected from the sewer system to ensure that the water from the roofs flows clearly visible across the square into the basins. And as a bonus, the Reformed Church gets a font for outdoor baptisms.

The project is completed in December 2013 and is nominated for the Dutch Water Board Prize in 2013 and for the international GreenTec Special Award.

What happened when the festivities were over? The Zadkine College, which was actively involved in the design process and also contributed to its maintenance, partially withdrew from the location Benthemplein. The Grafisch Lyceum has taken over the Zadkine College facility, but unfortunately not its role. This brings up the question of who owns the public space.

Meanwhile De Urbanisten still feels responsible for its brainchild and the water boards also inspect it regularly. It turns out that the materials used are not holding up to daily use by skaters and boot campers. That is learning by doing as well. Another concern is keeping the square clean: this is not a regular Roteb project, so who is responsible for its maintenance? And when? Because after heavy rain fall, the square is supposed to be hosed down, but this is not part of the municipal cleaning schedule.

Minor problems such as these do not alter the fact that the water square has become an exemplary project. It has been included as a standard measure in the recalibrated Water Plan and in Rotterdam's Adaptation Strategy. At the national level, too, the water square is considered a best practice. De Urbanisten recently completed a second water square in Tiel.

<u>Roles and Responsibilities</u>
Developing a complex challenge like a water square from an idea to a completed project requires a committed commissioner and a dedicated team. After all, its complexity transcends the traditional boundaries of spatial design.

How do you deal with flooding? What systems play a part? Rather than only the sewers and the rainwater systems, this project also involves the urban infrastructure that ensures the drainage of streets and squares to canals. Such a broad exploration requires a different approach to the design process: one that research by design can provide.

Characteristically, research by design also invests energy in dialogue. Sharing a design while it is not yet finished prevents a hermetic approach. It allows different players to participate and contribute to the plan's development.

The process of research by design has resulted in several outcomes. Not only in terms of the square itself: there have also been publications, exhibition contributions and a local and national policy instrument.

It is possible to unravel the process on the basis of the seven steps in the DTP Diagram (→p. 128). First, taking five steps from strategy to design. After a lengthy standoff the initiators returned to the concept stage and eventually moved to occupation and monitoring from there.

Reflection
Dutch planning is internationally known for its strong, spatial design concepts that influence the actions of many parties and continue to exert their influence for a long time. Andreas Faludi called them planning doctrines.[158] Is the Energetic Odyssey of the IABR 2016 such a planning doctrine? According to Dirk Sijmons, who developed the project with Maarten Hajer, it is even more than that: 'This plan also breaks the spell of the crisis of the imagination.'

Research by design provides a setting, a backdrop for a colourful group of actors that meet in an often completely new context. Thus, it provides the imagination with common ground, with a context in which every participant can make a contribution to the concrete development of prototypes. Stakeholders know themselves to be part of a comprehensive framework of ambitions and goals.

In the Energetic Odyssey project, the composition of the coalition was deliberately made the subject of a design. The range of participants was continuously evaluated and much effort was put into finding the right balance in the group of participants. For participants contribute four different values: money, knowledge, time and charisma.

158
Faludi, who came up with the term, defines a planning doctrine as a cohesive spatial planning concept that combines design and organizational aspects. Examples that still continue to exert their influence today are the Green Heart and the Randstad.

It is especially important not to underestimate the latter. The development of an initiative can sprout wings with the support of charismatic individuals or organizations. Members of the royal family that open a museum, a former vice president that warns of climate change and one of the best football players in history that gives his name to an initiative that introduces football in urban areas. The contribution Shell made to the project for the production of renewable energy on the North Sea is of the same order: it won other parties over.

Time, in most cases contributed by volunteers, is important as well. In the early stages, when it is unclear whether prototypes will work and be successful, it is often only disinterested contributions that make breathing life into a concrete realization possible. Driving forces for success like knowledge and money speak for themselves.

Actors not only join because they want to make a contribution, they hope to profit by their joining as well. Win prestige, for example. Both individuals and companies value their images. By investing time in the realization of prototypical projects, they acquire prestige they can capitalize elsewhere. In addition, participation often provides actors with knowledge: research by design is a source of innovation and leads to ideas, insights and technology. Sometimes there is even money to be made straight away.

When realizing pilots, it is therefore important to consider questions such as: Who invests what, and who profits in what way? Who takes risks and who walks away with a profit? Unless this is properly balanced, it will create inequality within the coalition.

Part 3 is about the dynamics inside the consolidation points of the DTP Diagram: strategy, idea, concept, project.[159] To enter the next stage, it is important to close every research by design stage with a clear consolidation. How far have we come? What does the idea look like at its most concrete? This is important to find out whether all actors have arrived at the same point in the process and also whether they see opportunities for a continuation. Do the new players that are brought in have new knowledge, but similar desires and ambitions? Who is likely to opt out of the process because their part is played out?

The creation of the water square involved a colourful procession of actors that succeeded one another during the various stages of the design process. The designers turned out to be the stabilizing factor and this is often the case in such processes. Whereas governments and participating advisors come and go, designers and their designs monitor the progress and development of the idea into a project. Thus, design is also of great importance to the continuity.

If intermediate steps are clearly marked, disagreements between actors come to light early and facilitate a timely intervention. In the case of Buiksloterham, this appears to have been neglected. What was overlooked was that the ambitions of the developers and the primary initiators were more advanced than those of the new players, including the

159

See Part 2, Chapter
'The DTP Diagram' →p. 126.

future end users. This resulted in the classic plan development situation in which users feel that their needs and desires are not being met by the combined developers.

The example of Zeekracht shows that a compelling and inspiring idea can be raised to a more concrete level by other designers. It also shows how research by design contributes to knowledge development: *2050 – An Energetic Odyssey* demonstrates that a grid is a better carrier than the ring structure proposed by Zeekracht.

In the consolidation points on the left in the Diagram – involving strategy, idea and concept – the process is deliberately more focused on inspiration than in subsequent points. As the process progresses – around the definition of the project and the further designing – the steps become smaller. The rich variety of new insights and prototypes decreases as precision and complexity increase.

Gradually, the focus shifts to technological development. This requires the introduction of new players with the necessary knowledge. Consultants give way to contractors and engineers. All that time, the design carefully preserves the earlier-established ideas and communicates them to the new parties. The design becomes more or less the memory of the project. The way it has been recorded in images and text is therefore of the utmost importance.

Now that the engineers are in, what about the lawyers? The opportunities uncovered by research by design often meet with rules that have been designed to mitigate risks. Some of these risks have been reduced considerably by new technology and can be reduced even further by clever connections and combinations in the near future. To address the challenges generated by the energy transition, the circular economy and healthy living, both the system and the players who work with it will have to find new rules and new mutual relations.

A good idea is a comprehensive idea that is aimed at a point far away on the horizon, but has an eye for the here and now at the same time: it provides a concrete translation that brings hope and confidence in the actual achievability of the comprehensive idea.

A single water square does not mean we will be able to keep our feet dry – that will take much more drastic and complex measures – but it does create the confidence that it is indeed possible to realize these new typologies and that the city can in fact be organized in a way that will prevent peak rainfall from causing flooding in the near future. Innovations therefore benefit from realized pilots or prototypes.

In contrast with the small scale, at which it is relatively easy to test innovations, is the large scale at which they actually (have to) have an impact. That scale is the region. The region has a different size and significance in every situation and in the context of every problem, but generally speaking, the region is at least the size of ten to 15 municipalities. The region is comparable with the range of the average commuter who takes an hour to get to work from home by car. The region is the level at which the Netherlands is both urban and rural: densification generates urban problems that can only be solved in the rural space, and vice versa.

Research by design is able to connect these scale levels in a logical and meaningful way. Showing the small aspects of the large and the large aspects of the small, designers can not only give people hopes and dreams, but also the confidence to take small steps. Healthy urbanization begins in the here and now.

resilient infrastructure

Natuurderij — Deventer (NL)

Agriculture and livestock farming turn out to be effective and inexpensive ways to manage nature along rivers that have been redeveloped to prevent flooding. At Natuurderij Keizersrande, a biodynamic farmer herds cows in the river foreland.

The Keizersrande estate is part of the Natura 2000 nature reserve north of the city of Deventer. Birds like the endangered godwit, the curlew and the lapwing breed in its wetlands and meadows. The area is the property of the IJssellandschap Foundation, an independent organization that has been managing nature reserves and estates around Deventer since the thirteenth century.

In recent years, the rivers in the area have been widened to reduce flood risks to the city of Deventer. This widening comes with high demands in terms of maintenance. At the same time, the nature management in this area has to meet strict requirements. An experienced farmer was found to be the best possible candidate for the job of combining the two challenges. She started a commercial yet sustainable business on what was called a Natuurderij (nature farm) and took over the nature preservation from the responsible authority.

In 1995, the Dutch dikes were almost breached because of prolonged rainfall and abundant meltwater pouring in from Germany, and 250,000 people were evacuated. Though the incident ended well, the country was forced to face the facts: dike improvement alone was not going to be enough to stop the water. The rivers needed more space to be able to handle excess water and to allow the water levels to drop.

In 2007, the central government launched a national programme called Room for the River to widen rivers in dozens of places and realize more nature reserves and recreational areas at the same time. The idea – to flood polders and farmland deliberately – was not uncontroversial. Did rivers actually have to be able to cope with peak levels comprising 16,000 m3 of water, as experts in the Deventer area demanded? And was it not wiser to improve the dikes after all?

One of the areas where the river had to be redeveloped was the Keizerswaard and the Stobbewaard.

■ farm (connection between
   estate and river)

▨ flood area (high):
   meadow

⠂ flood area (low):
   grazing

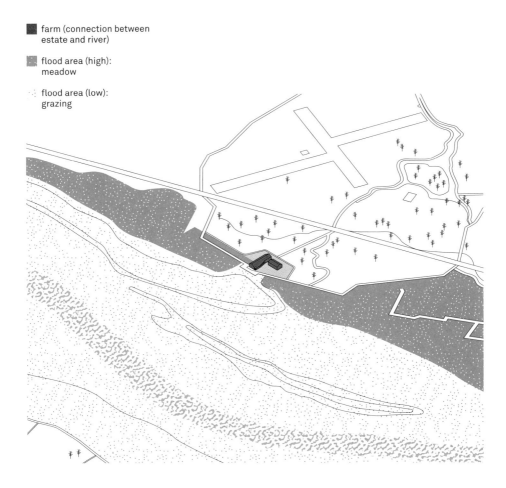

fig. 102 — Dynamic nature
management

Wide trenches along the river would ensure that the
water level in Deventer would drop by 12 cm at high
tide. The project was commissioned by the water boards,
which commissioned a builder to perform the work.
Central government supported the IJssellandschap
Foundation, the owner of the land, which was responsible for its upkeep.

   Director Jaap Starkenburg engaged landscape architects Noël van Dooren, Ruut van Paridon and Karen de
Groot at an early stage. They mapped the details of the
estate and its surroundings meticulously and then proposed to erect a building on the river side of the dike in
order to reconnect the river and the estate.

'For this project, I wanted to find a new, sustainable
balance between farming and nature,' says Starkenburg,
who trained as a biologist himself. For inspiration he
visited areas along the Loire River in France in which
livestock farming has always remained extensive and

agriculture and the management of the river foreland are traditionally combined.

The study *Boeren voor de natuur* (Farming for Nature) by research institute Alterra (Wageningen University) was influential as well.[160] In sum, the report states that agriculture has to benefit nature and the landscape. In the past, farmers always had a share in the management of nature. Agriculture and nature reserves became strictly separated only after the intensification of agriculture.

Next, they conceived a plan to build a farm on the river foreland and have a farmer manage the area. Room for the River programme director Ingwer de Boer was up for the idea, even though building in the river foreland was not at all in keeping with the plans he was supposed to carry out. And building in a nature reserve is usually off limits, in fact it is officially not even allowed. Still, all obstacles were overcome as De Boer also became convinced that the introduction of agriculture and livestock farming comprised the best way to tame the water.

'During the initial conversations about our contribution to Room for the River it became clear that traditional nature development is at odds with water safety requirements,' says Starkenburg. The water has to be able to

fig. 103 — Nature farm Keizersrande is built on concrete dams in the flood plains of the IJssel River

160

Boeren voor de natuur, Alterra (Wageningen University), 2013.

flood the land unhindered and having a lot of vegetation with trees and shrubs prevents that.

It is precisely at this point that farming could offer a solution. 'Grazing cattle keep the vegetation short,' says Annette Harberink. The enterprising biodynamic farmer considered the developments around the new estate to be 'a beautiful opportunity'. She managed several farms before and had been planning to start or take over a biodynamic dairy farm of her own before she applied for a job at Natuurderij Keizersrande and became one of the project's driving forces.

Together with Starkenburg and his foundation, Harberink changed the river foreland area into farmland with hayfields and meadows. The farm is on a mound, with a good view of the water level in the river foreland. The low-lying forelands accommodate 80 mature Meuse-Rhine-Yssel cows and 60 calves. The compact, red-and-white MRY cattle are characteristic of the region. They graze by the river and the manure from their stables keeps the land fertile.

These efforts not only created a water-resilient area, but also a varied landscape. The diversity of river and agricultural landscapes, complemented by newly planted trees, is attractive to animals such as the corncrake and the spotted crake. New footpaths and observation points make the area more accessible to nature lovers. They can download an App to learn more about nature management and the history of the landscape along the way. The farm also has a separate space for the education of pupils nearby and field trips are held in the area regularly.

The Natuurderij Keizersrande became a success thanks to a diverse coalition: central government drew up the plan, the water board of Groot Salland contracted the builders, the IJssellandschap Foundation hired designers to map the estate and now manages it together with a local entrepreneur.

This is a trend that is also visible elsewhere. The task of civil society organizations such as the IJssellandschap Foundation is to maintain nature and the landscape. And because this is expensive and labour intensive, they make strategic alliances like the one with farmer Annette Harberink.

Through her collaboration with IJssellandschap, Harberink got access to an area of 170 hectares. She lives off her business, from the milk and the meat of her cows, soon perhaps complemented by the income she can make by selling cheese and homemade beer. In addition,

fig. 104 — Following spread: Modern cowshed

the IJssellandschap Foundation pays her a compensation for ensuring that the area remains water resilient. Her cows keep the grass short, for example, she polls the willows and manages the grasslands and fields in a way that allows grassland birds to breed there. This is a lot cheaper than having the IJssellandschap Foundation either manage the area itself or outsource management to a commercial company.

What a farmer maintains a nature reserve that is an important link in the national river network

Where Deventer, the Netherlands

Design DAAD Architecten, Van Paridon x de Groot landschapsarchitecten

Realized 2014

Intervention widening the river and building a farm in a nature reserve

Also good for vital economy (an entrepreneur makes nature preservation profitable), healthy living (biodiversity) and sociocultural connectivity (education)

fig. 105 — View over the IJssel River from nature farm Keizersrande

resilient infrastructure

Cycling Commuters

A variety of business pockets lies on the southwestern flanks of the Amsterdam Metropolitan Area. Each and every one of them is a monofunctional industrial or commercial estate, accessible only by car. To create greater flexibility, these pockets are to be connected by a ring of modern buses and rapid cycling routes. This requires active participation by the businesses in the area.

The industrial and commercial estates of Waarderpolder in Haarlem, Beukenhorst and Schiphol in Haarlemmermeer and Riekerpolder in Amsterdam each have a unique personality and a different sort of user. Whereas Schiphol possesses the allure of an international hub, Riekerpolder and Beukenhorst – both only a few minutes away from Schiphol – struggle with a dearth of occupants and a lack of quality. Waarderpolder occupies a middle position.

What these estates have in common is that they originate from a time when housing and employment were strictly segregated. They consist of individuals lots and industrial buildings; little attention has been paid to the public space – and as a result they are falling behind. The new economy demands mixed environments, in which brainpower and craftsmanship work side by side, in which businesses benefit from each other's proximity, with housing and recreation within easy reach.

To make these remote industrial estates future-ready, it is imperative that they become part of a network. To this end a combination bus- and bicycle ring is to be built to connect them to one another and to the housing and recreation landscape between them. This route is to become the spatial support for all of these different areas. The starting point consists of the stops for the rapid-transit bus. Businesses that currently hold real-estate

fig. 106 — A transformation of working environments around junctions

positions there are to be given a significant role in the densification of construction and the improvement of public space.

As businesses with a different kind of employee are coming in and accessibility by public transport and bicycle is improving, fewer car parks are needed. As compensation, businesses are to be allowed to build on their car parks adjacent to the bus stops. They are also to be allowed to top up their buildings with apartments, work places or public facilities.

The infrastructure profile is to be restructured from top to bottom. The wide motorways are to be transformed into bicycle paths and dedicated bus lanes. Less infrastructure also creates more space for greenery.

Designer Chloe Charetton

Academy Amsterdam

Design Atelier SouthWest Works!

Where Amsterdam Metropolitan Area, the Netherlands

Lecturers Marco Broekman, Roel van Gerwen, Harm Veenenbos

resilient infrastructure

Densification around the Slow Lane

Eindhoven grew out of a series of villages, linked by a radiating network of roadways. Following the devastation of the Second World War, the city centre was rebuilt with a massive amount of automobile-oriented infrastructure. Current growth ambitions and climate objectives demand densification based on sustainable mobility. Linking this densification to the cycling infrastructure would allow the city to grow and simultaneously become greener.

Eindhoven's main attraction lies in the high-tech manufacturing industry, with companies such as Philips and ASML. These are usually not located in the city centre, but rather on campuses on the outskirts of the city, featuring a great deal of greenery. Examples include the High Tech Campus (the former Philips NatLab) on the south side of the city, the campus of Eindhoven University of Technology in the Dommeldal and the Ekkersrijt industrial and commercial estate. A high-quality cycling path was recently laid to link these areas, called the Slow Lane.

Because the bicycle is one of the most efficient means of transport in a high-density city, the Slow Lane is used as the foundation for densification. An analysis of the network produced three sites ripe for densification. Various housing models were tested here in relation to a mobility network primarily based on cycling traffic.

The first site is a metropolitan residential block six storeys high, in which cycling paths are, as it were, woven into the block itself and terminate at the front door, in order to make the use of the bicycle more appealing. A second site consists of several smaller residential volumes oriented to a specific target audience, focused on healthy living and (cycling) mobility: athletic expats and young families. A third site is oriented towards (young) elderly people who wish to live in the city yet want to maintain a connection to the countryside of Brabant.

The phasing and interchangeability of the various densification models has been discussed in consultation with relevant stakeholders.

Designers Shelly van Gogh, Tianyi Xue, Xiaohui Zhong

Academy Tilburg

Design Atelier Eindhoven The Mobility Challenge

Where Eindhoven, the Netherlands

Lecturers Maurizio Scarciglia, Marieke Kums

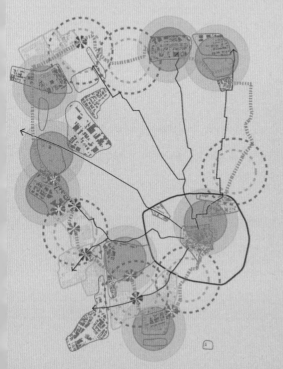

fig. 107 — Riding bicycles in the Slow lane

renewable energy

Energy Workplace — Friesland (NL)

Active and well-informed citizens are crucially important to the transition to renewable energy. Energy Workplace Fryslân is the lubricant between individual cooperatives and other energy initiatives in Friesland.

The people of Friesland like do things together. At the end of 2015 Friesland, with a population of less than 650,000 inhabitants, counted 37 energy cooperatives. That means the province is ahead of the pack, nationally.[161] And three-quarters of these collectives were less than two years old – so their number is on the rise.

People establish energy cooperatives to jointly insulate their homes or to purchase or produce renewable energy. This form of collaboration might well be decisive in the transition from fossil fuels to renewable energy. The support of the local community is essential, because people are familiar with the local situation and can provide a social basis for sometimes unpopular measures.[162]

Yet many bottom-up initiatives do not last for long. In many cases, initiators appear to lack a clear picture of the steps they need to take to bring their plans to fruition.[163] To change this the Energy Workshop Friesland, an initiative of sustainability organizations supported financially by the province, was established in 2014.[164, 165]

The Energy Workshop supports local communities that take small-scale and local energy initiatives and helps them face any issues that may arise. How do you encourage knowledge sharing? And how do you increase the scale and thus the impact of successful local projects? How can you combine separate projects to create coalitions of people with similar ideas?

There have been initiatives for renewable energy in Friesland for a number of years. The first local wind turbines were built 40 years ago in Deersum, a village of close to 150 inhabitants that wanted to be self-sufficient.[166] In 2010, the Frisians experimented with the first pipeline to distribute biogas from cow manure over a larger area. Farmers in the area between Dokkum and Leeuwarden connected their businesses to it with

161
Lokale energiemonitor, 2015.

162
Towards an Integrated Energy Landscape, J. de Boer and Ch. Zuidema, 2013.

163
The Grassroots of Sustainable Transition: A Generic Approach to Describe Local Energy Initiatives in the Northern Netherlands, H. van der Blonk, B. Boschma et al., 2013.

164
Doarpswurk (improvement of the living conditions in the Frisian countryside), Friese Milieu Federatie, Netwerk Duurzame Dorpen and Ús Koöperaasje (promotes renewable energy).

165
Disclaimer: The author was closely involved in the development of working methods and experiments of the Energy Workshop an external advisor and designing researcher.

166
For the history of the Frisian energy cooperatives, see: Groene energie in Friesland, F. Bokser, 2012.

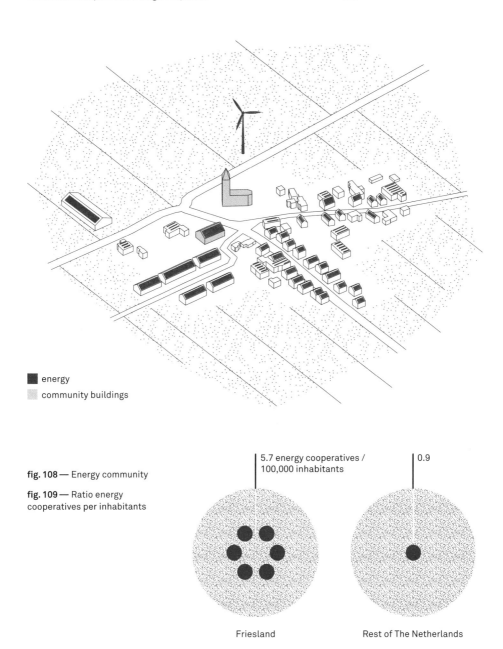

energy
community buildings

fig. 108 — Energy community

fig. 109 — Ratio energy
cooperatives per inhabitants

5.7 energy cooperatives /
100,000 inhabitants

0.9

Friesland   Rest of The Netherlands

fig. 110 — Following spread:
A meeting of the Energy Co-op

the intention of supplying 25,000 households with renewable gas.

Perhaps coincidentally, all this took place in the immediate vicinity of Raard, the village in which the Energy Workshop that connects sustainable initiatives across the province is now located.

'The technology isn't the problem,' says Jaap Koen Bijma, project manager at the Energy Workshop, about

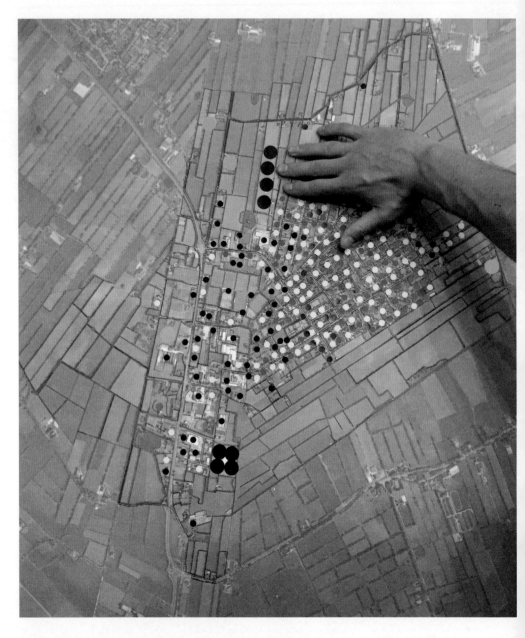

the kind of questions that end up on his plate. 'People know how to install solar panels, for example. Problems arise if a group of people wants to do something together.' People who want to buy a wind turbine or build a solar farm together soon come across financial, legal, planning or organizational problems.

fig. 111 — Energy locations

The Energy Workshop helps them over hurdles such as these. The project of energy cooperative Ekon illustrates how. It wanted to fit 1,200 solar panels on the shed of potato farmer Fokke Fokkema from Slappeterp to provide a maximum of 150 households with renewable energy. Ekon developed the financial model together with the Energy Workshop.

A couple of farmers came up with the first money. The *Fûns Skjinne Fryske Enerzjy* (Clean Frisian Energy Fund) underwrote the risks, the Bank Nederlandse Gemeenten refinanced the project. Once it had been realized, residents could buy solar panels, with a minimum of three. To avoid speculation, deposits were linked to energy need. Bijma: 'People want to see first before they dare invest. Once the panels are up there, they are willing to consider buying stock.'

In the context of this type of established collaboration and consultation, the Frisians like to refer to their strong sense of community, the *mienskip*. This is not a formal collaboration, but rather a partnership that involves the entire community. Famous examples are the 11-city skating race and winning Leeuwarden the nomination for Cultural Capital of Europe of 2018. Both were organized by the local *mienskip*.

The village of Reduzum shows that this strong sense of community can also promote the energy transition. On behalf of the community, workgroups have already built homes, a columbarium at the cemetery and an extra floor to the school. A wind turbine followed in 1994. The village population had been shrinking for years and the income from the wind turbine was to guarantee the village's future viability.

The turbine cost half a million guilders (340,000 euros) at the time. The villagers raised 200,000 guilders themselves by issuing some 250 certificates of interest representing values ranging from 100 to 10,000 guilders. They complemented this with a favourable 'green' loan from the local bank and with government subsidies. They recovered the costs in eight years and in the next 12 years it earned them a real income of 61,000 euros. That money goes into the 'turbine pot' and is used for investments in, for example, solar panels on the roof of the primary school, the insulation of the sports canteen or LED lighting in a new housing estate. Wind turbines may often be controversial elsewhere, but the people here work hard towards buying a bigger one.

And yet, despite the sense of community, the energy transition goes slowly in Friesland. Many local initiatives go wrong due to intractable political obstacles. Take Reduzum once again, where the number of residents

that wanted a larger wind turbine was in the majority.
Yet they did not get one, because the province would
not give permission for any new onshore wind turbines. Similarly, municipalities are not always open to
initiatives from 'their' cooperatives or active residents'
organizations.

To a large extent, political resistance and the local
uncertainty that follows from it arise because the perspectives are difficult to concretize. A spatial design can
change that and accelerate the process.[167] What are the
alternatives, for example, if wind turbines are not an
option? And how will they change the Frisian landscape?

That is why in addition to legal and financial support,
the Energy Workshop also offers procedural and substantive support. It helps groups to formulate a long-term
vision, for example, write a business plan or make assessments of the implications and opportunities of plans for
the landscape. Designers are therefore part of the team.

To accelerate implementation, the Energy Workshop
has been organizing villages in so-called communities of
practice since 2015. That way, they can exchange knowledge about energy efficiency, energy production through
solar panels and entire energy-neutral villages. Together
with a Master's candidate from Wageningen University,
the villages Harkema, Heeg, Baard and Wijnjewoude
have used this format to conduct a pilot study into the
spatial impact of the ambition to make a village energy-
neutral. The study resulted in a method with which
the villages themselves can feed and monitor the costs,
energy mix and spatial implications of their long term
energy objectives in local energy scenarios.

Together with a Master's candidate in urbanism from
Delft University of Technology, eight other villages
mapped their demand and supply of electricity, heat and
residual materials and thus formulated regional energy
scenarios for 2050[168]. All of the villages concluded that
it is valuable to spatially concretize energy ambitions,
because this works as a catalyst. Images and design
scenarios undeniably contribute to the concretization
of the spatial consequences and facilitate the selection
process. Customized interactive design methods that
match the ambitions of the village are essential. Meanwhile the Province of Drenthe has also started to work
with communities of practice to increase the success
rate of its solar power cooperatives.[169]

167

'Towards the Energy Transition in
Fryslân'. In: *Investigating the Spatial
Impacts of the Energy Transition
at the Local Scale,* H. Dijkman,
2015 (Masterthesis Wageningen
University & Research).

168

'Empower the energy landscape
of Friesland', A. Galama,
2016 (Master Thesis Delft
University of Technology).

169

'€ 100.000 voor Drentse
zonnecoöperaties'. At:
www.energieplus.nl, 15 July 2016.

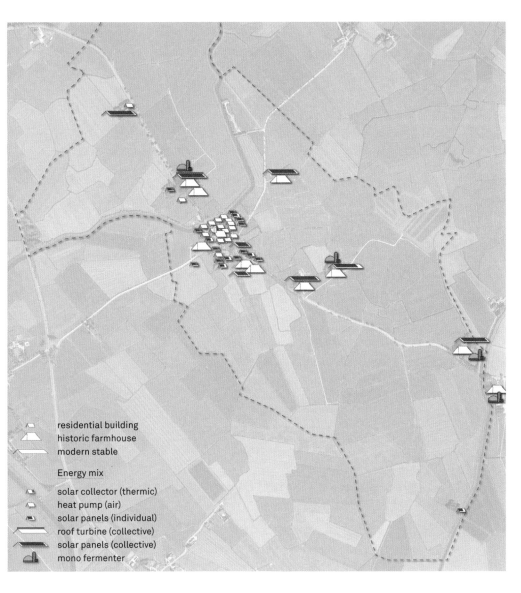

residential building
historic farmhouse
modern stable

Energy mix

solar collector (thermic)
heat pump (air)
solar panels (individual)
roof turbine (collective)
solar panels (collective)
mono fermenter

fig. 112 — Baard 2050,
Energy-neutral village

What a knowledge platform that
supports citizens and local organizations
in achieving the energy transition

Where Province of Friesland, the Netherlands

Realized 2014 (ongoing)

Intervention creation of communities
of practice

Also good for vital economy
(cooperatives keep money in the
community), sociocultural connectivity
(encouraging local ownership)

renewable energy

Regional Eco-Station

The food chain from farmer to consumer is long and makes an enormous footprint. A system oriented to the regional market could save significant energy. In Zuidhorn, two designers examined the energy transition in our food chain in an attempt to push farmers, consumers and the authorities into action. First, the demand side:

Zuidhorn is willing to accelerate the transition to an energy system with a smaller footprint, but each party has its own arguments against taking any concrete steps just yet. Farmers are at the mercy of the international market and struggle with low prices for their products, which means they are unable to invest in transition. Consumers do not immediately see the urgency – food is mainly supposed to be cheap and easily available. The municipal government, with its top-down set of instruments, is not equipped to activate local residents. And the environmental work group that aims to forge coalitions does not have the tools to get all the stakeholders around the table.

With a combination train station and ecological food centre, this design is aimed primarily at the demand side of the food chain. A large greenhouse serves as a station building, an allusion to the vast internal space of stations built during the Industrial Revolution. In this greenhouse, all facets of local production are given a place. Crops are grown under the gaze of train passengers and a greengrocer sells the farmers' produce. There is also a pick-up stand where commuters can collect their locally produced groceries when they get off the train.

This turns the local food chain into a part of people's daily routine. The efficient linkage of commuters, consumers and production streams also reduces energy use.

Consumers pay with a 'green card', a subscription that guarantees them local produce. The green cards also provide more security for the farmers. The eco-station reinforces the idea that (energy) consumption is not without obligation.

Designer Ronald Brunsting

Academy Groningen

Design Atelier Energietransitie Regio Groningen

Where Zuidhorn, the Netherlands

Lecturers Alex van Spijk, Sjoerd Betten

fig. 113 — The eco-station

renewable energy

Mixed Farming New-Style

What does a local food chain look like? And how does it actually work? A concrete visualization of these questions through design has awakened the enthusiasm of people in Zuidhorn. Two local projects have combined to focus on the energy chain as a whole. Below the eco-mound, which addresses the supply side.

Scale expansion in agriculture is reaching its limits. As a result of declining profit margins, farmers seem to have no other choice than to either scale up even further or quit altogether. Yet more and more farmers are returning to a mixed type of farming that produces for the local market or are combining their farming with the production of renewable energy. They are significantly reducing their ecological footprint by reducing transport journeys and by converting to electric farm vehicles.

The eco-mound harks back to an age-old form of human settlement – the mound or *terp* – in order to organize a new style of mixed farming. It connects a number of farmers, the village of Zuidhorn and various cycles. Flows of waste and leftover food from the village, for instance, are converted into energy on the eco-mound. This creates shorter chains, requiring much less energy.

A portion of the agricultural production serves as livestock feed. The livestock's excrement becomes the primary component of fertilizer for the fields and the cultivation of algae and fish. The heat produced by the cows contributes to the production of duckweed and algae. The eco-mound produces gas and heat thanks to the fermentation of the cutting waste of the crops and a portion of the fertilizer. A smart storage system ensures that heat and biogas are available year-round.

However, the eco-mound is not just for production via functional cycles. It is also aimed at guiding consumers and at restoring the connection between production and food, in the process making our food chains more transparent once again.

Designer Omar Smids

Academy Groningen

Design Atelier Energietransitie Regio Groningen [Groningen Energy Transition District]

Where Zuidhorn, the Netherlands

Lecturers Alex van Spijk, Sjoerd Betten

fig. 114 — Eco mound

material cycle

Do-It-Yourself — Liverpool (GB)

The remaining residents of a rundown neighbourhood in Liverpool resisted the demolition of their homes. They set up a Trust and went to work themselves: hence the title *Do it Yourself*. Together with a group of young designers they made their own streets liveable again, the rest of Granby followed suit.

Late 2015, a non-artist won the prestigious British Turner Prize for the first time in 31 years. Assemble, a London collective of young designers, received the award for the refurbishment of working-class neighbourhood Granby Four Streets in Liverpool. A 'ground-up approach to regeneration, city planning and development in opposition to corporate gentrification,' said the jury.[170]

Assemble worked closely together with residents of the Four Streets (Beaconsfield, Cairns, Jermyn and Ducie), which comprised Victorian terraced housing typical of the late nineteenth century: brick dwellings that follow the height differences of the street.

A group of active residents managed to stop the decline that started in the course of the last century and enlisted the help of an unconventional design studio to do so. Together they found an alternative to demolition.

Liverpool was a major port city at the time this working-class neighbourhood was built. Besides workers, the ten streets with brick workers' houses accommodated migrants from across Europe, craftsmen and administrative port officials. Later, the area became one of the country's first black communities.

The port deteriorated in the course of the twentieth century and in the 1970s the southern part was closed down. This led to violent unrest in the neighbourhood, culminating in racial riots in 1981. In heavy fighting with police, cars and buildings caught fire and hundreds of people were arrested. The Granby Triangle became a no-go area. Four Streets was no longer kept clean and one shop after another closed its door. Residents moved away from Granby. Homes were torn down and grounds became wastelands. The area reached rock bottom when only 20 residents were left. But those residents did not

170
'Urban Regenerators *Assemble* Become First "Non-Artists" to Win Turner Prize', *The Guardian*, 7 December 2015.

171
In 2002, Labour Minister John Prescott launched a plan that was to revive the failing housing markets of the Midlands and Northern England in 15 years. According to critics, this all too often foretold demolition. In 2011 David Cameron's conservative government stopped financing the plan.

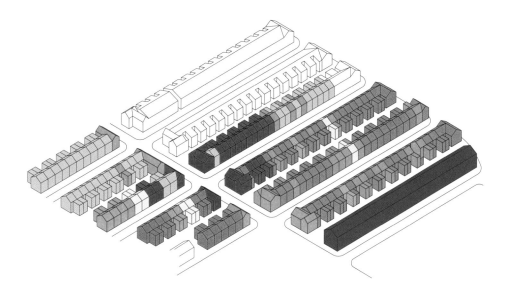

Owner	private	shared ownership	rental
Granby Community Land Trust	✕	5	5
Terrace 21 (co-op)	✕	12	✕
Plus Dane	✕	9	30 (3 new)
Liverpool Mutual Home	9	18	61
Liverpool City Council	5	✕	✕
Private (individual) home occupants	44	✕	✕

■ CLT (*Granby Community Land Trust*)

■ LMH (*Liverpool Mutual Homes*)

Plus Dane

Private (local residents)

Liverpool's City Council's innovative Homes for a Pound

RSL

■ Steinbeck Studios (new development)

fig. 115 — Hybrid (1:1) development model

fig. 116 — The multi-phase redevelopment program of the different houses has been executed by multiple actors

fig. 117 — Following spread: Ducie Street

give up hope and united as early as 1993 to prevent the announced definitive demolition of their neighbourhood.

It had happened before; slums had been cleared across the country after the war. Until the mid-1970s, 160,000 people moved to the suburbs in Liverpool alone. Early this century, the government once again launched large-scale renovation and demolition plans for areas where the housing market had failed.[171]

The Four Streets, the last of Granby's ten streets, were
under threat as well.

fig. 118 — Delivery buildings CLT
on Cairns Street

Resident tried to breathe new life into their neighbourhood themselves: they planted trees, put planters
on the street and grew ivy against dilapidated buildings.
They painted abandoned houses. And they organized a
neighbourhood market on every first Saturday of the
month. Gradually more people began to care for Granby.

The tide turned around 2011. Heritage Organization
Empty Homes had picked up on the four remaining
streets of the Granby Triangle and politicians were
becoming more aware of refurbishing options and resident initiatives. The residents of Granby improved their
bargaining position by setting up their own Community
Land Trust, a legal status that combines individual property rights with collective land ownership.

Meanwhile, Empty Homes had acquainted them with
Steinbeck Studios, a social investor from Jersey that
puts money into the refurbishment of neighbourhoods
of cultural and historical value. Steinbeck Studios not
only offered financial support, but also helped the Trust
to professionalize. The Trust meetings moved from the
picnic table to an office on 48th Cairns Street. Together,
Steinbeck Studios and the Trust wrote a business plan,

fig. 119 — Jermyn Street
(Homes for a Pound)

fig. 120 — Mantle made out
of recycled materials from
Granby (Assemble)

fig. 121 — Following spread:
Cairns Street. Left future winter
garden. Right remains occupied

negotiated with the municipality and made agreements with property owners.

In 2012, Steinbeck Studios introduced the Trust to Assemble, a group of young architects, designers and other creatives. They had united shortly after their graduation to build temporary cinema Cineroleum in an abandoned petroleum station. They describe themselves as a collective that works at the intersection of art, architecture and design.

Assemble's neighbourhood approach contrasts hugely with post-war urban renewal practices. These had been quite heavy-handed in the past, with dwellings simply torn down and replaced by generic single-family dwellings. Asking residents what they wanted simply was not done – they had already been moved to the outskirts anyway. But even today, dwellings in the Granby area are modernized and standardized without much attention to the residents and the way they use their homes.

The Assemble people took their time. They asked all residents what they wanted for the neighbourhood and for their home and took the gathered information back to the drawing board. From the high ceilings and large windows to the mantel pieces and the built-in cabinets, the doorknobs and the tall trees by the road: whenever possible, the designers repaired the houses and the

streets and they renewed old elements together with the
residents.

fig. 122 — Interior of
finished CLT house

Once the city council had transferred ten properties on
Four Streets to the Trust in 2014, the inhabitants got to
manage and let them. Their refurbishment topped the
agenda of the Trust. Most importantly, the houses had to
remain affordable. Half of them are now let at 104
pounds per week.[172] A system of shared ownership was
devised for the owner-occupied housing: buyers paid
80 per cent of property's value and paid off the remaining 20 per cent in the form of rent. As a result, houses
whose renovation cost 120,000 pounds could be sold for
99,000 pounds. If real estate prices rise, the profits will
flow back to the Trust and thus to the neighbourhood.

The ten houses proved a taste of what was in store.
Not much later, other parts of the Four Streets were also
given a makeover. In Beaconsfield Street housing association Plus Dane refurbished 24 houses and built three
new ones. Landlord Liverpool Mutual Home repaired
47 properties in Cairns Street and Jermyn Street. A local
housing association refurbished in different locations.
Starters could enlist for the Homes for a Pound programme: for 1 pound they could buy a property in poor
condition to refurbish themselves.[173]

172

The average one-bedroom dwelling
outside the Liverpool city centre
costs 460 pounds per month,
www.numbeo.com (July 2016).

173

Private home owners refurbish a
shell property to their own liking.
In the Netherlands, Rotterdam
was the first to provide such
'renovator's dreams'. Also see:
'Do-It-Yourself Assemblages
in Rotterdam', B. Boonstra and
W. Lofvers. In: *disP.– The Planning
Review*, Beitske Boonstra &
Willemijn Lofvers (2017) Rotterdam: Do-It-Yourself Assemblages
in Urban Regeneration, disP
- The Planting Review, 53:1, 6-17.

fig. 123 — Granby Workshop

In the summer of 2015, the Granby Workshop opened in empty shop premises on the corner of Granby and Cairns Street to sell handmade furniture, printed fabrics and other products, often made from waste materials. Its proceeds flow back to the neighbourhood.

When Assemble received the call about being shortlisted for the Turner Prize, it immediately called the residents of the Four Streets to ask whether they were up for all the attention. Did they not think it strange that though they, the residents, had been working at the neighbourhood for 25 years, Assemble, which had only joined in a couple of years ago, was being nominated? Assemble was willing to reject the nomination if that's what the residents wanted.

But that's not what the residents wanted. They felt honoured by the attention, they said. It was an affirmation of years of work. Once it had received the award, Assemble announced it would use the £ 25,000 in prize money for the construction of a winter garden in the ruins of two houses – a meeting place for the neighbourhood. The plans show how sunlight is admitted into the building through a glass roof. Granby proves that an area can effectively be upgraded from the ground up and in consultation with the residents.

What designers and residents joined forces to revive a rundown neighbourhood

Where Liverpool, Great Britain

Design Assemble

Realized 2016

Intervention designers talked to all residents and attuned renovation plans to their wishes for the neighbourhood

Also good for vital economy (new industriousness), sociocultural connectivity (cohesion in the neighbourhood)

material cycle

Industrial Area Gets Polder-bank and Own Currency

Spaanse Polder was built 75 years ago to supplement the transit market, as a place for the industrial sector, linked to the flow of freight from the port. Today many businesses are part of (worldwide) chains disconnected from the area. These chains can, after analysing the businesses and their flows, be redirected towards other businesses in the area. A local currency helps in this.

Spaanse Polder originally had a clear organization of sectors (food, logistics, manufacturing) and business sizes. The current picture is much more diffuse: sectors and business sizes have become mixed.

Three major size categories can be identified among them, each with a different importance and a different link to the area: the small business dependent on the local market for its customer base, the medium-sized business, often a family business with strong local roots with a network in the wider region, and finally the multinational or the multi-chain conglomerate that has the largest footprint but is least connected to the area in terms of its customers.

Today these businesses are often situated alongside one another by coincidence. As an organizing strategy for redevelopment, the question arises what added value this proximity can produce, for instance in the interaction of flows of energy or products. The design incorporates a number of functions intended to enable the businesses to join forces; this primarily involves the reuse of flows of leftover food.

The main entrance of the site will feature a representative loading station for the wholesale and multi-chain corporations, complete with storage and assembly spaces. This removes the logistics from the site and makes space available for

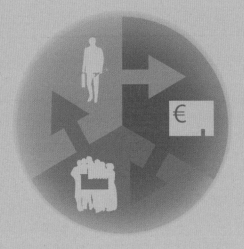

fig. 124 — Synergy logo

development. The automobile and demolition businesses will be situated along a single street, making it easier to purchase and recycle common materials, attract personnel, share tools or knowledge and produce joint marketing. Another example is the processing of leftover food from the wholesale market into ready-made meals for businesses in Spaanse Polder.

The new services will trade using a local currency, the Polder Peseta. The added value created will therefore benefit the whole area. The joint polder bank will make new local investments possible once more.

This project applies an organization strategy of conditions and impulses. The spatial context is linked to the actors' trading perspectives. Connecting these systems of networks leads to resilience for the area and a potential for regeneration.

Designer Floris Schiferli

Academy Rotterdam

Design Atelier Food Hub Spaanse Polder

Where Rotterdam, the Netherlands

Lecturers Thijs van Bijsterveldt, Willemijn Lofvers

material cycle

Renewable City

In the next 15 years, thousands of homes will be replaced or radically renovated in Rotterdam-Zuid. If this endeavour is considered from the perspective of the circular economy, waste flows can be put to use as valuable resources. These new flows have an impact on various places in the city and in various sectors.

The construction sector is the largest producer of waste in the Netherlands; it generates 26 million tonnes of waste, about 40 per cent of the total. Of this waste, 90 per cent is reused for embankments or for foundations in road building. This literally buries the accumulated value of these products underground. Can a design for a circular construction chain bring about change in this destruction of capital? And can this construction chain also provide opportunities for the regeneration of the Port of Rotterdam?

Rotterdam's construction challenge consists primarily of the regeneration of existing sections of the city. The municipal government's housing plan Woonvisie refers to 20,000 homes in need of replacement or radical renovation. A large proportion of these are in neighbourhoods in Rotterdam-Zuid. Three sites illustrate the impact of a circular construction chain on Rotterdam-Zuid's urban development.

The design takes advantage of the large quantities of bio-based materials already being shipped in through the Port of Rotterdam, where they are processed into intermediate or final products. These are transported to the Waalhaven docks, as is the flow of construction waste out of the city. There these two flows are converted into new construction materials or other high-quality applications – for instance construction materials based on hemp, loam, shells and lumber. This creates a new ecosystem of enterprises, large and small, in the circular economy at the Waalhaven docks.

The new materials produced here are used in the regeneration of existing neighbourhoods in Rotterdam, such as Carnisse. The circular construction chain also has an impact on a variety of Rotterdammers: the dockworkers, the producers of bio-based materials and the residents of the regenerated neighbourhoods.

Designers Ashwin Karis, Freek van Riet
Academy Rotterdam
Design Atelier Afval als bron
Where Rotterdam, the Netherlands
Docent Dirk van Peijpe, Floris Schiferli

fig. 125 — New production environments in the Waalhaven harbour

vital economy

Industrial Curator — Arnhem (NL)

The company Schipper Bosch is the owner, developer, landlord and manager of industrial estate Kleefse Waard in Arnhem. Being in charge itself allows the company to safeguard the quality, cultural and historical value and sustainable and innovative character of the industrial estate.

The foundation of Kleefse Waard, a 90-ha industrial estate in the north of Arnhem, was laid in August 1942 under the watchful eye of the German oppressor. The factory of the Arnhem Kunstzijde Unie produced straw cellulose and cell fibres here for years.[174] The company later became part of paint and varnish multinational AkzoNobel. In 2003 Schipper Bosch bought the greater part of the grounds. The project developer and investor turned Kleefse Waard into a sustainable and innovative industrial estate for the clean-tech sector: companies that focus on innovations in energy and environmental technology.

'The DNA of the area appealed to us. In the time of Akzo it was a campus for production, learning and innovation,' says Femke Berendsen, communication advisor at Schipper Bosch. 'Once we'd bought it we immediately began to think about spatial interventions and a future-oriented, varied programme.' To Schipper Bosch this involves more than merely renting out work spaces. The company wants to create an actual community on the fenced off and secured industrial estate, which is in environmental category 5, the highest but one in terms of environmental impact.[175]

The estate has shared facilities, from meeting rooms to electric cars, there are innovation hubs, meeting spaces and educational programmes, and between working, learning and innovating employees can take part in boot camps, socialize during a networking reception or have a meatball sandwich in the restaurant. In short: industrial estate Kleefse Waard wants to become the best clean-tech business park in the Netherlands.

Over the first few years, Schipper Bosch was mainly busy cleaning up and redeveloping the area. The company invested in the buildings and in the needs of the

174
'Kleefse Waard Goud Waard 1943-1993', AKZO, 1993.

175
On an environmental category 5 site, the production of paint and varnishes, chemicals, artificial fertilizer, fireworks, electricity and pharmaceutical raw materials is allowed as well as ship and aircraft building. Only oil refineries, carbon electrodes factories, pig iron and steel mills and power plants are in a higher category.

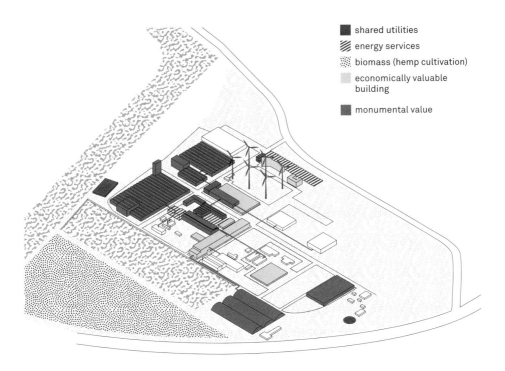

shared utilities

energy services

biomass (hemp cultivation)

economically valuable building

monumental value

fig. 126 — Shared ammenities

fig. 127 — Following spread: Small wind turbine park

existing tenants. In 2008 the founder of Schipper Bosch, Michel Schoonderbeek, approached West 8 Urban Design & Landscape Architecture to draw up a master plan, because the ideas of Schipper Bosch clashed with those of the municipality.

The municipality, which owns the remainder of the land, wanted to divide the industrial estate into plots in order to sell them. Schipper Bosch, on the other hand, wanted to remain the owner and create a collective estate with shared functions, because it believed in the combination of knowledge, industry, innovation and culture.

West 8 had to combine these divergent ideas. The office was provided with a number of starting points: environmental standards had to allow all industry, the existing infrastructure (pipelines, energy, connection to water, rail, road) had to be preserved and even extended and it had to be possible for all logistic and industrial processes to take place on the premises.

Thanks to West 8's master plan, the industrial estate now actually looks like a country estate, with refurbished monumental brick buildings surrounded by greenery. The above-ground pipelines provide the estate with an old-fashioned industrial atmosphere, while the sleek graphic design places it firmly in the twenty-first

century. The corporate colour orange is repeated in the
buildings, the logo and the furniture.

fig. 128 — De Waard restaurant

But Schipper Bosch's design role is more about content than about form. As the owner, the company tries
to fathom what it is the tenants want, to be able to
support them. All the necessary knowledge is at hand
since Schipper Bosch employs project developers
as well as architects, designers, strategists and communication experts. Schipper Bosch also has shares
in different companies, such as Weltevree (design
products), Platowood (wood refinement), RhineTech
(metal), The New Motion (charging solutions for electric
vehicles) and the Greenhouse, an incubator for clean-
tech start-ups. Cross-fertilization takes place on the
industrial estate as well: a restaurant or square may for
example be furnished by Weltevree or a new building
may use sustainable timber from Platowood and steel
from RhineTech.

Schipper Bosch calls itself an area curator. 'We not only
develop and manage the real estate, but we are also
concerned with the broader strategy of the estate. We
closely monitor the rental properties, to ensure that we
can safeguard and develop the quality, the historical
value and the sustainable and innovative character of

fig. 129 — Networking event
Charging square

the estate and its users,' says Mendel Robbers, who is responsible for design and strategy. In an area development context, Schipper Bosch focuses on quality and sustainability rather than on short-term returns or profit maximization. Essentially, Schipper Bosch buys properties and areas to preserve them.

Industrial estate Kleefse Waard has its own management, but is still part of Schipper Bosch. Profits are reinvested in the site on the basis of the philosophy that a well-managed industrial estate makes more money in the long run.

The estate comprises heavy industry and some companies work with hazardous substances. For safety reasons, it is fenced off and secured. That is why some companies settle here deliberately. Other companies are attracted by the combination of manufacturing facilities and knowledge-intensive businesses. Together with Schipper Bosch, large and small clean-tech companies and various educational institutions and governments work on the circular economy. The site is already self-sufficient in terms of wastewater treatment, but wants to be independent in terms of renewable energy as well.

Schipper Bosch actively approaches companies if it feels they would flourish on the estate. TÜV Rheinland Nederland, for example, was invited to come to Arnhem. Schipper Bosch managed to convince TÜV by offering the company a bespoke design trajectory for its future housing.

It is important that the activities of the companies on the estate fit together. Femke Berendsen: 'We work hard to provide the amenities and activities necessary to create a community of companies that inspire each other, for example through the exchange of knowledge.' There is the Powerlab for innovation in the energy sector, for example, there are monthly master classes and there is a bi-annual Green Industry Event. Recently an innovation hub for energy and environmental technology moved to the estate as well. Here trainees, interns and students from HAN University of Applied Sciences work on corporate challenges with the aim to improve the connection between educational institutes and the business world.

Owing to its emphasis on community and knowledge exchange, Kleefse Waard industrial estate stands out among standard estates and draws companies that need collectivity and synergy. It is an approach that works well in other places, too, for example at the Philips

fig. 130 — The central axis of Kleefse Waard

High Tech Campus, at Strijp S in Eindhoven and at the Chemelot Campus for chemical innovation in Geleen and the transformed industrial area 22@ in Barcelona.

The corporate culture and directorial approach of the family-owned Schipper Bosch have determined the success of the Kleefse Waard industrial estate. Through its intensive involvement, it left its mark on everything to do with design: refurbishments, house style, layout, communication and outdoor space. But as an area curator, the company especially used design to programme and organize. The project developer combines a long-term strategy with a hands-on approach. Because it comprises different disciplines, the company can furthermore respond quickly to changes and requirements.

What transformation of an industrial estate with a strong directorial approach by a project developer and investor

Where Arnhem, the Netherlands

Design Schipper Bosch, West 8 and others

Period 2003 (ongoing)

Intervention a synergetic estate for the clean-tech industry with space for meeting and knowledge exchange

Also good for resilient infrastructure (self-sufficient in waste water treatment), renewable energy (plans for in-house green energy production) and sociocultural connectivity (exchange between businesses and educational institutes)

vital economy

Public Waterfronts

The Zaanstreek owes its name and its economy to the River Zaan. Products from the area were transported to the surroundings and beyond. Yet this ancient industry has little future left. And the new economy is placing new demands on its environment. This means the businesses along the Zaan have to give the riverbanks back to all the residents of the area.

In the past, the banks of the Zaan were steadily privatized by factories and the villas of rich industrialists. However, the new economy, oriented towards knowledge, innovation and services, requires a well-managed public space, high-quality public facilities and recreational potential. Can the banks of the Zaan become that kind of public space?

Instituting a regulation that every (re)development along the Zaan must be linked to a development in public space means residents are, bit by bit, getting the banks of the Zaan back.

Every spot along the Zaan is being looked at in regard to what kind of programme it might accommodate, and what kind of public space this would require. From Wormerveer to the Hembrug area,

this generates seven proposals, which not only make visible the qualities being added but also the roles the various parties along the Zaan can play in this process.

The former Brokking factory north of Wormerveer, for instance, is to be transformed into a hotel with a view of the Zaan and the landscape of peat meadows. Floating terraces will be placed in front of the hotel to increase the experience. A walking path runs from the hotel to the existing yacht marina.

The businesses at the Hembrug area are also given a role in the public space, making them more visible. Currently they are often positioned with their backs to the water; the designer flips this round: their access is now via the riverbank and via the water. The new access becomes both a billboard and a public path.

Designer Marie Séon
Academy Amsterdam
Design Atelier Zaans Next Economy
Where Zaanstad, the Netherlands
Lecturers Marco Broekman,
Dingeman Deijs, Rik de Visser

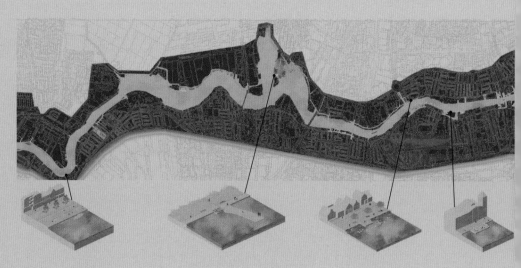

fig. 131 — Zaans Public Space

vital economy

Iconic Industrial Road

All kinds of flows run through Spaanse Polder. For some the industrial estate is the destination; others are simply passing through. The flows are to be reorganized to become visible in the public space. So that the users of the area can find one another more easily.

Spaanse Polder is a variegated industrial estate, where various industries are randomly distributed. They all have their specific flows of goods, personnel, suppliers and commercial clients. These routinely find their way, but for consumers looking for a specific business this is not such a simple task.

Recreational users also criss-cross the area, as the cycling route between Rotterdam and Midden Delfland – between the city and countryside – runs through it. Little of this is visible, however.

A programme of requirements, which the route is meant to meet, is compiled for each user. Subsequently the public space is organized and designed to make the various flows identifiable.

The freight flow requires unimpeded movement, few obstacles and sufficient room to turn a lorry round. For employees, daily bottlenecks need to be removed, and sufficient comfortable car parks provided. The recreational routes, for the sake of safety, must run along dedicated cycle paths. For consumers, wayfinding is extremely important, which can mean that business may be relocated and rearranged based on new sightlines.

Interventions in the infrastructure improve the clarity of the area. Some flows are conjoined, others separated. The profile of the roadways is to be adapted for their function – unimpeded passage, for instance, or a turning loop for lorries.

Where flows overlap or cross, interventions are implemented to reinforce this encounter. This creates new typologies such as the Industrieweg (Industrial Road), with iconic overhead wires, and the Flow Fly-over, where one can experience the landscape under the motorway.

Designer Chris van Nimwegen
Academy Rotterdam
Design Atelier Food Hub
Spaanse Polder
Where Rotterdam, the Netherlands
Lecturers Thijs van Bijsterveld,
Willemijn Lofvers

fig. 132 — Agroduct

healthy living

Biodiverse City — Eindhoven (NL)

The worlds of plants and animals are on the decline, even in cities. A landscaping business in Eindhoven is trying to counteract this by creating urban nature – garden by garden, house by house. But it takes more than that. Biodiversity ought to be an integrated part of the design process: there should be a landscape gardener in every team.

Global biodiversity is deteriorating rapidly. The decline has harmful effects on our ecosystems, agricultural production and food security; on drug production and the quality of air and water. Scientists and policymakers agree that something needs to be done about it. We usually associate biodiversity with protecting and connecting natural and agricultural areas and much less with nature in the city. However, more than half of the world's population lives in cities and biodiversity makes an important contribution to a healthy urban environment.

A research team at the University of Glasgow that analysed public health in 268 urban areas in England found a direct relationship with the presence of parks and woods. The larger the green zone, the greater its positive impact on public health. More green meant a longer life and fewer suicides.[176] A Japanese study demonstrated that the elderly live longer if they live near a park.[177] And Danish and Canadian researchers found that the proximity of parks has a negative effect on obesity.[178]

In 2009, the municipality of Eindhoven presented a biodiversity action plan. Because biodiversity improves people's health and quality of life, makes the city more attractive to residents and visitors, increases (urban) agricultural production, can prevent flooding and safeguards water and air quality, Eindhoven is trying to increase the number of plant and animal species in the city. For example by connecting the city and the countryside with green areas, introducing low-traffic streets, adding greenery to industrial estates, constructing ponds and wildlife tunnels and encouraging guerrilla gardening and green roofing through subsidies.

176

A Comparison of Green Space Indicators for Epidemiological Research, R. Mitchell, T. Astell-Burt, T. and E.A. Richardson, 2011.

177

'Urban Residential Environments and Senior Citizens', *Journal of Epidemiology and Community Health*, 2002.

178

Beetje natuur, grote invloed, IVN, 2014.

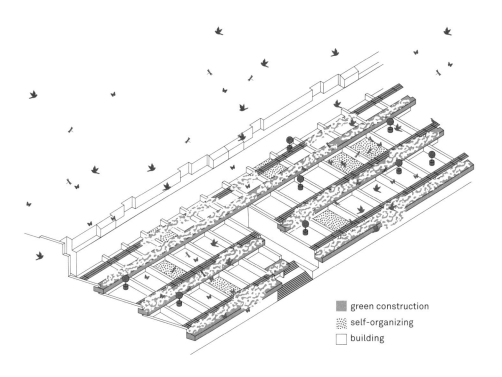

green construction
self-organizing
building

fig. 133 — Growing ecosystem

Nature makes the city more comfortable to live in, says Eindhoven, and citizens can contribute by protecting flora and fauna as well as by choosing to make their gardens greener rather than turn them into large, paved surfaces.[179] The city calls on its citizens, businesses and organizations to participate. It has created an online 'map of biodiversity opportunities' that shows which plant and animal species live in the city and where, and that explains how people can arrange a garden or plot in such a way that it will attract a variety of animal species such as the Northern crested newt, hedgehog and polecat.[180]

A good example of a green building is the Medina in the centre of Eindhoven, close to entertainment area Stratumseind and the inner ring. The design by English architect Neave Brown includes 73 apartments, 250 parking spaces and 2,000 m2 of retail space. The complex features stacked green terraces that give it a lush Mediterranean look. Easy on the eye, but also good for biodiversity, air quality and the reduction of noise and excess rain water.

But soon after its completion in 2003, it turned out that the contents of the planters, terraces and pergolas

179

Actieplan Biodiversiteit Eindhoven; Alpenwatersalamander als ambassadeur, Municipality of Eindhoven, 2009.

180

Map of biodiversity opportunities: bit.ly/29Zk9ny.

were not well-chosen. The promised green wealth proved an arid, barren desert. In 2004 the owner-occupier's association therefore took matters into its own hands and asked Eindhoven landscaping company Soontiëns to create a new design.

'Something that often goes wrong in the design of green buildings or sites is that people fail to take specific climatic and soil conditions into account and as a result, plants die quickly,' says director Martijn van de Loo. He argues that biodiversity is location specific, after all one cannot simply draw any green into a design. Local soil conditions, flora and fauna, climate and ecological structure have to be taken into consideration. This takes research, substantive knowledge, experience and early collaboration among specialists: ecologists, biologists, hydrologists, civil engineers and urban planners.[181] Van de Loo: 'I advocate an integrated approach to the design of green buildings. The landscape designer is involved from the beginning and is preferably part of the construction team.'

Soontiëns Hoveniers specializes in urban nature. Martijn van de Loo and codirector Jeroen Soontiëns give lectures, initiate urban green projects and design public green areas and parks. They have also created several urban pick-your-own gardens and community kitchen gardens and designed a community garden for the campus of the University of Technology.

Soontiëns is one of the very few hands-on landscaping companies that is also involved in theoretical research and plan development. The company developed a system for vertical guerrilla gardens, for example. Eye-catching projects in Eindhoven include a green bus shelter and street lighting in hanging flower baskets. Soontiëns is committed to the improvement of biodiversity and the experience of nature in the city and wants to make people aware of the value of urban nature. This starts with visibility.

In that context, the Medina makes for good publicity. The terraces are now richly overgrown, as was promised in the sales brochure. The landscaping company introduced different species of green to attract birds, insects and butterflies. Thick hedges and hardy annuals offer protection to birds; butterflies are attracted to flowering plants and provisions for caterpillars have also been included.

There are now more than 20 species of butterfly in this tiny piece of city, whereas it is increasingly difficult for butterflies to survive in the Netherlands at all. In addition, some 15 species of birds nest here. The Medina

181

'Essay biodiversiteit', Loo, M. van der, Snep, R. and Soontiëns, M. In: *Duurzame landschapsarchitectuur – essays en praktijkvoorbeelden*, Blauwdruk Wageningen, 2015.

fig. 134 — Roof gardens Medina in Eindhoven, Soontiëns Hoveniers

fig. 135 — Following spread: Roof gardens Medina in Eindhoven, Soontiëns Hoveniers

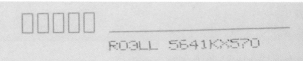

ROELL 5641KXS70

Neave Brown
...yne Road
...2YY

mobile: 0044 774...

10 June 2014

Dear Martijn

It was a great pleasure to meet you at the event at Medina.

✗   'You are a bigger man than I am, Martijn Loo'.

I was amazed to see the planting, vines and creepers, bushes, and trees you had done - the landscape you have created. Architects have visions of the future of their buildings and are generally disappointed. Here you had understood and gone beyond my dreams - been more creative than I could have imagined.

I am impressed   - that you have a programme (requiring persistence)
- that you have defined public, semipublic and private areas
- that you have controlled scale and enclosure
- that you have such beautiful planting.

I had written: 'The section arrived quickly - a garden throughout: continuous-public, semi public, and private, it mounts floor by floor from street level to roof against an urban wall as hard on the road side as soft on the other' - and you have done it.

There was a question about the upper balcony fronts and the penthouse terrace edge. I put the timbers there in the hope that vines could grow - realising there would be a problems with density and enclosure - but hoped that it could be managed with pruning - but I am totally ignorant of how and what can be done. I would love vines to grow all along the penthouses' rails but made no provision for planting, for for the trellises to the back wall at both ends to become vine covered - a 'pergola'. One can hope too much.

Just my comments - but I cannot believe the quality and care and the extent of the achievement - the amazing contribution of your work to the quality of - the building - the environment - Eindhoven.

Yours sincerely

Neave

✗ 'You're a better man thenI am, Gunga Din'- Kipling- known by all-

182

Also see: *Het weer in de stad. Hoe ontwerp het stadsklimaat bepaalt,* S. Lenzholzer, 2013.

contributes to biodiversity, but also to climate adaptation. The terraces absorb rain water and as a result the sewers are less burdened during heavy rainfall. The shade and the evaporation of the plants also ensure that the building and its immediate surroundings remain cool. This prevents the Urban Heat Island (UHI) effect from occurring here.[182]

But no matter how beautiful the Medina is, a single green building does not create a biodiverse, green city. How can you connect individual projects and start an actual system change? 'People have to see that it matters,' says Van de Loo. It can involve more than green buildings or guerrilla gardens: 'There are many ways to green an urban environment, also inexpensive ones. Unfortunately, as yet there are not enough architects and clients that integrate green in the design. It still makes builders anxious and architects think in built structures rather than in growing structures.'

The city can be a pioneer by making the creation of new nature preconditional to new development plans. That would be a good way to complement the 'map of biodiversity opportunities' and subsidies for guerrilla gardens and green roofs.

What stacked green terraces of an apartment complex enhance biodiversity in the city, improve air quality and promote the comfort of residents

Where Eindhoven, the Netherlands

Design Soontiëns Hoveniers

Realized 2004

Intervention at the request of the residents a landscaping company created a new green design for the decoration of the building

Also good for resilient infrastructure (greenery keeps cool and absorbs rainwater) and sociocultural connectivity (joint maintenance)

fig. 136 — Personal contribution

healthy living

Pioneering Sports Factories

During the step-by-step development of a new residential district at the edge of Arnhem's city centre, mobile sports facilities are to be installed. In this way the designers aim to create dynamism and local identity. Which parties and partners are needed to establish these pioneers?

On the southeast side of Arnhem's city centre, on the banks of the Rhine, a former industrial area is making way for an urban residential district. This process is unfolding step by step: the pace depends on the investors and developers. The character and the identity of the site, as proposed in the design, will therefore have to wait.

During the development process, iconic objects are to be installed in the district, called sports factories. These are small mobile structures containing sports facilities. The kinds of sport vary, depending on the situation at the moment. Is the Coberco factory – a piece of industrial heritage that has waited 13 years for a new use – suitable for indoor climbing? Can a workers' residential neighbourhood slated for demolition serve as a playing field for paintball? And why not turn a sand landscape into a motocross course – it would only take a day's worth of shovelling.

In each of these interventions, the iconic sports factory becomes the visible, connecting element. During the transition period, all kinds of collectives can adopt the sports factories and use them to practise their sport – such as sport leagues, businesses or groups of future residents. This builds a community on site even before the district has been fully developed. Ultimately the result will be a series of permanent sports facilities along the banks of the Rhine.

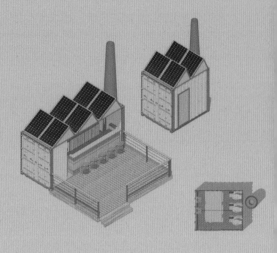

fig. 137 — Mobile service

Designers Jan-Laurens van der Horst and Marcel Plomp

Academy Arnhem

Design Atelier Sport en bewegen in de openbare ruimte

Where Arnhem, the Netherlands

Lecturers Bas Driessen, Thijs van Spaandonk

healthy living

The Elderly Take to the Streets

The Arnhem district of Elderveld dates from the 1970s and 1980s. Its population is getting older and becoming steadily less mobile. The declining quality of the public space and the rising lack of social safety and security are exacerbating the problem. The designers went looking for ways to get people out of their houses again.

How do you get the older residents of Elderveld to exercise more in the open air? The analysis by the designers reveals that facilities are located too far away to be reachable on foot and that the quality of the public space is deteriorating. Causes include budget cutbacks on maintenance and slow-traffic routes that are felt to be socially unsafe and insecure, because they run behind the houses.

Another trend is that more and more services are being offered to older people at home. People can have groceries and meals delivered, and visitation schemes are available for medical care and companionship.

In order to turn this development around, the design proposes an intricate network of flexible everyday facilities in the various neighbourhoods. This literally drags the elderly residents over the threshold: there is always a cluster of facilities within walking distance. An app will be released to let local residents know what is available in the clusters and what services they can use. The clusters will include such features as a coffeehouse, a flexible medical clinic with a GP one day and a physical therapist, for instance, another day, and the elderly can have their mail or groceries delivered there. This creates nearby-care instead of home-care.

For their research the designers sought repeated contact with stakeholders in the area. They presented their ideas at a meeting of the residents association, conducted interviews with residents and obtained information from a local association devoted to promoting physical exercise, 'Elderveld in beweging' ['Elderveld in motion' - the Dutch word for exercise also means motion]. As a result, the design is a concrete response to the genuine needs of the district - elements of the design can be implemented immediately.

Designers Harm Diesvelt and Diederik Mulder

Academy Arnhem

Design Atelier Sport en bewegen II

Where Arnhem, the Netherlands

Lecturers Bas Driessen, Thijs van Spaandonk

sociocultural connectivity

Broedstraten — Amsterdam-Noord (NL)

In the Broedstraten in Amsterdam, residents, artists and entrepreneurs work together in theatre plays, street parades, a world restaurant, a neighbourhood market, a sewing studio and many other projects. These connect the residents and make the neighbourhood more social and lively.

In 2009, Mira ter Braak, Maaike Poppegaai and their team founded the Broedstraten, five streets in Amsterdam-Noord in which artists and residents set up projects with themes such as fashion, theatre, market, colours and music. The name 'Broedstraat' is a variation of 'Broedplaats': the name of an abandoned building that is temporarily occupied by artists. But according to Poppegaai, 'broedplaatsen' – 'breeding grounds' – are often introspective. 'We wanted to be accessible and make connections between artists and residents in these streets.'

Broedstraten is a foundation that is active in working class neighbourhoods such as De Banne, Vogelbuurt, Tuindorp Nieuwendam and Tuindorp Oostzaan. Of old, this is where dockworkers and factory workers lived and where everyone knew everyone. That social cohesion is gone and the neighbourhoods now face high vacancy rates, unemployment, poverty and social exclusion. New residents – mostly migrants, artists and students – are drawn to the area by its inexpensive housing, but there is hardly any contact between them and the original residents. The idea behind Broedstraten is to create social cohesion and cultural connectivity by coupling artists to their neighbours.

Ter Braak and Poppegaai are originally an interior decorator and a social geographer. They were involved in the Noorderparkkamer, a cultural meeting place for and by the neighbourhood in the Noorderpark, and saw opportunities for the socially vulnerable neighbourhoods of Amsterdam-Noord. Subsidies from the city, a housing association and the Oranjefonds enabled them to establish the Broedstraten foundation.

As quartermasters they encourage participation, promote the development of residents and try to strengthen social cohesion in the neighbourhood – but they do not

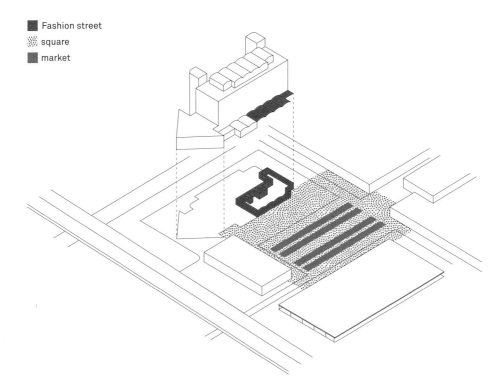

■ Fashion street
░ square
▓ market

fig. 138 — Activating vacant buildings

want to be called welfare workers. Poppegaai: 'We don't solve any problems – there are other institutions to do that. If you have debts, we refer you to debt counselling. We don't look at problems, we look at opportunities. What is someone's talent? What can they do?' The starting point of Broedstraten is that everyone can participate.

They found artists, photographers, film makers, designers and musicians in their own network and by making an appeal to the people. Later, new people joined indirectly. It was important that the artists were open to working with their neighbours and to being inspired by the neighbourhood. A group of theatre makers in Theaterstraat (Zonneplein), for example, made portraits of the elderly residents resulting in a play called 'Echte Mensen' (Real People). Afterwards they entered into conversation with the audience and with the portrayed people. In Muziekstraat (Leeuwerikstraat) a director started a neighbourhood choir for everyone to sing in, whether they were talented or not. This way, activities that brought people together emerged in every Broedstraat.

The quartermasters were offered (temporary) space in abandoned buildings that belonged to housing associations and the city, like an empty garage, a flower pavilion and outdated dwellings or shop premises. 'Being in the

fig. 139 — Following spread: Buikslotermeerplein

middle of the neighbourhood was of key importance,' says Poppegaai. 'They have to be spots that are lively already, where people can just walk in.'

fig. 140 — Office units and student workshop

Once they had found those locations, the Broedstraten project was launched. The quartermasters did not carry out extensive preliminary studies. 'There are already shelves and shelves of books about the problems in disadvantages areas. The problem is that nobody does anything about them,' says Poppegaai: 'We could have done research first and made analyses, but we chose an active approach and just got on with it.'

Thus, in 2010 Kleurenstraat was launched from a garage in a condemned apartment building in De Banne, simply by opening the door and offering the children a place to do crafts. On the first Wednesday afternoon there were no less than 20 children waiting, raring to go. On other days a neighbour ran a thrift shop from the premises. Kleurenstraat continued even after the garage had been demolished. Visual artists, photographers and filmmakers work on annually recurring projects and new activities in the street, in abandoned buildings or in (temporary) rented locations.

Another example is Modestraat (first on Volendammerweg, now on Buikslotermeerplein), where Mira ter Braak is quartermaster. This is where coffee corner

fig. 141 — Fashion street in a former Chinese restaurant

Pleur en de Koek is, where people can buy coffee and cake as well as the mug from which they drink or the vintage chair on which they sit. Modestraat also features an exchange shop, a hairdresser's, a dance studio, a sewing studio and a knitting lab. Ter Braak: 'Three people found ten knitting machines for sale on the Internet and launched the lab. That's easy to do in Modestraat.'

The products that the residents and designers make here together, such as screen-printed textiles and jewellery, are now sold throughout the city. The monthly World Restaurant, in which 50 local chefs with a variety of backgrounds cook meals, is also well-known. Some have become professional caterers and now work at festivals and events.

But it was not smooth sailing all the way. The quartermasters encountered resistance as well. Poppegaai says the market vendors that work on Mosplein, where a traditional goods market has been taking place since 1920, could do without her decorative market stalls in Van der Pekstraat that sold home-made products supplied by local residents.

'They tried to stop us by all means. They saw us as competition. The only thing we could do was enter into conversation with them: How can we tie our market up with yours?' A successful joint mother's day action allowed mutual trust to gradually develop. Today, the

fig. 142 — Following spread: The Fashion street has many different functions

two markets have even been integrated to create the Pekmarkt. Several local entrepreneurs that were previously on benefits opened a stall and now run shops in the street. The bicycle mechanic even has two shops, Poppegaai says proudly.

The Broedstraten are of course about more than one or two neighbourhood businesses. Local residents gradually began to self-organize, allowing the quartermasters to take a step back. The dynamics between creative entrepreneurs and residents leads to shared interests, increased social cohesion, a varied cultural life and a more pleasant neighbourhood. Entrepreneurship in the area furthermore received a new impulse and abandoned properties were given a (temporarily) new destination.

The question is how sustainable these initiatives are. The Broedstraten were established in 2009 during the economic crisis. Housing associations were happy to cooperate because their vacant properties were given a practical use that was even good for the neighbourhood. But the situation has changed: temporary contracts expire, the housing market has picked up and the vacancy rate is declining.

Its dependence on government subsidies makes the foundation vulnerable and that is why it is looking for new partners. But sponsors and funding bodies require measurable results, data analysis and a business-like attitude and it is difficult to demonstrate and measure social added value and benefits. The two quartermasters see more in a partnership between creative city makers and the business world. One possibility is a partnership with companies that would send their commercially skilled employees on secondment to the Broedstraten. Discussions with progressive financial companies are ongoing already.

What couple artists and residents in
vulnerable neighbourhoods to promote
quality of life and social cohesion

Where Amsterdam-Noord, the Netherlands

Design Mira ter Braak/
Stichting de Broedstraten

Realized 2009 (ongoing)

Intervention provide spaces in streets
with high vacancy rates to artists
and residents for joint initiatives

Also good for vital economy
(encourage enterprise) and healthy
living (cooking and eating together)

fig. 143 — A hairdresser
on the Fashion street

sociocultural connectivity

Cluttered Modernism

In de district of Vrieheide, residents have constantly adapted their houses, and as a result many modernist residential blocks have become unrecognizable. This contributes to the cluttered quality of the district and a negative trend in property values. Only collective interests can persuade residents that renovation is worthwhile.

The Heerlen district of Vrieheide was built in the 1960s, commissioned by the Vascomij company, which went bankrupt in 1967. The rental units then passed to various landlords until the tenants were offered the opportunity to buy their homes in 1980. From that point on, the residents enjoyed the freedom to adapt and expand their homes according to their own ideas and budgets. One resident added romantic elements, another closed off his balcony, a third enclosed his entire garden with walls and a roof. All kinds of materials and styles were used. This contributed to the district now looks cluttered and dilapidated.

Radical renovation is needed, but this can only take place if the residents actively take part. They have to be persuaded of a collective interest. Various interests can qualify, such as collective energy generation, a collective laundry, local food production and energy-neutral renovation. For each intervention, the savings or profits generated by collective organizing for an individual household are explained.

The role of the designer in this process is different from that of a traditional architect. The designer draws up an inventory of the skills already available in the district that can be put to use for the various interventions. Are there residents, for instance, who can do remodelling work, or have experience with gardening or with providing care for the elderly?

This allows the designer to demonstrate how the collective can contribute to the improvement of the district people live in; the creation of a community and an increase in property values go hand in hand.

Designer Bert Schellekens
Academy Maastricht
Design Atelier Ontwerplab Vrieheide
Where Heerlen, the Netherlands
Lecturers Jules Beckers,
Marco Broekman, Niek Bisscheroux

The Original

Libero Forbiera

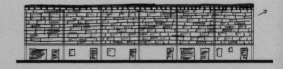

Bie-Heide

Vrei-Heid

fig. 144 — Freedom of choice at the block level

sociocultural connectivity

Upscaled Pop-Ups

The southern portion of Arnhem's city centre is wedged between the true city centre and the Rijnkade. The area lacks spatial cohesion and its residents have little to do with one another. Many plans have been proposed for the area, but they have all come to naught. Now a more intensive use of the public space aims to create cohesion.

The area was built during post-war reconstruction, and while it could form a pleasant link between the shopping district and the Rijnkade with its riverfront terraces, it primarily works as a barrier. There are shops, apartments and large offices for government agencies such as the Province of Gelderland and the Public Prosecution Service, which means the area attracts very diverse visitors.

Many plans were proposed for the area over the past several years. The most well-known is the megalomaniac Rijnboog, which, overtaken by the economic crisis, never got off the drawing board.

The starting point for the transformation of the public space advocated by the designers involves several successful pop-up initiatives in public space and in vacant buildings. These initiatives prove that activities can emerge without real estate development. Florentijn Hofman's Aardvark, for example, became a playground. The roof of a little-used parking garage is turned into a roof garden several months a year.

The designers want to add facilities for sports and exercise in various locations, which will make the public space more lively; this already happens on an incidental basis now. The facilities will be adapted to the requirements of current residents. The employee unions of the government agencies, for instance, are building a driving range along the Rhine, using golf balls made of compressed fish food. Beach volleyball pitches will be located on the quayside and a swimming pool will be constructed in the river, at the initiative of local hospitality venues. In collaboration with two gyms a square is to be transformed into an outdoor fitness centre.

Designers Bouke Nijland
and Niels Leijte

Academy Arnhem

Design Atelier Sport en bewegen
in de openbare ruimte

Where Arnhem, the Netherlands

Lecturers Bas Driessen,
Thijs van Spaandonk

fig. 145 — The Rijnkade is permanently transformed into a city beach with sports and games facilities

Conclusions

What has it brought us, three years of research into the future of urban regions and the role research by design can play in it? No ready-made solutions, but rather a set of instruments that can be used to tackle intractable problems. And more than 50 inspiring Practical Examples.

This final part draws conclusions. First, design thinking is placed in a wider perspective, which includes attention to the dangers of efficiency and to the benefits of equations with two unknowns.

The Chapter 'What and Where' discusses the need to think beyond location and zooms in on scale problems and the potential of probing.

Next is an extensive discussion of experiences with the three models – the DTP Diagram, the ICCI Model and the C3 Cube.

Finally, we take one last look at new and old coalitions. Because ultimately, people will have to make the changes. Research by design that fails to convince people is good for nothing.

A Design Can Also Be a Question

We live in the age of cities. We are born in them and we die in them, we work, play and live in them, they protect and mould us. Many people love the city, even if that love is mixed with annoyance and sometimes, actually, dislike. But even the people that deliberately choose to live in the countryside depend on the city.

The fact that people are closely connected with the city means we have no choice but to bend the city to our will. What we want are cities with vital economies and clean air, with places for us to meet, with space for participation and consultation and with infrastructure that is safe. Cities that are resilient enough to face adversity, cities with circular material flows and renewable energy.

The world is full of lists ranking cities in terms of their success as an innovative city, healthy city, green city, happy city, resilient city, circular city, sustainable city, low carbon city, liveable city or sponge city. Universities and knowledge centres also address these and related

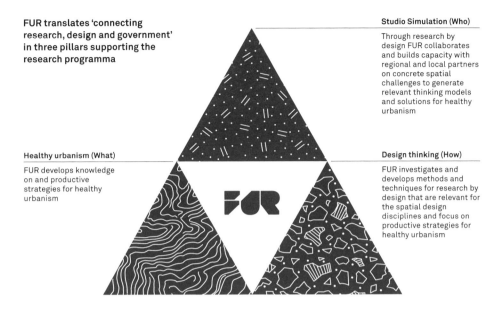

FUR translates 'connecting research, design and government' in three pillars supporting the research programma

Studio Simulation (Who)

Through research by design FUR collaborates and builds capacity with regional and local partners on concrete spatial challenges to generate relevant thinking models and solutions for healthy urbanism

Healthy urbanism (What)

FUR develops knowledge on and productive strategies for healthy urbanism

Design thinking (How)

FUR investigates and develops methods and techniques for research by design that are relevant for the spatial design disciplines and focus on productive strategies for healthy urbanism

fig. 146 — The triangle healthy urbanity (What), design thinking (How) and design ateliers with local partners (Who)

themes and develop a wealth of insights. This naturally raises the question of what the research group Future Urban Regions has been able to add.

The main objective of the research group was not only to increase the theoretical knowledge on healthy urbanity, but also to help with concrete problems and questions that play an important part at the local and regional levels, to find answers to questions about what demands healthy urbanity makes of buildings, streets, cities and regions and what role spatial design can and should play in realizing them.

FUR's focus follows logically from its genesis. The research group goes back to the *Action Agenda Architecture and Spatial Design 2013-2016*. In this document, central government captured its intention to 'strengthen the connection between education, research and government'. The objective was not only to provide designers with the skills they needed for their new social role, but emphatically also to support regional and local stakeholders facing design challenges.

The six Dutch Academies of Architecture that took on the challenge established a research group to specifically focus on research by design. Next, the research group was provided with a substantive framework by focusing it on healthy urbanity. In other words: first came the 'who', then came the 'how' and finally the 'what'. That is, although in the reverse order, exactly the structure this book follows.

FUR considers developing and understanding the way the city is used as an essential addition to research by design: designers should

not only have eyes for the space, but also for the environmental performance of the city and its economic potential and level of sociocultural
participation.

In other words, research by design combines classical spatial
challenges with an analysis of use in the wider sense to create new
urban typologies. In many areas, these offer new starting points for
design disciplines concerning the landscape, the city and the building.

The Increased Importance of Design

What do Apple, Pepsi, Philips, Kia Motors, 3M and Johnson & Johnson
have in common? All of these companies have appointed a Chief
Design Officer (CDO). At the highest administrative level, this person is
responsible for roles and tasks the Chief Marketing Officer previously
delegated to lower-ranked Design Executives.

The reason for such an appointment seems simple: excellently
designed products sell themselves. But even more important is the fact
that designers understand the needs and desires of consumers and that
they are able to identify and create new products and services.[183]
Balancing on the edge of reason and instinct, their design thinking is
sharply focused on the future.

CDO's can oversee all design initiatives within the organization. Their
responsibilities extend from the design of user experiences and pack-
aging to spatial, industrial and graphic design. Advertising, marketing
and engineering are frequently among their job responsibilities as well.
Essentially, a CDO weighs qualitative and quantitative factors.

This business trend is increasingly being copied. In the spring of
2016, Helsinki was one of the first cities in the world to appoint a CDO.
Design knowledge, digitization and interactivity are becoming an
integrated part of urban development. 'The main objective is to transform the city into a functional environment for everyone; for citizens
and companies – for all users of the city.'[184]

These examples clearly show that the notion of the importance of
design enjoys growing support in our society. And this goes beyond the
traditional notion of spatial design, it also involves a different design
attitude. Designers are learning not to immediately think in solutions;
the best solutions, especially to strategic problems, are often more
specialized questions.

Efficiency Can also Be Dangerous

Over and over again, the transition challenges that must
be met to improve the performance of the city raise the
question: Which coalition of actors will it take to achieve
the transition? The activities of FUR therefore actually
take place in the intermediate space between three
pivotal questions: What is healthy urbanity? How can
transition challenges be designed? What kind of people
will it take to achieve the goals?

183
'What is behind the Rise of the
Chief Design Officer?', M. Stuhl. At:
www.forbes.com, November 2014.

184
'City of Helsinki Among the
First in the World to Hire Chief
Design Officer', R. Murto. At:
www.helsinkidesignweek.com,
16 May 2016.

The research therefore focused on the development of productive strategies, methods and instruments that, through design, can establish connections between questions.

The performance of the city improves if systems are connected, made more efficient and if linear processes are transformed into circular chains. However, there are limits to the degree to which we can make urban ecosystems more efficient and smart. 'Ecosystems always include some degree of redundancy, a kind of overcapacity. This redundancy is also important to the city, by this we mean that a city continues to function, even if one of its systems is not (fully) working.'[185]

Perhaps we should look for what Lebanese-Canadian thinker Nassim Taleb calls the 'antifragile'.[186] He uses the term to refer to the property that a system grows stronger by undergoing disturbances and turbulence – like a human body after it has been vaccinated. This is something beyond robustness or resilience. It is still unclear which interventions work for cities, but to begin with, design can help test their fragility and antifragility.

Dichotomies

More and more often, commissioning governments emphatically choose a position amid the partners. This creates both a wider view of the problems and solutions that seem more hybrid and sometimes even diffuse.

Strikingly, answers to 'What?', 'How?' and 'Who?' in both the Practical Examples presented in this book and in the results of the FUR Ateliers each comprise their own dichotomy. The *what* question requires the combined action of centralized and decentralized solutions. The *how* question stretches between desk research and fieldwork. And the *who* question is looking for answers that can either be top-down or bottom-up.

The balance between top-down and bottom-up is partly determined by the context. In the existing city, the dependency of stakeholders is substantial and this lends itself more to bottom-up solutions, while it seems technical top-down solutions are often more called for in rural areas. But not always. Take the energy transition: centralized collective solutions on a large scale are often much cheaper than decentralized individual initiatives. But strikingly, the German *Energiewende* has taken place from bottom up. The strategic intervention of the national government offered individual initiatives the opportunity to play a part in addressing the challenge of the energy transition. This caused a huge acceleration and turned individuals into stakeholders in the transition from fossil to renewable energy. Both of these solutions have their own benefits and also result in completely different design challenges.

185
'Nieuwe coalities maken stad veerkrachtig', interview with Ellen van Bueren, Professor of Urban Development Management at Delft University of Technology. At: www.mastercitydeveloper.nl, March 2016.

186
Antifragile: Things That Gain from Disorder, N. Taleb, 2012.

Equations with Two Unknowns
Research by design often turns out to revolve around equations with
two unknowns. Once the answer to the *what* question is known, the
follow-up questions enter the picture: *how* is the issue to be addressed
and *who* will work on it.

Take, for example, the water square in Rotterdam.[187] This city has
always faced water storage and drainage design challenges, but only
engineers addressed them – they were simply not on the spatial designers' agenda. The opposite applied to squares: they were considered
typical spatial challenges. It was only when the question of how
citizens could benefit from the temporary storage of water was asked
that a new typology could emerge through the collaboration of the
two disciplines.

A similar equation with two unknowns emerges once the *how* is
known. If you know *how* to optimize a system, then the obvious next
question to designers is to identify *what* possible solutions there are and
then examine *who* will form a coalition. This is what happened in the
example of London's High Streets, where Mark Brearley used mapping
as a research method to determine what had to be done and which
parties that would take for a variety of locations.[188]

The same thing seems to apply to the *who*: once the coalition is
known, the research is aimed at exploring the common interest, which
results in the leading question of *what*, as well as *how* and which
method to use to work together towards a solution. This variation is
found, for example, in 'Energy Workplace – Friesland', which supports
local corporations and initiatives in a procedural way.[189]

What and Where

FUR distinguishes six themes in relation to urban transitional challenges: resilient infrastructure, renewable energy, material cycles, vital
economy, healthy living and sociocultural connectivity. This division
is based on a substantive analysis of the wider field of healthy urbanity, but was also inspired by practical considerations: six academies
participated in the research group, each of them with its own intrinsic
focus.

The themes are of course interconnected, since the six
of them have the city as a common factor. You can see
the six perspectives as different entrances to the same
building. The artist entrance, the stage tower and the
main entrance each provide a different view of the same
hall.

The overlap proved to be an advantage: interventions
related to one theme made positive contributions to
other themes as well. Analysis of the Practical Examples discussed in this book showed that an intervention
exerted influence on an average of 3.5 themes.

187
See Part 3, Chapter
'A Metabolic Square' →p. 208.

188
See Practical Example
'High Streets – London' →p. 170.

189
See Practical Example
'Energy Workplace – Friesland'
→p. 226.

Metabolism

Generations of designers have literally learned their profession through transfer. They build on the work of their predecessors, which in turn learn the profession from the generation before them.

Cities have been designed on this basis for centuries. No matter how valuable the tradition is, it does not really reflect the way urban designs are used. While we find it very normal that product designs include extensive testing of user experiences, urban design hardly ever includes such testing. The metabolic approach intends to change that.

Studying the underlying flows teaches us how the city is used and safeguards that we also look at the system as a whole, rather than at spatial expression alone. This approach ensures that we can gradually restore the balance between interventions in the urban system and the spatial design.

The addition of the social metabolism to the originally mainly physical notion of metabolism turns out to be a productive way to create a richer picture of the challenges, but also presupposes a new way of working.

It does need mentioning that any metabolic detour eventually has to reconnect to the representation of the space. In research by design processes, spatial concretization is sometimes long in coming, which is asking a lot from both the designers and other stakeholders.

Think beyond the Location

In system challenges, it is advisable to keep the location of the design intervention open. The FUR design atelier about wastewater started with the question of how to recover nutrients from the sewer and what spatial interventions doing so would take.[190] As it turned out, two different approaches were possible: separate the sewage into a solid and a liquid fraction or release the central sewage system and apply a hybrid solution.

The first possible solution generates mainly technological challenges: How can a nutrient-rich liquid fraction be used as a raw material for agricultural production? And how can the solid fraction of the waste flow be coupled to other organic residual flows, such as GFT, and what typological changes of dwellings and neighbourhoods does that require?

The second possibility focuses on a combination of a sewer system for the city centre and water treatment fields at the neighbourhood level and is more about the actors. How can coalitions of residents in collaboration with the wastewater company organize a more sustainable sanitation of the city? Who invests and who receives the profits – in other words: who owns the nutrients? And only then does the question come up: What does this system change mean to the spatial layout of the city and how it will turn out?

The stakeholders found out that choosing the urban system as a starting point for the solving of a spatial problem provided them with a new angle. Generally,

190
See design Atelier 'Waste as a Resource' (Appendix 1) →p. 303.

neighbourhood renewal is considered an exclusively spatial problem, but here the transition challenge of the urban system is guiding
and that creates opportunities for greater dynamics and other spatial
designs at the neighbourhood level.

With that, this design atelier convincingly demonstrates that typological innovation can be separate from location. In fact, working on the
basis of the system appears to be a lot smarter than taking a location as
the starting point for a spatial development.

The energy transition in Leiden shows a similar development.[191] During the mapping of the heat flows, researchers found that the Port of
Rotterdam was discharging large quantities of heat into the New Water-
way and that the quantity discharged far exceeded the quantity used in
the immediate vicinity. The construction of a regional heating network
makes it possible to distribute the released heat to the region.

A next step was deciding on the precise location of the heat pipes.
It soon became clear that this infrastructure could have a spatial impact
similar to that of car and railway infrastructures: by planning future
urban extensions in accordance with the heat pipes, the energy infrastructure will determine the shape of the city, rather than the other way
around.

In the future, the network could switch from residual heat (generated by fossil energy) to sustainable geothermal energy. This requires
drilling and the optimal distance between drilling locations turned out
to be about 1.5 km. Connecting the bores to the regional heat network
creates nodes between the horizontal heat network and the vertical part
of the network that is used to drill for geothermal heat at thousands of
metres below ground level.

Nodes such as these have a double role: they pump hot water to the
neighbourhood and cool water back to the port. The return water must
be as cold as possible, so as much energy is extracted as possible. The
nodes will thus have a heat surplus that can be used to heat cycle paths,
squares and sports fields in the city. This creates opportunities for new
urban typologies based on the analysis of the production, distribution
and nodes of the heat infrastructure.

Scales and Sounds

In the initial stage, it is important not to determine the scale of (spatial)
interventions too soon. It will only become clear whether the challenge
requires a landscape, urban or built response later in the process. This
requires designers that are sufficiently flexible to work at different scale
levels and to bring different actors together to face a challenge.

Additionally, the metabolic approach raises the risk of
ongoing up-scaling. Because flows move across all scale
levels and are thus also visible in drains and on street
corners, sounding proved a good way to keep the design
grounded in a concrete and literal sense.

One of the FUR designers worked with this sounding
technique for the Metropolitan Region

191

See practical example
'What If-scenarios – Leiden'
→p. 148. For more information
about the heat network, see
*Zuid-Holland op St(r)oom!; Ruimte
voor de energietransitie*, 2013.

Amsterdam-Zuidwest.[192] The area extends from the Port of Amsterdam, via Schiphol Airport to Greenport Aalsmeer and functions as a hub for people, materials and goods. In order to analyse an area of this magnitude in a short period of time, researchers carried out soundings of typically urban fabrics in different locations. Together, they give an impression of the flows as a whole.

The advantage is that this makes the scale imaginable and concrete. The disadvantage is that it takes an effort to rise to a higher scale level and that the larger system runs the risk of being overlooked.

When designing a single object, upscaling looks easier, but this is only allowed if the results are explicitly tested on other scale levels. This was managed, for example, by the design atelier that focused on the obsolete Eindhoven Canal.[193] The developed toolbox with cultural and technological approaches could also be used in other places and at other times. By clustering and ranking the interventions, scenarios were created that helped the involved stakeholders to determine their next step.

Working with Models

Research by design is increasingly used to explore spatial challenges, rather than only to solve spatial problems. Rightly so, because it allows the development of alternatives, the realization of frameworks and the creation of high-quality integrated solutions. The next question is how to translate the sustainability promises of the transition challenges into practical solutions.

FUR, too, found that there are various ways in which designers can contribute to representation, argumentation and decision making. To use that power and to fulfil their changing social role, it is desirable for designers to develop new, complementary skills. To this end, educational institutions can provide more space for research by design and lay the foundation for a lifelong learning attitude. Also promising in this regard are the 'communities of practice' on energy, established in the north of the country: here, designers continue to receive expert feedback.

Research by design is not a non-committal academic exercise. FUR has taken the initiative to make the approach more imitable and to place it in a tradition of design as an instrument for knowledge development. But this cannot be more than an initial impetus. The development, testing and use of the methods of research by design requires further exploration, to take the field of study to the next level and to strengthen the social role and position of the designer.

192

See design atelier 'South West Works!' (Appendix 1) →**p. 305**.

193

See design atelier 'Water Works' (Appendix 1) →**p. 297**.

194

See Part 2 →**p. 128**.

The DTP Diagram has Proven Its Usefulness

Research by design can make a difference in cases where parties are looking for strategies, ideas or concepts together. Perhaps the most useful model that FUR tested in practice turned out to be the diagram that explains the Design Thinking Process.[194]

FUR mainly conducted research into the first four stages of this model, from the strategy stage to the project stage. After that it became less interesting, because once the designers are in the project stage they know very well what to do, that is what they have trained for.

The DTP Diagram provides all actors with an understanding of the stage the research by design process is in. In addition, it connects the attitudes of the different actors (ranging from neutral to realizing) to the extent in which the design is practically applicable (ranging from imaginable to usable).

If the attitudes of actors in a coalition towards an issue differ greatly, this is a risk to the success of the process. If some are merely interested in an idea while others are already willing to invest in it, this is a problem. Provided it is well-executed, research by design can help ensure that everyone involved is on the same page. The objective of the process is that all stakeholders end up at the same point eventually, so that they can enter the next stage together.

Formulating and monitoring common interests and holding coalitions together requires special process management skills of designers. If they do not have any, or if the process is too complex, they can also outsource process management to specialists and thus widen and professionalize the design coalition.

The ICCI Model is Under Development

Working on the metabolism of the city requires the assessment and evaluation of its performance, rather than only of specific locations. This 'de-spatialization' of design challenges not only makes high demands on designers (and thus on educational institutes), but also on the actors that are part of the coalition. To address this challenge, FUR has tested various techniques, paying particular attention to ways to get from one stage of the DTP Diagram to the next.

To this end, FUR developed the ICCI Model and tested it a first time. As it turns out it is useful and workable to explain the transition from one stage to the next in four steps: Inform, Combine, Choose and Implement. The first two steps are taken to generate all kinds of possibilities (divergence), from which choices are made in the last two steps (convergence). Steps three and four are connected to the development of scenarios based on the knowledge developed in step one and two. Scenario development can be used to extrapolate the obtained information.

It is important that all of the four steps are taken together with all of the involved actors. And that is not easy, because it is unclear how much time this will take. Fixing the amount of time each step can take in advance has only met with limited success so far.

The C3 Cube as a Checkpoint

A third model that FUR used is the Complete City Cube that connects the dimensions of actors (citizens, companies and governments) with three pillars of sustainable urbanity (economics, sociocultural connectivity and ecology). This consistency is examined at three scale levels: the street, the city and the region.

Using the C3 Cube makes it possible to determine whether all subjects are in the picture at every stage. Does the coalition of actors correspond with the purpose of the challenge? Are all of the perspectives still relevant? And how will the challenge impact the three scale levels?

Once the project definition is established, the objective of the design challenge is evident, the scale of the challenge is clear and the planning, the budgets and the involved actors are known. The challenge, in other words, has become a commission.

To gain an understanding of the way challenges develop, the students' design proposals were tested using the C3 Cube at the start and at the end of the design atelier.

A first conclusion is that none of the design proposals was limited to a single scale level and that almost all of them not only impacted the primary theme they focused on, but other healthy urbanity themes as well. As expected, they were all multidisciplinary and cross-border proposals. This obliged the students to collaborate and use an inclusive approach. None of the design proposals was developed in a straightforward, unambiguous process.

The design ateliers confirmed our view that designers can play an important part in addressing wicked problems. This is not an uncomplicated, easy-to-deal-with or solitary task, however, but one that requires multidisciplinary cooperation, patience, reflection and perseverance.

Design Skills

Especially in the beginning of the process, which is about strategies, ideas and concepts, not all of the actors and other stakeholders are able to understand the means that designers generally use to exchange and transfer information. Blueprints, for example, should not be used in the early stages. People cannot read such drawings or they think the end result will be 'exactly like the drawing'. But more importantly, initially their attitudes are only neutral or interested and a drawing will not convince them to embrace the problem and join in its solving.

In the early stages of the research by design, it is mostly narrative techniques and images that work well. Films, magazines and other creative forms of communication proved to be more effective than the traditional means of communicating design products.

It is also clear that the concreteness and precision of drawings and representations have to increase as the project stage approaches. This requires a more true-to-nature portrayal of the context, more detailed visualizations and more realistic lighting and material expression. Traditional means such as master plans, working drawings and detail drawings can be used later in the process, they are roughly effective from the project stage.

FUR developed alternative techniques to provide the actors with the information they need to transition to a next stage. For the students of the Academies of Architecture, FUR organized master classes to explore the possibilities of storytelling, mapping, scenario planning and other techniques.

Though FUR has a model of the way to transition from one stage to another, it is as yet unclear which instruments are needed at which stage of the process. This requires additional research.
In any case, research by design not only requires knowledge of the spatial consequences of transition challenges, but also, for example, of financial and legal aspects of the transition and the opportunities that actors have to participate in them. Designers do not always feel at home in this world.

In some cases they manage to actually fathom the financial and legal aspects and derive productive spatial strategies from them. But it is probably more efficient to choose an alternative approach and to teach designers how to involve external experts in the process.

Beyond Institutionalization

'Designing Makes You Understand' read a telling headline of an article by the University of Wageningen about the role of design in regional planning.[195] Research by design initiates communication and interaction, achieves insights and understanding and creates support and commitment. In addition, it underpins joint image formation and idea development and it promotes the collaboration, network creation and decision making that can speed up spatial developments.

Though there is a lot of talk about new coalitions for working on the city in the Netherlands, the country remains highly institutionalized. Traditional players continue to dominate as the commissioners of research by design. Though it is increasingly possible to get not only the Ministry of Infrastructure and the Environment but also the Ministry of Economic Affairs round the table, the objective is also to interest pension funds, insurers and other major companies in research by design.

The Energetic Odyssey that the IABR made to explore possibilities of using the North Sea for wind farming is promising. Oil companies, network operators and investment firms were part of that coalition.[196]

Coalitions often change over the course of a process. Some actors simply play a larger role in a particular development stage of the project than others. Research by design can also send a coalition in a direction that requires new players.

Research by design can contribute to the identification of those new players. The initiative Hackable City in Buiksloterham, for example, explores the possibility of upscaling individual initiatives and looks for ways to use them to influence the institutional world.[197] Initially,

195

'Design Makes You Understand—Mapping the Contributions of Designing to Regional Planning and Development', A. Kempenaar et al. In: *Landscape and Urban Planning* 149, 2016.

196

See Part 3, Chapter 'An Alliance on the North Sea'
→p. 202.

197

See Part 3, Chapter 'Alternative Area Development'
→p. 205.

its emphasis was on the use of technology, but it has become clear that the role social aspects play is at least as important.

Citizens

The biggest task facing research by design is the structural involvement of citizens in the renewal of the city, and not only the highly educated, progressive elite, but also the disadvantaged immigrants and disillusioned retirees. The Netherlands Institute for Social Research expressly warns of the danger of large groups being side-lined.[198] During the IABR 2016's final debate, sociologist Arnold Reijndorp pointed out that research by design seems particularly interested in the special and spectacular and has far less interest in the ordinary and the everyday.

A case in point is an English project in Granby Four Streets, a poor black neighbourhood in Liverpool that was due for demolition in the 1990s. The salvation of the neighbourhood started with local involvement and much later a London design team placed itself in the service of the active residents' community. It won the design team the Turner Prize and they used the £ 25,000 in prize money to build a meeting place for the neighbourhood.[199]

Students of the Academy of Architecture in Arnhem succeeded in involving the elderly residents of the Elderveld neighbourhood in their plans and they also managed to win the municipal Sports Department of Arnhem over to their side.[200] Unfortunately, the Urban Development department has been unwilling to play ball so far.

Increasing Complexity

Coalitions are formed on both sides of the table, both on the side of those bestowing the commission and that of those receiving it. This hardly makes the relations more transparent.

On the side of the commissioners, we see a process of clustering and clotting: coalitions of commissioners and initiators emerge on the basis of common interests and goals. That is not without risk. If a coalition of three commissioners formulates a single assignment, in practice it often turns out to actually combine three problems. In that case it is up to the designers to analyse, for example using the DTP Diagram, shared interests and to translate them into one single challenge. However, this challenge is still likely to address multiple disciplines and therefore be more complex than a challenge formulated by an individual commissioner.

These more complex questions lead to the circumstance that commissioners increasingly seek each other out to form design collectives and multidisciplinary partnerships. Particularly in collaborations without a clear hierarchical structure, personal commitment can play a key role.

Designers are increasingly acting as commissioners themselves, as well, especially in circular experiments.

198

Niet buiten de burger rekenen; Over randvoorwaarden voor burgerbetrokkenheid in het nieuwe omgevingsbestel, The Netherlands Institute for Social Research, 2016.

200

See Design Proposal 'The Elderly Take to the Streets' →p. 267.

199

See Practical Example 'Do-it-yourself – Liverpool' →p. 236.

In Buiksloterham, for example, both the individual initiators and the driving forces behind the various CPO's are quite often architects. Due to their background, they are ideally able to think about new urban typologies such as heat hubs, bio digesters, worm hotels and glasshouses for food manufacturing, and about the opportunities these offer to reintroduce functions into the city that are currently largely located in the country.

In Conclusion

Research by design requires controllability and transparency. Spatial designers must be able to justify their use of sources and their application of methods.

We hope this book helps to strengthen the faith in research by design that actors – from citizens to the CEO's at multinationals and from civil servants to city makers – already have.

Because it is our deep belief that research by design can help find answers to the wicked problems we face and that it can contribute to a more beautiful, healthy, sustainable and fair world.

Appendices

I: The 18 Design Ateliers

Resilient Infrastructure

— 2013/2014 Eindhoven 2050

— 2014/2015 Water Works

— 2015/2016 Eindhoven: the Mobility Challenge

Renewable Energy

— 2013/2014 The Energy Transition in the Groningen Region

— 2014/2015 Energy Transition and Healthy Ageing

— 2015/2016 Energy: Transition and Transformation 2016

Material Cycle

— 2013/2014 Food Hub Spaanse Polder

— 2014/2015 De Grondstoffenfabriek
(The Raw Materials Factory)

— 2015/2016 Afval als bron (Waste as a Source)

Vital Economy

— 2013/2014 De levensloopbestendige stad
(The Age-Proof City)

— 2014/2015 Zaans Next Economy

— 2015/2016 South West Works!

Healthy Living

— 2013/2014 De ecologische stad (The Ecological City)

— 2014/2015 Sport en beweging in de openbare ruimte
(Sports and Exercise in Public Places)

— 2015/2016 Sport en bewegen II

Sociocultural Connectivity

— 2013/2014 Ontwerplab Vrieheide (design Lab Vrieheide)

— 2014/2015 Verbonden in Parkstad (Connected in Parkstad)

— 2015/2016 Parkstad verbindt (Parkstad Connects)

resilient infrastructure (2013-2014)

Eindhoven 2050

With nearly three times as many patents per capita as Silicon Valley, Eindhoven is the most innovative city in the world. How can technology and design help this modest and not very attractive city to transform into one that can hold on to its future generations?

The objective of this design atelier was formulated together with the municipality: rather than about the prediction of the future, it is about the exploration of ambitions for several fundamental domains and subsequently about the formulation of a strategic spatial agenda – reasoning retroactively from a hypothesized future.

To follow up on the somewhat non-committal studies, two pilot projects were formulated. The first comprises the transformation of Eindhoven Central Station into the city's Central District. Though the station will continue to be an important location in the future, its brick appearance is no longer significant. How can this efficient transfer machine fill the part of the 'Eindhoven city of design, light and innovation' showpiece?

A less monumental pilot project comprises experiments with 'citizen streets'. Technological developments in the field of self-driving cars will have major spatial consequences and many streets will lose their mobility-related function. This offers opportunities to enhance the quality of life in old neighbourhoods. How can we return the vacant space to the community in a sensible manner? Will residents take over the management of the area or can we create other forms of organization so people can jointly contribute to the substantive ambitions of the city?

The atelier clearly explains that design research in combination with social and economic explorations form an important instrument to develop the city of the future in a process of co-creation through new alliances. The future has just begun.

Academy Master of Architecture // Master of Urbanism – Fontys School of Fine and Performing Arts

Year 2013-2014

Where Eindhoven, the Netherlands

Researcher Caro van de Venne

Students Bob van der A, Ahmed Al-Mallak, Qian Bao, Tom Billingham, Diana Bokovaia, Jochem van Boxtel, Patricia Calvino, Jiexin Cheng, Cees Donkers, Mohammed Elagiry, Jing Feng, Yu Han, Irena Itova, Javier Leyba, Rong Lin, Gijs Maas, Dolf Nijsen, Hong Liu, Tao Lv, Shenqi Wang, Yong Wang, Yongzhi Wang, Sidney van Well, Rob van der Wijst

Lecturers Jason Hilgefort, Caro van de Venne

Also involved in teaching Pnina Avidar, Reinout Crinche, Cees Donkers, Marc Glaudemans

Stakeholders Municipality of Eindhoven Solange Beekman (Head Urban Planning Department), Mary Ann Schreurs (Alderperson Innovation, Culture and Public Space), Lucien Panken (Strategy Department), Camille Wildeboer Schut (Strategy Department)

resilient infrastructure (2014-2015)

Water Works

Water has been causing problems in the Eindhoven region for many years. The area floods due to heavy rainfall, while agriculture faces water shortages and the waste water system needs readjusting. At the same time an originally important body of water, the 14-km-long Eindhoven Canal, has fallen into disuse. Is it possible to give it a new function and simultaneously make it a starting point for the further examination of the opportunities and problems of Brabant's water systems?

Which interventions contribute to a more resilient water system for this Brabant region, the city of Eindhoven and the canal itself? What are the spatial aspects of a possible transition? And which stakeholders can we approach in this context? The area is too large and complex for the municipality of Eindhoven alone.

The research by design is divided into four phases. In the first phase, students literally and figuratively map the canal. In the second phase, they develop separate concepts for possible transformation themes, from idea to spatial development. After an intensive scenario planning workshop, these are transformed into coherent strategies. In the final phase, the most promising scenario is investigated in detail.

By themselves the concepts are insufficiently realistic, but taken together sequentially they form development scenarios in which the one project benefits from the other, thus creating an exciting spatial and programmatic diversity. The resulting scenarios pull unexpected stakeholders into the picture.

The energy company emerges as a major stakeholder. Water purification and agricultural businesses and other commercial parties can join in with them. The use of scenario planning techniques not only leads to a broadened and enriched challenge, but also to a more flexible approach to metropolitan problems and to a follow-up project for the transformation of the canal zone area.

Academy Master of Architecture //
Master of Urbanism – Fontys School
of Fine and Performing Arts

Year 2014-2015

Where Eindhoven, the Netherlands

Researcher Marieke Kums

Students Joske van Breugel,
Co van Griensven, Li Gubai,
Lieke van den Heuvel,
Liudmila Neykova, Joeri Schutte,
Daan Steeghs, Jessica Stoop,
Joyce Verstijnen, Pim Wagemakers

Lecturer Jason Hilgefort

Also involved in teaching
Marc Glaudemans (MA+U)

Stakeholders Municipality of Eindhoven
Solange Beekman (Head Urban Planning
Department), Karel Beljaars (Landscape
Ecologist), Luuk Postmes (Senior Project
Manager Advisor Water), Ellen van Rosmalen
(Supervision Areas of Natural Beauty)

resilient infrastructure (2015-2016)

Eindhoven:
The Mobility Challenge

Eindhoven wants to accommodate an extra 70,000 residents by 2050 (an increase of 30 per cent). This will inevitably lead to an increase in buildings, facilities and mobility. However, the city wants to sharply reduce car traffic prior to 2050 to achieve carbon neutrality. How can we make specific locations more compact in a responsible manner and at the same time improve mobility in the entire city?

Students carry out research into compaction models at two very different locations. The first location comprises the campuses that are situated on the outskirts of the city and that provide 'Nederland Innovatieland' with a spring board. These are mostly located along highways and are poorly connected to the rest of the city. At the same time they have a high potential for urban densification, there are many jobs and there is sufficient space.

The city is already working on a project called Slow Lanes: an urban network of bicycle routes in and around the city meant to connect the campuses. Having mapped the existing networks, buildings and facilities comprehensively, the students are now able to indicate three locations where the potential for urban densification around a Slow Lane is the most promising. They examine what urban (residential) areas will look like when bicycles are the main (or only) means of transport.

The second densification location builds on the design atelier Water Works, which focused on the area around the Eindhoven Canal. The location is attractive because of its central location in the city, yet it is also an isolated place: a hole, as it where, in Eindhoven's current (public) mobility network. Additionally, the magnitude of this private area makes it difficult to access the right (group) of stakeholders.

The students address two problems coherently: that of the disused infrastructure of the Eindhoven Canal and that of large, partly disused and unattractive car parks. They start with temporary use and the money they make facilitates a more permanent redevelopment of the area when coupled with investments in better connections to the existing public mobility network. This way, the area will not only become attractive as an inner-city residential location, but the mobility of the city as a whole is improved as well.

Academy Master of Architecture //
Master of Urbanism – Fontys School
of Fine and Performing Arts

Year 2015-2016

Where Eindhoven, the Netherlands

Researcher Marieke Kums

Students Johan van den Boom,
Shelly van Gogh, Anton van Hooft,
Joeri Schutte, Tianyi Xue, Xiaohui Zhong

Lecturer Maurizio Scarciglia

Also involved in teaching
Marc Glaudemans (Academy of Tilburg)

Stakeholders Municipality of Eindhoven
Frans Dijstelbloem (Cultivator-Advisor
Healthy Urbanization), Kristy Gilsing
(Programme Manager Housing)

renewable energy (2013-2014)

The Energy Transition in the Groningen Region

The urgency of the energy transition is felt more acutely in Groningen than in the rest of the Netherlands. The impact of gas extraction is beginning to manifest aboveground in the form of earthquakes. They cause a lot of damage to the already shrinking communities. In Groningen, the energy transition not only represents an ecological topic, but is also a socioeconomic issue.

In this design atelier, students examine what the energy transition means to spatial planning. How, for example, can we use the *trias energetica* as a reason for new design proposals? What impact will this have on spatial programmes such as food production, mobility, housing, work

and industry? And what impact does the energy transition have on the scale of the building, the block, the neighbourhood, the district, the city and the region?

Students make an analysis of the local and regional energy potential. They subsequently develop scenarios for representative locations in the region and create spatial designs for these locations. The choice of location is free, the only condition being that they are in the Groningen region. The resulting transformation proposals pertain to, among other locations, Lageland, Drielanden, the Suikerunie grounds, rwzi Garmerwolde and Zuidhorn. Some students focus on a more generically applicable design.

The designs provide a concrete representation of the energy transition that can be used to inform the various stakeholders in the region and possibly even stir them to play a part themselves.

Academy Academy of Architecture –
Hanze University of Applied Sciences

Year 2013-2014

Where Groningen, the Netherlands

Researchers Sandra van Assen,
Clemens Bernardt

Students Ronald Brunsting, Tom Prins,
Nina Schouwman, Marcel Schuurs,
Omar Smids, Guido Tits

Lecturers Alex van Spijk, Sjoerd Betten

Also involved in teaching Victor Ackerman
(Coordinator Design Studies Academy
of Groningen), Gert ter Haar (Director
Academy of Groningen), Jan Jongert
(Winter workshop Academy)

Stakeholders Jan Buiten (Senior Planner
Province of Groningen), Paul Corzaan
(Renewable Energy Municipality
of Groningen), Jan Martijn Eekhof
(Urban Planner Municipality of
Groningen), Aniëlla van den Heuvel
(Trainee Grolab Municipality of Groningen),
Martin Klooster (Environmental Department
Municipality of Groningen), Jola Meijer
(Suikerunie grounds), Linda Noorman
(Architect Province of Groningen),
Alex van Oost (Programme Manager
Hanze University of Applied Sciences
Groningen), Mieke Oostra (Lecturer
NoorderRuimte), Tjerk Ruimschotel
(supervisor Urban Planning),
Tineke van der Schoor (Member District

Water Board of Noorderzijlvest and
Project Manager NoorderRuimte),
Edward Sie (Groningen Region),
Martien Visser (Lector NoorderRuimte)

renewable energy (2014-2015)

The Energy Transition and Healthy Ageing

The way we live, produce food and travel has a huge impact on our energy demands. This means that the energy transition is almost impossible without radical lifestyle changes. Stakeholders, experts, designers and users need to adopt new roles and attitudes.

Discussions with stakeholders lead to questions such as: What do energy interventions mean to districts, how can they contribute to healthy aging and how will they affect people's daily routines?

On the basis of activities ranging from a scenario development master class, discussions with stakeholders and intensive workshops, students couple acquired knowledge about energy flows to two specific locations: the districts Selwerd and Europapark, both in the city of Groningen.

This leads to very different proposals. Some will change people's daily routines, for example a design for a sustainable mobility hub. Others map the energy potential at the district level. And there are proposals for the transformation of housing blocks. Thus, research by design brings together local, regional and individual issues and opportunities.

Academy Master of Architecture //
Master of Urbanism – Fontys School
of Fine and Performing Arts

Year 2014-2015

Where Groningen, the Netherlands

Researchers Sandra van Assen,
Clemens Bernardt

Students Ronald Brunsting,
Douwe Drijfhout, Yerun Karabey,
Chris Pekel, Simone Poel,
Omar Smids, Thomas Steensma,
Guido Tits, Mark Venema, Tom de Vries

Lecturers Alex van Spijk, Rene Heijne

Also involved in teaching Victor Ackerman (coordinator design teaching, Academy of Architecture - Hanze University of Applied Sciences), Gert ter Haar (director, Academy of Architecture - Hanze University of Applied Sciences), Sabine Meier (Lector, Academy of Architecture – Hanze University of Applied Sciences), Bettina van der Hoven (University of Groningen, Healthy Ageing), Christian Zuidema (University of Groningen, assistant professor Planning)

Stakeholders Jan Buiten (senior planner Groningen province), Eva Bennen and Thijmen Hordijk (Wijkbedrijf Selwerd), Wouter van Bolhuis (Groningen Municipality), Harry Bouma (chairman platform Euroborg), Arnold van Calker (Development Sports centre Eurpopapark), Paul Corzaan (sustainable energy Groningen municipality), Anton Drost (Harbour master), Jan Martijn Eekhof (Urban planning municipality of Groningen), Frans Epping (Noorderpoort housing), Aniëlla van den Heuvel (trainee Grolab, Groningen municipality), Jan Nijhoff (project management Europapark Groningen municipality), Emiel Galetska (Water authority Hunze en Aa), Martin Klooster (Warmtestad / Groningen municipality), Linda Noorman (provincial architect Groningen), Tjerk Ruimschotel (senior planner Groningen municipality), Jasper Schweigmann (planner Groningen province), Mark van Maanen (project leade Europapark Groningen municipality), Geerlinde Rutgers (Mediacentrale), Henk Scholten (Architect De Linie Zuid), various residents Europapark and Selwerd, Mariel Vos (Neighbourhood vegetable garden council company Selwerd), District council Selwerd, Boukelien Woltjer (Zorg in de wijk, ZINN)

renewable energy (2015-2016

Energy: Transition and Transformation 2016

The energy transition is not only about the integration of wind turbines in the landscape or about filling roofs with solar panels. The transition from fossil fuel to renewable resources impacts all aspects of our daily lives. It changes the way we deal with mobility, food consumption, consumer behaviour and so on. Conversely, the same thing is true: the choices people make in their daily lives partly determine whether the transition to a renewable energy supply has a chance of succeeding.

That is why students that take part in this design atelier literally visit the districts. The aim is to actively involve the residents of the Groningen district of Paddepoel in the development of scenarios for their own habitat. The assumption is that the resilience of the district will increase as its inhabitants are offered guidelines for action. To familiarize the residents with the transition challenge, the students have a place to work in the district at their disposal during the project: a vacant storefront.

One of the ways the students acquire knowledge of and insights into the relationship between the energy transition and social agendas is by analysing exemplary projects. Subsequently, they identify the potential in the Paddepoel district. On this basis, they make choices about the further development of specific proposals and scenario's for different locations in Paddepoel together with the stakeholders.

The students present their end results to all people involved in the districts. Strikingly, designs that might well be judged too shallow in the classroom are sometimes very popular in the field, because they are accessible and easy to understand. Also, organizational or business models sometimes prove more useful than spatial plans.

Academy Academy of Architecture – Hanze University of Applied Sciences

Year 2015-2016

Where Groningen, the Netherlands

Researcher Sandra van Assen, Clemens Bernardt

Students Douwe Drijfhout, Yerun Karabey, Boukje Klaver, Chris Pekel, Thomas Rosema, Mark Venema

Lecturers Sandra van Assen, Alex van Spijk

Also involved in teaching Clemens Bernhardt (theory), Sjoerd Betten (architecture), Wouter van Bolhuis (project leader Energy Groningen municipality), Petra de Braal (kasus.nu, Social Capital), Jochem de Koster (coordinator Academy of Architecture – Hanze University of

Applied Sciences), Jelmer Pijlman (E&E, IABR), Karin Peeters (Territoria, supervisor district laboratory), Annet Ritsema (Specht, IABR), Martien Visser (lector Hanze University of Applied Scieces Energy systems), Christian Zuidema (University of Groningen, assistant professor Planning)

Stakeholders Jan Buiten (senior urban planner Groningen Province), Jan Martijn Eekhof (supervisor urban planning Groningen municipality), Els Struiving (Paddepoel Energiek Foundation, ambassador Grunneger Power), Jasper Schweigmann (urban planner Groningen municipality), Henk Jan Falkenaar (WIJS Atelier), Harald Hilbrants (WIJS atelier), Anne Huizenga (Grunneger Power), Anne Kraanen (WIJS Atelier), various residents, shopkeepers and entrepreneurs from the Paddepoel district

material cycle (2013-2014)

Food Hub Spaanse Polder

The growing world population and its rising prosperity ensure that the demand for food continues to grow. The food industry makes heavy demands on space, climate and water and energy supplies and inefficient handling and transport furthermore produce lots of waste.

Previously, production and transportation of food were among the main ingredients used in the organization of a city. Today, the production and processing of food have been relocated outside the city to ever larger, monofunctional and technocratic production environments. In reaction, we see the emergence of local and regional production and distribution.

In Rotterdam initiatives such as 'Eetbaar Rotterdam', 'Rotterdamse Oogst' or 'Uit Je Eigen Stad' examine how the food flows can be programmed into the city in a visible manner. The number of organic supermarkets and restaurants that focus on cooking with local produce is increasing rapidly.

The municipality wonders to what extent food flows can also be used to improve the quality of both the city itself and the relationship between city and countryside. In other words, can the city, especially its outskirts, benefit spatially and programmatically from a regionalization of the food chain? The municipality proposed a case study in the Spaanse Polder district that might answer this research question.

The Spaanse Polder includes one of the largest urban industrial estates in the Netherlands. It already accommodates many companies that are part of global food chains. At a national level, the area is easily accessible by the A20 and A13 motorways, the Delfshavense Schie Canal and (potentially) the railway, but on a local and regional scale, it is an island between city and countryside.

The atelier examines how the Spaanse Polder can be transformed into a Food Hub for Rotterdam, for example by spatial clustering, the closing of cycles, and new forms of mixed use and transport.

The students develop scenarios to exploit the regional position of the area and strengthen the connection between the city and the countryside. The end product is a joint area strategy for the development of the Spaanse Polder that includes designs made by the students on the basis of individual sub-assignments.

Academy Rotterdam Academy of
Architecture and Urban Design –
Rotterdam University of Applied Sciences

Year 2013-2014

Where Rotterdam, the Netherlands

Researcher Willemijn Lofvers

Students Barend Mense,
Chris van Nimwegen and Floris Schiferli

Lecturers Thijs van Bijsterveldt,
Willemijn Lofvers

Also involved in teaching
Wesley Leeman and Christian Rommelse
(Rotterdam Academy of Architecture and
Urban Design), Sharon Janmaat-Bouw
(Municipality of Rotterdam), Dirk Sijmons
(IABR 2014, H+N+S), Jan Willem van der
Schans (Eetbaar Rotterdam/ Wageningen
University), (Market Superintendent/
marktmeester) Bart (Groothandelsmarkt)
and Studio Marco Vermeulen

Stakeholders Municipality of Rotterdam
Annemieke Fontein and Sander Klaassen
(Space and Housing Department)

material cycle (2014-2015)

De grondstoffenfabriek (The Raw Materials Factory)

There is a lot of research into the improvement of the wastewater chain, but the spatial implications of, for example, disconnecting or decentralizing systems are barely interpreted. Can we turn wastewater chains into resource factories for a circular economy? Is it possible to correlate urban development and the circular economy more closely? This atelier uses analysis and design to explore possible answers to these questions.

The students gather existing knowledge about historical and new water technologies. On that basis, they outline new spatial solutions for The Resource Factory. The system analysis of Rotterdam's wastewater results in the selection of locations where scenarios can be applied.

This results in concrete proposals for the Rotterdam system as a whole and for specific locations such as the abandoned Marconi Towers in the area Merwe-Vierhavens, the Tarwewijk in Rotterdam-Zuid and an existing waste treatment plant. At the lowest scale level, separation at the source results in renewal of the typology of the single-family dwelling and the walk-up flat.

The atelier shows that system innovations can give new meanings to the city, the district and the dwelling. Another conclusion is that such innovations are unrelated to locations, for they result from the research question and the research into the possibilities, and not the other way around.

To conclude, it appears that sustainable sanitation does not necessarily require either a central or a local-decentralized system. In many cases hybrid systems, in which individuals contribute to the public interest, and vice versa, work better.

Academy Rotterdam Academy of
Architecture and Urban Design –
Rotterdam University of Applied Sciences

Year 2014-2015

Where Rotterdam, the Netherlands

Researcher Willemijn Lofvers

Students Wander Hendriks,
Nicky van der Kooij, Cécilia Miedema,
Bram van Ooijen, Emma Westerduin

Lecturers Florian Boer, Willemijn Lofvers

Also involved in teaching Steven Delva
(delva Landscape Architects), Bas van Eijk
(rinew/Evides), Charlotte van Erp and
Stefan Geilvoet (Transition Waste Water
to Resource), Eric Frijters (FUR/Fabric),
Fransje Hooimeijer (Delft University
of Technology), Christian Salewski
(ETH Zurich), Wouter Veldhuis (Rotterdam
Academy of Architecture and Urban Design/
must Stedenbouw), Loes van der Linden
(Municipality of Rotterdam),
Andre Rodenburg (Interdelta), Jaap de Ron
(The Schieland and De Krimpenerwaard
Regional Water Authority), Wolbert van Dijk
(Urban and Landscape Design),
David Dooghe (Deltametropool Foundation),
Marieke Kums (FUR/Studio Maks), Chris van
Langen (Rotterdam Academy of Architecture
and Urban Design), Dirk van Peijpe
(De Urbanisten), Margit Schuster (Rotterdam
Academy of Architecture and Urban Design)

Stakeholders Municipality of Rotterdam
John Jacobs (Water Management),
Sander Klaassen (Urban
Planning Department)

material cycle (2015-2016)

Afval als bron (Waste as a Source)

One of the key points of the circular economy is that we stop thinking in terms of waste and start thinking in terms of resources. Our current linear economy – in which resources undergo production and consumption to end as bothersome waste that needs treatment – has to be transformed into a circular economy that focuses on the reuse and recovery of resources.

This atelier examines the spatial possibilities of a waste-oriented circular district economy in the old districts in Rotterdam-Zuid. In this context, the city is understood as a marketplace for materials and resources.

Students trace the producers, processors and buyers of waste, identify the composition and size of waste flows and examine what infrastructure the supply,

collection and treatment of waste requires. In short, they look for the value of waste, the potentials of flows and the right economy of scale for treatment and reuse.

In the second phase, the students examine the positioning of the design challenge and specific local research. The third stage involves taking decisions with respect to an integrated design. In the fourth phase, to conclude, they act accordingly.

The students develop five design proposals on different scales and for different locations. In Rotterdam-Zuid, plans are developed for the Maashaven and Waalhaven, the AVR waste processing plant, Carnisselande and the Afrikaanderplein.

Academy Rotterdam Academy of
Architecture and Urban Design – Rotterdam
University of Applied Sciences

Year 2015-2016

Where Rotterdam, the Netherlands

Researcher Willemijn Lofvers

Students Hidde van der Grind,
Daniël Grobecker, Wander Hendriks,
Ashwin Karis, Ruud van Leeuwen,
Christian Quist, Freek van Riet

Lecturers Dirk van Peijpe,
Floris Schiferli

Also involved in teaching Maarten Gielen
(Rotor), Aetzel Griffioen (Vakmanstad),
Jan Jongert (Superuse), Hans Jungerius
(explorer), Joris Maltha (Catalogtree),
Ad Muller (AVR), Florence Slob
(Van Ganzewinkel, Circularity Centre),
Jeroen Visschers (Rotterdam Academy
of Architecture and Urban Design)

Stakeholders Municipality of Rotterdam
Sander Klaassen (Urban Planning
Department), Stijnie Lohof
(Senior Urban Planner Zuid)

vital economy (2013-2014)

De levensloopbestendige stad (The Age-Proof City)

Though ageing is often considered a problem, the fact that we live longer also creates many opportunities. Provided, that is, that districts and dwellings are age-proofed. What urban amenities and architectural solutions does that require? And how can they benefit the economy?

To find answers to these questions, this atelier follows two lines of thought. The first departs from the notion that cyclists and pedestrians spend more than motorists. Realizing the spatial dominance of slow traffic, however, requires the drastic redesign of the city streets.

The second line looks further into the future, to when people will live to be 150 years old. What will that mean to our working lives? Will we still have a single profession, for example, or perhaps two or even three careers consecutively? And what will this mean to the educational system? It requires a new urban typology that connects lifelong learning with a new housing philosophy.

Students start individually and work on their own research. Though they are free to choose which location they examine, they cover the whole city relatively well. For example, there are transformation proposals to make the Rivierenbuurt more sustainable, to revise the road profiles of Nieuw-West and learning and living are literally projected along and in the Amsterdam canals.

The results of individual projects are bundled at the end of the atelier and made available to all stakeholders. Thus, a general problem – making cities age-proof – is translated into themes that are relevant to Amsterdam.

Academy Academy of Architecture – Amsterdam University of the Arts

Year 2013-2014

Where Amsterdam, the Netherlands

Researcher Boris Hocks

Students Ricsi van Beek, Rob Brink, Milda Grabauskaite, Atir Ahmad Khan, Bram van den Heuvel, Nico Lang, Kristina Petrauskaite, Albane Poirier-Clerc, Patrick Roegiers, Pim van Tol, Michiel Zegers

Lecturers Boris Hocks, Kamiel Klaasse

Also involved in teaching Arjan Klok (Academy of Architecture – Amsterdam University of the Arts, Head of Urban Planning), Marco Broekman (fur Researcher)

Stakeholders Eva Gladek (Metabolicalab), Kai van Hasselt (Shinsekai Analyses), Maurits de Hoog (Municipality of Amsterdam Space and Sustainability Department), Marco van Steekelenburg (Province of Zuid-Holland), Thomas Straatemeier (Goudappel Coffeng)

vital economy (2014-2015)

Zaans Next Economy

The economic growth of Zaanstad fails to keep up with that of Amsterdam and the rest of the metropolitan region. Its housing and industry are closely interwoven and this makes it difficult to meet environmental requirements. In addition, Zaanstad is almost completely surrounded by protected areas.

This design atelier addresses how strategic interventions in the city or in the landscape can trigger a new economy and concurrently use the potential of the Zaanstreek as a mixed residential, work and recreational area.

In the first part of the atelier, students examine the local economy, the history of the economy, the relationship between living and working, the hospitality economy and the economy of the landscape. This gives them insight into the DNA of the region and the way the Zaan area has repeatedly reinvented itself over the centuries.

The analysis of spatial tasks and challenges provides the students with a basis for the development of a spatial strategy in the second part, when they further develop separate sections. The proposed strategies differ greatly. A first group combines major infrastructural intervention with the clustering of spatial and economic activities. A second group focuses on acupunctural interventions to enhance the spatioeconomic structure.

A third group analyses the urban ecosystem, reveals the underlying links and exposes new potential in relation to other economic sectors (crossovers). The fourth and last group focuses on interventions on the level of the structure or system to create opportunities for a new economy, for example by changing the environmental contours.

Academy Academy of Architecture – Amsterdam University of the Arts

Year 2014-2015

Where Zaanstreek, the Netherlands

Researcher Marco Broekman

Students Kim Baake, Frank den Boer, Jelmar Brouwer, Hein Coumou, Floris Grondman, Michiel Homs, Jacco Jansen, Kim Kool, Mirte van Laarhoven, Willemijn van Manen, Katarina Noteberg, Marie Séon, Mark Spaan, Mark van Vilsteren, Frank Vonk, Brigitta van Weeren

Lecturers Marco Broekman, Dingeman Deijs, Rik de Visser

Also involved in teaching Arjan Klok (Academy of Architecture – Amsterdam University of the Arts) and Maike van Stiphout (Academy of Architecture – Amsterdam University of the Arts)

Stakeholders Municipality of Zaanstad – Jan Heijink, Mirte Rozemond, Gert Peter Vos; Province of Noord-Holland– Ton Bossink, Jurjen Tjarks; Broedplaats aan de Zaan – Albert Groothuizen, Ellen Holleman, AadVerburg; Municipality of Amsterdam Space and Sustainability Department – Eric van der Kooij; UvA, Economic Board Amsterdam – Zef Hemel

vital economy (2015-2016)

South West Works!

Nationally, the Metropolitan Region Amsterdam (MRA) is an important economic motor and internationally, it belongs to the sub top. The ambitions of parties in the MRA are to belong to the top global city regions and further expand their position as the motor of Dutch economy.

To the southwest of the MRA are economic hubs such as Schiphol, Hoofddorp Beukenhorst, Zuidas, the Port of Amsterdam and Greenport. This area has become fragmented over time, creating a limited working landscape.

The area combines several landscape types: polder, peatland meadow, port, forest, airport, city, Greenport and so on. Strengthening these diverse landscape qualities could be the basis for the creation of high-quality working and living environments, and thus for attracting talent.

Students examine how local spatial interventions in the working landscape of MRA-Zuidwest can lead to the improved quality of the whole and thus to the enhancement of the competitiveness of the region. They draw up a 'strategic master plan' for the urban landscape: however they start out on a small scale by analysing seven concrete working locations.

On the basis of these analyses, they develop various scenarios. The scenarios further develop sites or subsections that are of strategic importance to the success of the vision. The students' visions take the short, medium and long term into account. At several moments during the process, individual projects are linked together by literally drawing them onto a map, thus showing correlations and dependencies.

Academy Academy of Architecture – Amsterdam University of the Arts

Year 2015-2016

Where Metropolitan Region Amsterdam-Zuidwest, the Netherlands

Researcher Marco Broekman

Students Ziega van den Berk, Chloe Charreton, Roeland Meek, Anne Nieuwenhuijs, Paul Plambeck, Thomas Wolfs

Lecturers Marco Broekman, Roel van Gerwen, Harm Veenenbos

Also involved in teaching Merten Nefs (Deltametropool Foundation), Willem van Winden (Lector Amsterdam Knowledge Economy)

Stakeholders Municipality of Amsterdam Space and Sustainability – Helga van der Haagen, Hans van der Made, Arjen Nieuwenhuizen; Municipality of Amsterdam Economic Affairs – William Stokman; Municipality of Haarlemmermeer – Joost van Faassen; Schiphol – Tom Goemans, Maurits Schaafsma

healthy living (2013-2014)

De ecologische stad
(The Ecological City)

Green areas are often nothing more than patches used to fill in the residual spaces between infrastructure and buildings. In such cases, urban greenery has no other function than just being green. However, greenery can contribute to the quality of the city in many other ways. As a storage area for peak precipitation for example, or as a cooling element in case of great heat, as a space for a whole range of human activities and as a habitat for all kinds of animals.

This atelier is located in the post-war district of Presikhaaf, a former problem district. The district consists of a series of monofunctional groups of housing. Both the public space and the dwellings need a major quality impulse.

Presikhaaf is located exactly halfway between the Veluwe and the foreland of the IJssel River. This location offers opportunities for turning the district into a link in the chain of the national green belt (EHS). At the same time, its location beneath the lateral moraines of the Veluwe causes flooding during heavy rainfall. Based on ecological structures, students develop scenarios for the district.

First, the students carefully map the district's current condition on the basis of the layer approach (underground, networks and occupation). They then analyse developments that may be important in the future, such as the completion of the A15 motorway, a possible additional train station in the district and the development of the High Frequency Railway Programme.

This analysis has to lead to starting points for a design proposal. Four different spatial scenarios are developed that together demonstrate a whole range of possibilities. To ensure the relevance of the design proposals, the students enter into a dialogue with stakeholders

at various levels and produce a film that explains the design proposals.

Academy ArtEZ Academy of Architecture, Arnhem

Year 2013-2014

Where Arnhem, the Netherlands

Researcher Ady Steketee

Students Ludo van Dijken, Jeffrey Floor, Marcel van der Kroef, Renee Lugers, Frans Rubertus, Lean Sas, Lion Schreven, Youri Vijzelman, Lisa Wagemans

Lecturers Bas Driessen, Thijs van Spaandonk

Also involved in teaching Gerd-Jan Oud (ArtEZ), Ina Post (Illustrator Course)

Stakeholder Christine Paris (Ecologist)

healthy living (2014-2015)

Sport en beweging
in de openbare ruimte
(Sports and Exercise
in Public Space)

In the Netherlands, practicing sports was until recently a mostly institutionalized activity. You were a member of a sports club and you went to a gym or a pitch. These places are not part of the public space: if there are no club activities, their gates or doors are locked. In recent years, individual sports such as running, cycling, parkour and boot camp have boomed. These are sports that, conversely, do take place in the public space.

The students examine the added value sports and the public space can have to each other. How can we design a public space that both enhances the visibility of the way sportspeople currently use it and that invites other people to take part in sports? In addition, the students also examine how sports, as a programme, can be a reason for the (re)design of the public space and for area development in general.

Students begin with a broad investigation into the relationship between sport and spatial design. They analyse international examples ranging from the scale of the whole city (for example, the Olympic

Games) to that of a catalogue of sporting equipment for public spaces.

Then they switch to Arnhem. How sports-loving is Arnhem and what sports-oriented policies does the city implement? The sports landscape of Arnhem is carefully mapped. Using the abundant research material, they subsequently make proposals for four different places in Arnhem that are all situated around the city centre and that currently all represent missing links in the public space chain. They are Stadsblokken-Meinerswijk, Zuidelijke Binnenstad, Klarendal and Centrum Oost.

The students were explicitly asked to find and access relevant stakeholders for their proposal. The input these give helps them to accentuate the proposals. The results are presented in a film and in a magazine.

Academy ArtEZ Academy of Architecture, Arnhem

Year 2014-2015

Where Arnhem, the Netherlands

Researcher Ady Steketee

Students Jasper van den Bogaard, Jorik Dijker, Jan Laurens van der Horst, Teun Leene, Niels Leijte, Bouke Nijland, Marcel Plomp, Bas Rollerman

Lecturers Bas Driessen, Thijs van Spaandonk

Also involved in teaching Ko Jacobs (ArtEZ Academy of Architecture, Arnhem)

Stakeholders Sjaak Aarden (Municipality of Arnhem), Peter Blankestijn (Gap2), Noëlle Bus (De Leuke Linde), Yosser Dekker (Roofgarden Arnhem), Kars Deutekom (Rose's Lounge Bar), Regina Florisson (Municipality of Arnhem), Geert Geurken (Sports Department Municipality of Arnhem), Thijs Groenewegen (Studio Halfvol), Lucas Hullegie (Sports Department Municipality of Arnhem), Marlies van der Marel, Erik Metz (Rowing Club Jason), Brigitte Muller (National Sports Centre Papendal), Harry Popken (Municipality of Arnhem), Henk van Ramshorst (Housing Association Volkshuisvesting Arnhem), Kirsten van Rijen (Municipality of Arnhem), Freek Roffel (Atelierbeheer Slak Foundation)

healthy living (2015-2016)

Sport en bewegen II (Sports and Exercise II)

The Dutch health care system is under pressure and since the Dutch population is ageing, this will only get worse. The challenge is to make the population healthy and keep it that way. Physical exercise plays a major part in achieving this. The goal is to stimulate people to play sports more often and, more importantly, to stimulate them to incorporate more exercise in their daily routines.

The population of Arnhem cycles less than is average in the Netherlands. There is something to be gained here. Which part of Arnhem presents the greatest challenge? And why is that? Which target groups need the most attention, what measures can be taken and who needs to be involved?

The students analyse international reference projects in which public space and physical exercise are closely related. The subsequently bury themselves in studies and policy documents about the health of the population of Arnhem. They use the gained insights to select specific locations, specific programmes as well as the parties these involved.

In pairs, the students further develop a total of four area strategies. The developed proposals relate to Elderveld, the fast cycling route between Arnhem and Nijmegen, RijkersWoerd and the health care institutions in the Velperweg area.

The students enter into discussion with the stakeholders in the early stages of the design process, for example by presenting their first proposals at a meeting of the residents' association. The stakeholders involved will also attend the presentation of the final results. The results are furthermore compiled in a magazine and a film to facilitate their further distribution.

Academy ArtEZ Academy of Architecture, Arnhem

Year 2015-2016

Where Arnhem, the Netherlands

Researcher Ady Steketee

Students Taco Bijleveld, Guus Blom,
Antoine Bowers, Kasper Brinkman,
Harm Diesvelt, Frank te Grotenhuis,
Diederik Mulder, Wim Spijker

Lecturers Bas Driessen,
Thijs van Spaandonk

Also involved in teaching Ko Jacobs
(ArtEZ Academy of Architecture,
Arnhem), Gerd-Jan Oud (ArtEZ
Academy of Architecture, Arnhem)

Stakeholders Harry Popken
(Advisor Sports Municipality of Arnhem),
Ron Stokkink (Elderveld in beweging)

sociocultural connectivity (2013-2014)

Ontwerplab Vrieheide (Design Lab Vrieheide)

The housing stock in Heerlen's Vrieheide district is in poor physical condition and this goes hand in hand with social problems, high unemployment and a growing number of illegal cannabis plantations. How can we stop the multiple – social, financial and energetical – devaluation this causes? And which spatial instrument can we use to achieve this?

Based on research and analyses, the students develop a strategy at the scale of the district and subsequently gear it to a dwelling prototype and to a public community building. They then reflect on the developed strategy and document their progress in digital logs.

The students recognize that the multiple problems cannot be solved by spatial interventions alone. The introduction into the area of new economic carriers that match the district's DNA is especially interesting. They not only provide work and income, but also instigate social and energetic innovation. 'Voedzaam Vrieheide' for example stimulates the transformation of overgrown ornamental green into carefully landscaped vegetable gardens. Re-Activate Vrieheide focuses on boosting the local economy by attracting external visitors and tourists. They can stay in abandoned houses and

mobile huts made of recycled building materials.

Vrieheide's clean-lined, white housing blocks have lost their uniformity due to individual interventions. To enhance community spirit, a renovation project is aimed at steering this fragmentation in the right direction. It introduces a *réanimation architecturale*: the original situation is revived.

With its emphasis on designing for preservation rather than for growth, the atelier creates new connections between the Province of Limburg, the municipality of Heerlen and the Academy of Architecture.

Academy Maastricht Academy
of Architecture, Zuyd

Year 2013-2014

Where Heerlen, the Netherlands

Researcher Marco Broekman

Students Wim Jansen, Nadine Nievergeld,
Bert Schellekens, Kaj Segers

Lecturers Jules Beckers (Teeken
Beckers Architecten), Niek Bisscheroux
(Maastricht Academy of Architecture,
Zuyd), Marco Broekman (FUR Researcher)

Stakeholders Joost van Daal
(Municipality of Heerlen, Project Manager
Area Development Vrieheide),
Thierry Goossens (Parkstad Limburg/
IBA Parkstad), Frans Janssen (Province of
Limburg), Rik Martens (Humblé Martens),
Nol Reverda (Lector Demographic
Shrinkage, Hogeschool Zuyd), Ronald Rovers
(Lector Built Environment and Regional
Development, Hogeschool Zuyd), Vrieheide
District Management Association,
police officer Peters (service number 3633)

sociocultural connectivity (2014-2015)

Verbonden in Parkstad (Connected in Parkstad)

The population of the region Parkstad Limburg is ageing and shrinking; many properties are unoccupied. Are there any spatial opportunities in this kind of urban region? Can familiarity with sociocultural connectivity prime the revitalization of buildings and urban regions?

The design atelier focuses on the east side of Heerlen's inner city, where many large complexes are abandoned. The outdoor space between the buildings is bleak, fragmented and unattractive. Any connections with the highly appreciated landscape and the Caumerbeek zone are lacking.

After a quick analysis of the location, the students produce a speculative sketch. They next formulate three questions that they submit to stakeholders and the inhabitants of the area. The answers are incorporated in subsequent speculations. The mapping of data in the fields of demography and social infrastructure provides important input.

The students examine three levels: the street, the city and the region. At the level of the street, they use the former Arcus College to show that the 1960s building relates better to the street when it is surrounded by a walled garden.

At the level of the city, they investigate the transformation of a former hospital tower. On the basis of a series of interviews, they propose to house both students and senior citizens in this building. Both the new typology and the redesign of the outdoor space stimulate meeting and shared use by the different target groups.

At the regional level, the students aim to transform the Amrath Hotel into housing for students mainly coming from Aachen. A strong mix of functions will literally draw them across the border.

Iba Parkstad will invite stakeholders and potential partners to the exhibition of the designs. Thus, the research by design has actually only just begun.

Academy Maastricht Academy of Architecture, Zuyd

Year 2014-2015

Where Maastricht, the Netherlands

Researcher Franz Ziegler

Students Femke van den Boorn, Thijs Geelen, Meghan van der Maas, Channa Mourmans, Roel Raeven

Lecturers Jules Beckers (Lecturer, Architect), Peter Defesche (Head Lecturer, Architect)

Also involved in teaching Rik Martens, Bas van der Pol (Coordinators)

Stakeholders iba Parkstad – Jo Coenen (Curator), Thierry Goosens en Roel Meertens (Urban Planners); Municipality – Nicole Simons (Heerlen) and Jake Wiersma (Maastricht); World of Walas (Concept Developer)

sociocultural connectivity (2015-2016)

Parkstad verbindt (Parkstad Connects)

Parkstad Limburg is one of the Dutch regions that is weighed down by the consequences of shrinkage: the number of residents is decreasing and businesses are leaving. In addition, this region is struggling with the infrastructural inheritance of a now mostly bankrupt economy. Parkstad Limburg has an abundance of roads that, due to their size, now increasingly form barriers between locations rather than connections.

A concrete example of this is Provincial Road N281. It has the profile of a motorway, but traffic intensity is low due to the fact that there is an actual motorway, the A76, running directly parallel to it. Thanks to the many exits – eight on a length of 11 km – many companies and large-scale stores settled along the N281.

In the future, the road has to become part of a new urban area. In addition, the Parkstad Limburg region emphatically focuses on urban centres across the border. To this end, it examines multimodal connections with cities such as Aachen.

In this design atelier, students work on a perspective for the N281. How can this road play a part in the revitalization of the region? They start with a thorough inventory of the travel behaviour of the inhabitants of Heerlen. How do they move through their city and region? Which means of transport and infrastructure do they use? And how does that influence the way the people of Heerlen feel connected to their region?

The students start from the hypothesis that the N281 is no longer needed for

car traffic. This creates room for experimentation and temporary programming.
They develop interventions for the various
areas that the N281 bisects. The results
will be presented at the IBA (International
Bauausstellung) Parkstad.

Academy Maastricht Academy
of Architecture, Zuyd

Year 2015-2016

Where Heerlen, the Netherlands

Researcher Franz Ziegler

Students Mick Dubois,
Channah Mourmans,
Leon Nypels

Lecturers Franz Ziegler,
Peter Defesch

II: Overview Practical Examples and positioning c3 Cube

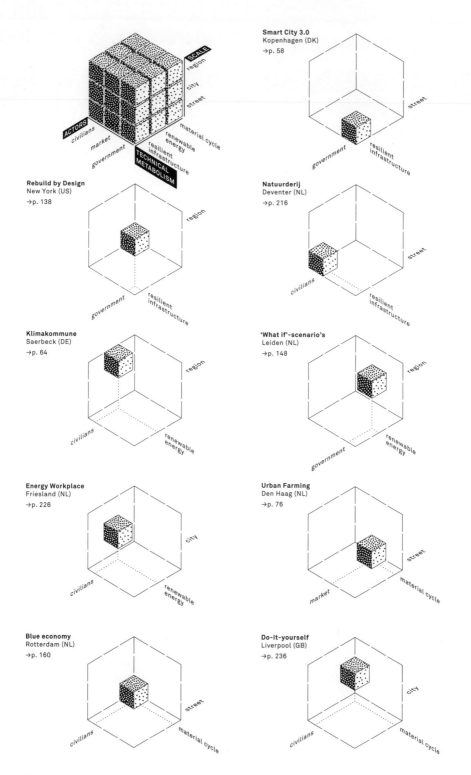

Smart City 3.0
Kopenhagen (DK)
→p. 58

Rebuild by Design
New York (US)
→p. 138

Natuurderij
Deventer (NL)
→p. 216

Klimakommune
Saerbeck (DE)
→p. 64

'What if'-scenario's
Leiden (NL)
→p. 148

Energy Workplace
Friesland (NL)
→p. 226

Urban Farming
Den Haag (NL)
→p. 76

Blue economy
Rotterdam (NL)
→p. 160

Do-it-yourself
Liverpool (GB)
→p. 236

Credits: Future Urban Regions, Catalogtree

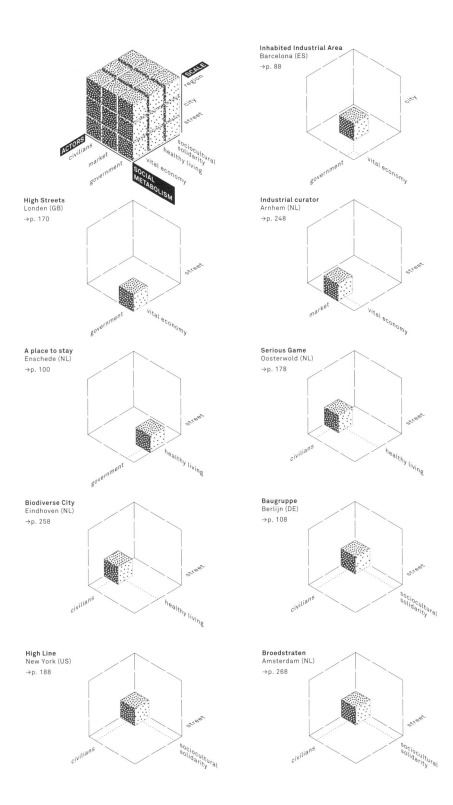

SCALE
region
city
street
ACTORS
civilians
market
government
sociocultural
solidarity
healthy living
vital economy
SOCIAL METABOLISM

Inhabited Industrial Area
Barcelona (ES)
→p. 88

city
government
vital economy

High Streets
Londen (GB)
→p. 170

street
government
vital economy

Industrial curator
Arnhem (NL)
→p. 248

street
market
vital economy

A place to stay
Enschede (NL)
→p. 100

street
government
healthy living

Serious Game
Oosterwold (NL)
→p. 178

street
civilians
healthy living

Biodiverse City
Eindhoven (NL)
→p. 258

street
civilians
healthy living

Baugruppe
Berlijn (DE)
→p. 108

street
civilians
sociocultural
solidarity

High Line
New York (US)
→p. 188

street
civilians
sociocultural
solidarity

Broedstraten
Amsterdam (NL)
→p. 268

street
civilians
sociocultural
solidarity

Image Credits

Portrait Sandra van Assen
— Annemarie Hoogwoud

Portrait Tijs van den Boomen
— Jan Banning

Portrait Marco Broekman
— Joost Bataille

Portrait Guido van Eijck
— Tino van den Berg (Autoexilio)

Portrait Eric Frijters
— Bas Driessen

Portrait Marieke Kums
— Evelien Kums

Portrait Willemijn Lofvers
— Annet Delfgaauw

Portrait Saskia Naafs
— anonymous

Portrait Thijs van Spaandonk
— Marcel Kampman

Portrait Ady Steketee
— Ady Steketee

Portrait Franz Ziegler
— Freek van Riet

fig. 1 — The nine planetary boundaries // Source: Steffen et al. Planetary Boundaries: Guiding human development on a changing planet, Science, 16 January 2015, bit.ly/planetaryboundaries, Redesign: Catalogtree →**p.29**

fig. 2 — The field of activity – four angles // Source: FABRICactions, Prix de Rome, 2010 / IABR, 2014, Redesign: Catalogtree →**p.32**

fig. 3 — Eleven essential values // Source: Kate Raworth: 'A Safe and Just Space for Humanity: can we live within the doughnut', Oxfam Discussion Paper, 2017, Redesign: Catalogtree →**p.36**

fig. 4 — The six FUR themes // Lectorate Future Urban Regions, Redesign: Catalogtree →**p.38**

fig. 5 — Real-time maintenance of public facilities // Thijs van Spaandonk, Catalogtree →**p.59**

fig. 6 — Ambitions CO_2 neutrality // Thijs van Spaandonk, Catalogtree →**p.59**

fig. 7 — Real time maintenance of public facilities // Copenhagen Solutions Lab, City of Copenhagen →**p.60**

fig. 8 — Wi-Fi points are installed in public areas. These are coupled to sensors for measuring the air quality, among other things // Copenhagen Solutions Lab, City of Copenhagen →**p.61**

fig. 9 — Continuous footpaths stay free of water // Joyce Verstijnen →**p.62**

fig. 10 — The new water system // Ziega van den Berk, Anne Nieuwenhuijs →**p.63**

fig. 11 — Embedding in the energy terrain // Thijs van Spaandonk, Catalogtree →**p.65**

fig. 12 — Production in relation to requirement // Thijs van Spaandonk, Catalogtree →**p.65**

fig. 13 — Former ammunition bunkers now function as carriers for new energy sources // Jannes Linders →**p.65**

fig. 14 — Energy park // Jannes Linders →**p.69**

fig. 15 — Biomass in the landscape // Jannes Linders →**p.69**

fig. 16 — Energy park // Jannes Linders →**p.72**

fig. 17 — Renewable energy and water purification combined in a bathing facility // Yerun Karabey, Mark Venema →**p.74**

fig. 18 — Duck weed nursery park // Douwe Drijfhout →**p.75**

fig. 19 — Revenue to need households // Thijs van Spaandonk, Catalogtree →**p.77**

fig. 20 — Stacked urban typologie // Thijs van Spaandonk, Catalogtree →**p.77**

fig. 21 — Section of the project // Space&Matter →**p.77**

fig. 22 — View from the greenhouse over The Hague // Martijn Zegwaard →**p.80**

fig. 23 — Detail of the connection between the greenhouse and the office building // Space&Matter →**p.81**

fig. 24 — View from the greenhouse to the offices // Martijn Zegwaard →**p.81**

fig. 25 — Largest rooftop farm in Europe // Martijn Zegwaard →**p.84**

fig. 26 — Water treatment greenhouse in a multicultural neighbourhood // Cécilia Miedema →**p.85**

fig. 27 — A symbiosis of water, food, energy and waste in Polderdrecht // Bram van Ooijen →**p.86**

fig. 28 — Reuse of office towers for water treatment // Wander Hendriks →**p.87**

fig. 29 — Rules for urban densification // Thijs van Spaandonk, Catalogtree →**p.89**

fig. 30 — Increase (percentage and total in 10 years) // Thijs van Spaandonk, Catalogtree →**p.89**

fig. 31 — Mixing scale and functions // Jannes Linders →**p.89**

fig. 32 — Battle in the neighbourhood // Jannes Linders →**p.92**

fig. 33 — Development of a lot // Jannes Linders →**p.93**

fig. 34 — Publicly accessible campus // Jannes Linders →**p.93**

Colophon

This publication was made possible through the generous support of the Creative Industries Fund NL and the Van Eesteren-Fluck & Van Lohuizen Foundation.

creative industries fund NL

EFL STICHTING

The publication is a cooperation between trancity×valiz and the Future Urban Regions lectorate, which is connected to the Dutch Academies of Architecture in Amsterdam, Arnhem, Groningen, Maastricht, Rotterdam, Tilburg. A separate Dutch edition is available.

Editors Tijs van den Boomen, Eric Frijters, Sandra van Assen, Marco Broekman

Image editing Willemijn Lofvers, Pia Pol

Photography Jannes Linders

Graphic Design Catalogtree

Translation In Other Words, D'Laine Camp, Jesse van der Hoeven, Maria van Tol

Proofreading Marianne Lahr

Production Pia Pol

Printing Wilco, Amersfoort (NL)

Publishers Simon Franke – Trancity, Pia Pol / Astrid Vorstermans – Valiz

www.trancity.nl
www.valiz.nl

ISBN 978-94-92095-33-6
English edition
ISBN 978-94-92095-32-9
Dutch edition

Future Urban Regions

The Future Urban Region lectorate explores urban (eco) systems and innovative design tools for the existing city. From a changing understanding of the use of space, it works to improve urban environmental performance, the economic situation, and/or socio-cultural participation. This agenda guides the assignments of (specific forms of) design research, which are commissioned by local and regional authorities, to be embedded in the education curriculum of the six Dutch Academies of Architecture.

trancity×valiz

trancity×valiz is a collaboration between two independent publishers that share a common understanding regarding the function of publications. Their books provide critical reflection and inter-disciplinary inspiration, and establish a connection between cultural disciplines and socio-economic issues. Publications on the city, urban change and the public domain are at the core of the collaboration between Trancity and Valiz.

International distribution:

BE/NL/LU Coen Sligting
www.coensligtingbookimport.nl

Centraal Boekhuis
www.centraal.boekhuis.nl

GB/IE Anagram
www.anagrambooks.com

Europe/Asia Idea Books
www.ideabooks.nl

Australia Perimeter Books
www.perimeterdistribution.com

USA D.A.P.
www.artbook.com

Individual orders
www.trancity.nl